WEARING THE CHEONGSAM

Dress cultures

Dress Cultures aims to foster innovative theoretical and methodological frameworks to understand how and why we dress, exploring the connections between clothing, commerce, and creativity in global contexts.

Published

Delft Blue to Denim Blue: Contemporary Dutch Fashion
edited by Anneke Smelik

Dressing for Austerity: Aspiration, Leisure and Fashion in Post War Britain
by Geraldine Biddle-Perry

Experimental Fashion: Performance Art, Carnival and the Grotesque Body
by Francesca Granata

Fashion in European Art: Dress and Identity, Politics and the Body, 1775–1925
edited by Justine De Young

Fashion in Multiple Chinas: Chinese Styles in the Transglobal Landscape
edited by Wessie Ling and Simona Segre Reinach

Modest Fashion: Styling Bodies, Mediating Faith
edited by Reina Lewis

Styling South Asian Youth Cultures: Fashion, Media and Society
edited by Lipi Begum, Rohit K. Dasgupta and Reina Lewis

Thinking Through Fashion: A Guide to Key Theorists
edited by Agnès Rocamora and Anneke Smelik

Veiling in Fashion: Space and the Hijab in Minority Communities
by Anna-Mari Almila

Wearing the Cheongsam: Dress and Culture in a Chinese Diaspora
by Cheryl Sim

Reina Lewis: reina.lewis@fashion.arts.ac.uk
Elizabeth Wilson: elizabethwilson.auth@gmail.com

WEARING THE CHEONGSAM

DRESS AND CULTURE IN A CHINESE DIASPORA

Cheryl Sim

BLOOMSBURY VISUAL ARTS
LONDON • NEW YORK • OXFORD • NEW DELHI • SYDNEY

BLOOMSBURY VISUAL ARTS
Bloomsbury Publishing Plc
50 Bedford Square, London, WC1B 3DP, UK
1385 Broadway, New York, NY 10018, USA

BLOOMSBURY, BLOOMSBURY VISUAL ARTS and the Diana logo are trademarks of
Bloomsbury Publishing Plc

First published in Great Britain 2019

Series design by BRILL
Cover image © Martin Brisson

A catalogue record for this book is available from the British Library.

A catalog record for this book is available from the Library of Congress.

ISBN: HB: 978-1-78831-081-9
       ePDF: 978-1-350-10986-5
       eBook: 978-1-350-10987-2

Series: Dress Cultures

Typeset by RefineCatch Limited, Bungay, Suffolk
Printed and bound in Great Britain

This book is dedicated to the memory of Charlotte Sim and David Tomas

CONTENTS

ILLUSTRATIONS

Figures

Plates

PREFACE

Figure 1 Charlotte Sim circa 1950s (Courtesy
Sim family collection)

In another life as a singer, I performed a concert wearing a vintage cheongsam.
It was floor length, sleeveless, and made from a silky print fabric of pink
flowers on a black background. Afterwards, a Chinese journalist approached
me to be a guest on her cable access television show about Chinese Canadians.
Being of mixed Chinese and Filipino heritage, I was amazed that she had
approached me, as all my life I had gone unrecognized as Chinese, whether
inside or outside the Chinese community. When I asked what had led her to
presume that I had Chinese heritage, she shrugged and said, "It was the dress."
It occurred to me at once that I had chosen this garment not only to promote
its exquisite beauty but also to represent and affirm a desire to connect with

my Chinese heritage, which had been lost out of a need to assimilate into dominant Canadian culture. Since then I have sought to deepen my understanding of what the cheongsam means to me and other women like me, who are second generation Canadian-born women of Chinese heritage.

I owe my love of the cheongsam to my paternal grandmother, Charlotte Sim (née King), who was born in 1906, during the last few years of the Qing dynasty (1644–1912). Her mother had bound feet and never learned to read or write. The fall of the Qing dynasty and the rise of the Republic Era (1912–49) ushered in a new vision for China—one of modernization. With it, the idea of the "modern" woman emerged, and a woman's place in society evolved. With the benefit of Charlotte's upper class status and her father's progressive attitude, she was the first woman in her family to receive a formal education. While the template of Charlotte's life was very much in keeping with the traditional roles of wife and mother, her life deeply informed my early feminist ideas. She was a well-respected entrepreneur, an influential member of her community, and she led many initiatives to improve women's lives. There was something else about her that made a deep and lasting impression on me, and that was her impeccable style. In my memories of her she almost always wore a cheongsam. Charlotte's dresses were mostly tailor made, her accessories chosen with great care, and every day until she got much older she tied her hair up in a neat chignon. In this spirit, Charlotte embodied substance and splendor, which has become an apt way of describing a feminist approach that I apply to my work as an artist and curator today. My engagement with the wearing of the cheongsam started early, without much reflection. But as my artistic and professional experiences led me to be become more politicized, wearing the cheongsam took on a deeper purpose. I needed to further understand the power dynamics of this garment, to divine its spirit and unlock its secrets. The best way for me to do this was to make the cheongsam the subject and object of an extensive art project. This book is the result of the research and the outcome of such a project.

Starting out, my medium of choice was video, as my television-saturated childhood demonstrated to me the myriad possibilities afforded by sound and moving image. My first job at the National Film Board of Canada also exposed me to the incredible work of pioneering film and video artists, such as Richard Fung, Mona Hatoum, and Trinh T. Minh Ha, who were exploring issues of "race," ethnicity, and sexuality through their personal stories. My first single-channel video work, *A Few Colourful Phrases*, produced in 1995, explored everything I wanted to say about growing up as a Canadian-born woman of color in the post-settler context of Canada through three commonly heard phrases: "If you don't mind me asking, where are you from?," "You know what they say about Oriental girls," and "Has anyone ever called you a banana?". The works that came after continued to explore and document the lives and experiences of women from a feminist and post-colonial perspective through a research-based methodology and an inter-genre, interdisciplinary, and auto-ethnographic approach. I began to employ a procedure of separating voice and image that would become a consistent feature in all of my videos—a critical strategy that would interrogate the gaze through the privileging of a woman's voice and words over her image. I also characterize my work as informed by a strategy of hybridity and "politicized sensuousness" that I will explain in more depth later on in this book. Since 2011, my work has expanded into an installation practice that combines multi-channel video, the creation of objects, audio montage, and site specificity. As an artist with a deep belief in the poetics of the art experience, I felt that inter-/multi-discplinary approaches in contemporary art, which can include video, photo, sound, painting, sculpture, text, and even space, could offer the visitor a crucial range of entry points to potentially deepen an appreciation and understanding of a subject, object, issue, or theory of interest. The prime motivation towards this shift was also due not only to my interest in further exploring the formal and historical aspects of the cheongsam, but to the desire to use it as a lens through which to study identity, ethnicity, and the diaspora condition of women of Chinese heritage in Canada. While I had created an experimental documentary in 2010 dedicated to the dress, its history, and its semiotic representation, I felt there was still so much to explore and say. The employment of visuals and sound through the video medium was a good start, but the desire became urgent to highlight the tactility of the dress, its activation on the body, and its charged physicality within the space of a meaningful site. I felt that art installation would be the most effective way to convey the multifaceted and complex story of the cheongsam and its analogous relationship to issues of identity. The cheongsam presented an irresistably rich object and subject to investigate the potential of art to access the more abstract and interstitial spaces of meaning. In this way, I employed art as a way to engage with the formal, theoretical, and affective aspects of the cheongsam, as it allowed me to treat these on a variety of levels and in a range of modes that I hoped would have significant impact and reach. The creative interpretation of this dress in the form of an exhibition of works allowed me to bring my passion for clothing, fashion, and style together with deeply personal questions about identity, belonging, and agency.

As this study of the cheongsam and its wearing practices is examined from an artist's view, it does not propose an exhaustive or conventional academic analysis, but rather offers a personal perspective informed by a qualititative methodological approach that includes ethnography, auto-ethnography, and historical research. Drawing on academic research on ethnic clothing and identity, theories and practices in contemporary art, and the chronicle of the creative process, this book is a hybrid, much in keeping with its subject and its author. It is hoped that it will be of benefit to readers engaged with a range of interests that can include fashion, diaspora studies, and contemporary art practice.

In the introduction that follows, I attempt to situate myself through an illustration of personal stories as well as key moments in Canada's growth as a nation, such as the establishment of the policy on multiculturalism, as a strategy for national identity formation. This contextual groundwork will set the scene for a larger discussion on what it was like to be born in Canada of Chinese heritage at a specific point in time. It will explain how many of us experienced the rejection or loss of a Chinese ethnic identity, but mostly it will explore how the recovery of such an identity might be channeled through the wearing of one very special dress.

ACKNOWLEDGMENTS

I would like to express my deep gratitude to all of the incredible people who have helped to make this book come to life.

Thank you to my parents, Victor and Rose, and my sister Lisa, for allowing me to bring your personal stories and photos into my artwork for all of these years. You will always provide me with great inspiration.

Merci to my partner Frédéric for his solid and loving support for everything I try.

I also want to express my sincere gratitude to the nineteen women who shared their personal experiences, as well as their ideas and feelings towards the cheongsam. These candid responses are the essence of this book and I am humbled by their generosity.

My sincere thanks to David Tomas and Monika Kin Gagnon, who have been instrumental in guiding my academic and artistic lives. I am very proud to call you my friends.

Thank you to Reina and Elizabeth of the Dress Cultures series, and Frances and Yvonne at Bloomsbury. I have thoroughly enjoyed this process and I feel very fortunate to have worked with such compassionate editors.

Finally, I wish to thank my grandmother Charlotte for providing me with such an impressive role model, a woman who forever embodies splendor and substance.

CHAPTER I
ONE SIZE DOES NOT FIT ALL

The cheongsam is by no means a simple garment. For all its beauty and elegance, the cheongsam has a dark side of contradictions that is the site of endless fascination. Wearing the cheongsam connects me with my grandmother and my Chinese family. It signals to others that I have Chinese ancestry as this is not always readily perceptible. Wearing the cheongsam can also be pleasurable, making me feel like a more regal version of myself. Perhaps most of all, wearing this dress allows me to channel an evolving sense of Chinese ethnicity and to make it part of an identity that is in constant production.

The cheongsam and its relevance to the lives of Canadian-born women of Chinese heritage provides a powerful vehicle through which to assess the state of the Chinese female diaspora in Canada, the second largest Chinese diaspora outside of Asia, after the United States. As populations continue to shift around the world, the study of ethnic clothing and its relationship with ethnicity and identity formation informs our understanding of the need for belonging and connection in a climate of advanced globalization and forced migration. How are concepts like nationality, ethnicity, "race," and gender formed, and who has the power to shape these? While I have always been convinced of the power of clothing to communicate messages, I had not fully understood why I was drawn to wearing a dress so charged with intense political and cultural readings. My inability to fully articulate these impulses catalyzed my interest in the study of wearing practices of the cheongsam by Canadian-born women of Chinese heritage.

Multiculturalism and the cheongsam

My mother was born in the small town of Kabankalan in the Philippines. My father was born in Swatow, China, and spent much of his childhood and adolescence in Hong Kong. They met at the University of Houston, Texas, and made their way to Canada in the late 1960s. In my mind, they were model immigrants, as they were ambitious, hard-working, knew how to speak English and were happy to adapt to Canadian culture and society. Changes to the Canadian Immigration Act at that time facilitated their applications to become Canadian citizens, which were eventually approved. I am their first child, born in Hamilton, Ontario, in 1971. That same year, Canada adopted multiculturalism as a policy, which according to the official Government of Canada website affirmed "the value and dignity of all Canadian citizens regardless of their racial or ethnic origins, their language, or their religious affiliation."[3] My parents embraced this message, as did many newly arrived immigrants to Canada at that time. But as I got older and became aware that I was different in Canadian society, multiculturalism's rosy statements started to ring hollow. The awareness of my difference started in kindergarten, where I attended a public school in the suburban town of Burlington, Ontario. One day our teacher gave us an exercise on what must have been something about how to categorize through a process of association and disassociation. She wanted to use eye color as a way to understand this concept and created a large chart with the words blue, green, hazel, and brown written down the left side of a pad of oversized, white chart paper. As each child was called upon, she or he was given a sticker that corresponded with their eye color. They were then required to go up to the chart and place the sticker next to the word that corresponded with their eye color. Blue-eyed children received blue stickers, green-eyed children were given green stickers, and so on. I waited patiently be part of the group of brown-eyed children, but my name was never called. When it seemed like the teacher was going to wrap up the exercise, I raised my hand. The teacher sighed, grabbed an orange sticker, attacked it with a black magic marker, and extended it to me. I slowly rose, feeling quite humiliated, and put my improvised sticker on a separate line—the one I supposed was for black-eyed children. From that point on, my difference was clearly articulated, and this incident would be the first of other racialized experiences I would encounter throughout my childhood. These would shape and motivate my wish to obscure my visible difference, and above all to be as "Canadian" as possible. Gradually I began to disown the signifiers of my difference. I complained about eating Chinese food and used a drugstore product to bleach my hair. Over time, I eschewed my ethnic heritages in an attempt to assimilate into dominant, white Canadian culture.

Throughout elementary and high school, with the almost daily questions that my appearance would raise, there was one consistent survival tactic that I adopted, and that was the careful and strategic selection of what to wear. Through consideration of a variety of factors, including the nature of an activity, its history, traditions, and current culture, I would put together an outfit that I hoped would grant me acceptance. When I was eight years old, I begged my parents for a pair of Roadrunner jeans and Cougar boots. These items were basic elements of Canadian pre-teen fashion in the late 1970s, and while I appreciated the style of these items, I also felt they would prompt my peers to see me as an average Canadian girl. I truly believe that clothing helped me to survive my insecurities about being visibly "ethnic" in a predominantly white society. Even if my appearance seemed out of place for some people, my negotiation of the right clothing for a given situation provided me with a sense of protection. In this way Bill Cunningham's famous quotation that "fashion is the armor to survive the reality of everyday life" is an idea that I continue to embrace to this day.

Coming out of adolescence, I found ways to come to terms with and celebrate my difference, and I have been empowered by what I have learned in the margins. But along the way, I most definitely lost a connection to my ethnic heritages which I contend is due in part to the double discourse articulated by the utopian rhetoric of Canadian multiculturalism. What I found from conducting this research is that I was not alone and that the contours of my early childhood story were quite simliar to those among the women I interviewed. How did people of color wind up in Canada? Since the early 1800s, immigration from settler nations was key to Canada's growth as earlier migrants from England and France were not providing enough population increase to satisfy economic goals in support of Canada's establishment as a nation. It is also important to note that the populations of aboriginal people across the country steadily diminished with the arrival of Europeans to North America in the mid-1500s. Efforts to dominate and control aboriginal communities—regarded as backward and inferior—were made through religious conversion, exploitation as slaves in the fur trade, the introduction of disease, displacement, unfair treaties, and state-sanctioned programs meant to force assimilation. In this way, Canada's early governments had clearly established a stance in regards to who would be part of this new nation and who would not. Immigrants to Canada from Western European countries were favored and laws and strategies to protect this preference stayed in place into the 1960s. Immigrants from Eastern Europe followed as a result of forced migration, largely based on the political and economic crises that befell countries after the Second World War. But immigrants from continents other than Europe only began to come in waves starting at the end of the 1960s when the government made efforts to de-racialize immigration laws and criteria for entering Canada, while maintaining a system of selectivity. Factors around ethnicity and country of origin were replaced by questions regarding skill, education, and training. But the cultivation of the idea that all immigrants might take part in Western prosperity was relatively new and not fully supported by Canada's more established citizens. The unequal perception of immigrants along ethnic and racialized terms was planted long ago with the treatment of aboriginal people, and later in the government's use of disposable migrant labor to build its infrastructural foundations. In his book *The Chinese in Canada* (1988), Peter S. Li presents a key example of how the instrumentalization of Chinese migrant workforces shaped attitudes towards immigration and people of color in Canada. The emigration of Chinese people began in the mid-nineteenth century due to famine, poverty, and economic instability caused by war and natural disaster. In order to better their chances of survival, waves of Chinese people were forced to leave China, landing in parts of Southeast Asia, Latin America, and North America. Li explains that in Canada, the arrival of the first wave of Chinese male emigrants came in response to the 1858 gold rush in Fraser Canyon, British Columbia. Settlements emerged and throughout the 1860s the Chinese were useful to the British settlers as they worked twice as hard for less pay than white men, and were tolerated as long as they did not claim citizenship or any other rights. Later on, from 1881 to 1885, as many as 17,000 Chinese men were brought to Canada through a "coolie trade," or indentured servitude, for the building of the Canadian Pacific Railway (CPR). The CPR was essential to Canada's union, with a transport link between both coasts that would provide a way for goods to be distributed across the country from its port in Vancouver. The CPR therefore played a paramount role in Canada's emergence as a commercial and political power. As a form of cheap labor, the Chinese were not credited for their contribution to Canada's emergence as a geographically unified nation, nor were they permitted the same rights as other immigrants at that time. The idea that they were unworthy of citizenship became entrenched and normalized in Canadian society early on.

By 1967, a campaign to attract new immigrants to Canada was launched to satisfy a need for more skilled labor to support Canada's economic boom. A points system was established, which allowed for immigrants from countries like China and India to be accepted. Led by Pierre Elliot Trudeau, a policy on multiculturalism was eventually proposed by the Liberal government to address the many issues and concerns that had arisen for the new nation, while maintaining Canada as a country of choice for immigration. On first view, the multiculturalism policy promoted Canada as an attractive and level playing field where immigrants from anywhere could access opportunity. However, as Eva Mackey points out in *The House of Difference: Cultural Politics and National Identity in Canada* (2002), the policy was more precisely a tool of nation building meant to:

> [. . .] respond to the range of complex and potentially dangerous conflicts in the cultural politics of Canadian nationalism, including the threat of Québec separatism, demands for recognition by immigrants and other minorities, and the need for immigrants to fuel prosperity. It also intersected with the need, seen as a natural "evolution" of nationhood, to construct a unified and distinct national identity to differentiate itself from the USA and Britain. (2002, p. 70)

The introduction of official multiculturalism was brought in to placate and diffuse the variety of urgent demands and claims made by established and newer citizens, while carving out a place of worldy distinction for this young country. Multiculturalism and Citizenship Canada even published a document in 1985 which described multiculturalism as "a great national bandage" meant to heal the "national fabric" (Mackey, 2002, p. 67). While the policy claimed that "all citizens can keep their identities," in practice, immigrants could do so only with the understanding that a dominant culture informed principally by Anglo-Saxon traditions and values was the norm and therefore to be practiced in public, everyday life. Despite the policy's aim to project an image of openness and "tolerance," I share Mackey's contention that it actually contributed to the articulation of difference and the reinforcement of unequal power relations between an immigrant "other" and a dominant Anglo-Saxon "national" culture. As she explains:

> The policy has been critiqued for maintaining the idea of British Canadians as the "norm," in relation to "multicultural" Canadians. In this construction of culture, we have a core Canadian national culture as a "whole way of life," and the "multicultures" exist as fragments of culture, only valued for the ways in which they contribute to this "whole way of life" of the national culture. (2002, p. 67)

She further illustrates this point by citing what C. Mullard calls "a 'three Ss' model of culture, which features 'saris, samosas and steel bands' in order to diffuse the 'three Rs': 'resistance, rebellion and rejection'" (2002, 67).

Mackey also cites Kogila Moodley's argument that Canadian multiculturalism "promotes a 'festive' aura of imagined consensus" (2002, 67). In other words, the celebration of ethnic food and dance is a non-threatening concession meant to appease people of color, or so-called "multicultural communities" who experience the effects of racialization and marginalization on a daily basis. Any public expression of ethnicity would be permitted on a specific occasion, and carefully controlled. The rest of the time, in public at least, the general population would conduct themselves in accordance with the customs and behavior indicated by dominant Anglo-Saxon Canadian culture. The desire I had as a child to assimilate in order to survive in Canadian society was not something I had invented. It was covertly enforced. I thought that if I could blend in, I would get along just fine.

What I have tried to do so far is to establish how state-sanctioned discourses, such as the policy on Canadian multiculturalism, articulated differences between a preferred dominant culture and an immigrant "other" in Canadian society as part of the nation-building project. These policies would have an effect on everyday attitudes towards people of color who were officially described as "visible minorities," that would range from racist taunts to physical violence. As I will show, experiences with racism are very common for Canadians born of immigrant "visible minority" parents. I will attempt to outline the significance of the experiences of second generation Canadian-born children of "visible minority" immigrants as it sheds light on how hegemonic forces compelled this generation to eschew their ethnic heritages, as I did, in an attempt to find acceptance in mainstream society.

While the immigrant experience in Canada has been well documented by academics such as Gerald Tulchinsky, with his 2008 book *Canada's Jews: A People's Story*, the 2011 book *The African Diaspora in Vancouver* by Gillian Creese, and Antona Fanella's 1999 ethnographic study *With Heart and Soul: Calgary's Italian Community*, the experience of the children of immigrants, in particular children of visible minority immigrants born in Canada, is still largely unexplored. A closer look at this particular group reveals a deeper understanding of not only the complexities of being "in between" but also the tactics and strategies employed by second generation Canadians to survive and thrive. One aspect of Canadian-born children of racialized immigrants that I argue is specific to second generation Canadians is the very notion of entitlement and the rights accorded by virtue of being born in Canada. As state rhetoric surrounding the multiculturalism policy was aimed at building a sense of national identity while surreptitiously defining the immigrant "other" from the dominant cultural majority, it would stand to reason that someone born in Canada would feel she/he had the edge over immigrants in terms of "rights" and privileges. As such, these veiled and problematic hierarchical distinctions recognizing settlers from immigrants are re-asserted between immigrants and Canadian-born children of immigrants. My own childhood survival instincts indicated that it was important to lay claim to my nationality, to say that I was Canadian, and to underscore and highlight that I was born in Canada. This would be an irrefutable fact to offer those who would question my location of birth and therefore my "place" in Canada. From my experience, this sense of a "national birthright" is a shared phenomenon amongst second generation Canadians and explains why there is great exasperation felt towards the continued asking of the question "Where are you from?" By way of an example from my own experience, in 1994 I was sending out an application for a grant to an arts council for my first art video *A Few Colorful Phrases*. Part of this video was about the very experience of being asked where I was from on a regular basis, despite having been born and raised in Canada. As if by some divine comedic intervention, the courier who came to pick up my envelope, a francophone Quebecois man of European heritage, actually asked me where I was from while I filled out the waybill. It was then that I was convinced beyond a shadow of a doubt that in mainstream culture people of color are not considered "from here." My desire, therefore, to assimilate into dominant culture was strongly motivated by the need to prove that, despite racialization, I was just as Canadian as the courier. The "where are you from?" question therefore revealed the underlying message that a racialized person of color must justify his or her presence in Canada. As a person in my early twenties, I felt this to be a racialized incident. Now I see that this person was, on a very general level, exhibiting his ignorance. My question then became one of a search for the roots of these attitudes. There are numerous cases of historically formed racialization in Canada, that include the experience of the first wave of Black people brought over as slaves in the late 1700s to build the city of Halifax, and of a second wave that arrived after escaping slavery in the United States during the late eighteenth and early nineteenth centuries. We can also note the internment of Japanese and Italian Canadians during the 1940s. And while very different in terms of narrative and scale, there is the ongoing cultural genocide of aboriginal peoples. Given my heritage, I was interested in the experience of the Chinese in Canada, who were subjected to large-scale attempts by the government to stave off and eventually stop the arrival of Chinese people to Canada altogether.

As Li (1988) explains, the early loss of control over Chinese immigration led to campaigns of anti-Asian xenophobia that shaped public, mainstream attitudes and perceptions of Chinese people and their Canadian-born children:

> Pseudo-scientific ideas about race were widely propagated during the colonial period, and the Chinese who went to British Columbia in the nineteenth century were immediately burdened with negative images and stereotypes. But it was the unequal conditions under which the Chinese were incorporated into the Canadian economy and society that gave new substance to racism. By the time Chinese labor was no longer required for the development of the west, anti-Orientalism had become a rallying principle that white politicians, labor unionists, workers, and employers alike could use to advance their immediate interests. As exclusion and segregation of the Chinese—politically, economically, and socially—became entrenched in Canadian society, the image of the Chinese as inferior was constantly reaffirmed and substantiated. (1988, p. 43)

This negative image of the Chinese was reinforced by Canadian legislation. The first major government action was the imposing of the first Chinese Immigration Act in 1885 which enforced a "head tax" of C$50 for every Chinese man, woman, or child arriving in Canada. Furthermore, as part of this Act, any Chinese person who took part in "the organization of any sort of court or tribunal, composed of Chinese persons, for the hearing and determination of any offence committed by a Chinese person" would be guilty of a misdemeanor, and subject to a fine of C$500, imprisonment for twelve months, or both. In 1900, the tax was increased to C$100 and then to C$500 in 1903. At this time, C$500 could buy two houses in Montreal, and this required sum effectively impoverished many Chinese. The head tax stayed in effect for thirty-eight years until 1923. The accumulated head taxes during this time amounted to C$23 million, which directly profited the Canadian government and provinces. Ironically, this amount was close to the cost of the construction of the western section of the Canadian Pacific Railway, built mainly by Chinese workers. In 1923, a second Immigration Act was implemented that replaced the head tax with an outright ban on most forms of Chinese immigration to Canada. In general, migration from most countries to Canada was controlled or restricted in some way, but only the Chinese were completely barred from immigration. As a result, families were separated for decades and this humiliating Act was finally repealed in 1947. However, independent Chinese immigration to Canada came only after the liberalization of the Canadian immigration policy in 1967. In the following passage, Li (1988) describes the impact of these legislations on Chinese-Canadians and their advancement in Canadian society.

> As long as Chinese-Canadians remain relatively few in number and confined to traditional immigrant enclaves in Canadian cities, they are tolerated as cultural novelties that help to celebrate Canada's multiculturalism and diversity. But as soon as Chinese-Canadians expand in number and excel economically and socially, their legitimate place in Canadian society comes into question, often on the superficial grounds that they represent a foreign culture with values and customs that are presumed to be incompatible with Canada's European traditions and established institutions. (1988, pp. 143–4)

Eva Mackey (2002) explored the opacity of the multiculturalism policy which effectively renders the "white" Canadian population blind to both the existence of a dominant culture and their privilege within it. She argued that because white Canadians buy into the government-led idea that they are "tolerant," they become oblivious to the reality of inequalities on the ground and in policy. In order to come to this conclusion, Mackey carried out field work in 1992, a period which saw a revitalization of the national identity question and the re-emergence of "identity politics" which coincided with the Canadian government's perception that there existed a "constitutional crisis." To mitigate the so-called crisis and to promote and reinforce a sense of Canadian identity, the government organized a campaign of festivities across Canada called "Canada 125." Mackey attended and studied these celebrations "designed to mobilise local people for patriotism and national unity" (2002, p. 7) as they offered a prime ethnographic opportunity to explore the "construction of national and local identities" (2002, p. 7). Her work entailed participant observation and interviews with people who attended these events as well as cultural workers and high-level bureaucrats involved in the "Canada 125" initiative. The results of her investigation and analysis allowed her to assemble a portrait of the attitudes of "ordinary" Canadians towards the concept of Canadian identity. Her study exposed some surprising truths for a country that promoted itself to the world as "open" and "tolerant." She explains:

One striking consistency in the interviews I did at small-town local festivals was the degree of anti-immigrant sentiment expressed in the language of populism, in a discourse of the oppressed and resistant "ordinary people." (1999, p. 33)

With this observation, a polemic was revealed between so-called "ordinary people" and immigrants that became particularly apparent when it came to the sharing of resources. Mackey asked white festival-goers to describe Canadian identity by posing a set of questions designed to gauge their reaction to the government's distribution of public money to help so-called "ethnic" communities organize special events. In general, the respondents believed that it was unfair to use "their" (public) money for these purposes. With these findings, Mackey concluded that while multiculturalism was an acceptable tool for promoting diversity on a superficial level, the true sharing of resources would come with serious reservations. Mackey's critical analysis further exposed the Canadian government's double message of promoting a multicultural face to the world while discreetly cultivating a culturally dominant one that is "unmarked, non-ethnic, and usually (a) white, '*Canadian*-Canadian' identity" (2002, p. 20). Rather than defending equality and plurality, the policy reinforced a model of normative national identity or a culture of "*Canadian*-Canadians," which failed to recognize that everyone in Canada, apart from aboriginal people, have arrived from somewhere else. Furthermore, the concept of the *Canadian*-Canadian ideal is inherently flawed because of the linguistic fracture line that is a result of English and French settler history that goes back to the founding of Canada. In this way, it is revealed that Canada never was, as in the case of all nation states, a homogenous and "purely" united culture, and the idea of a nation state is but a utopian one. Government rhetoric such as that surrounding multiculturalism reinforces dominant cultural norms through the structural forces of schools, government programs such as "Canada 125," and other cultural institutions, such as the Canadian Broadcasting Corporation (CBC) and the National Film Board of Canada (NFB) effectively telling us what "Canadian" is and looks like. The observations made by Li and Mackey support the hypothesis that a dominant Canadian culture has been formed and is reinforced by a range of hegemonic tools. What I contend is that the concept of an ideal Canadian has greatly impacted the children of immigrants born in Canada (second generation Canadians) and the connection that they have as adults, with their ethnic heritages.

In her thesis, *Ethnic Identity and Heritage Language Ability in Second Generation Canadians in Toronto* (2005), Bonnie Mah examines the link between heritage language, ethnic identity, and a sense of belonging to the community associated with one's ethnicity. The authors in her review of the literature found that the loss of heritage language, what they call the "language shift," contributes in a significant way to the "loss of ethnic identity, cultural fragmentation and 'non-authentic' expressions of ethnicity" (2005, p. 3). My experience as a Canadian-born daughter of visible minority immigrants demonstrated that the attempt to assimilate into dominant culture indeed resulted in the loss of heritage language(s) skills and this deficiency in turn compromised my sense of connection to my ethnic origins. The loss of language caused by an attempt at assimilation instilled a true feeling of distance from my Chinese roots, emphasized by my mixed heritage appearance. According to my research, this feeling of distance from one's ethnic heritage is particularly common for people of color in Canada. Scholar Farha Shariff shares my preoccupation with the importance of studying Canadian-born children of visible minority immigrants, as they are the first generation to be born in Canada as a result of major waves of immigration from non-European countries, and can tell us much about the formation of ethnic and national identities in the context of Canada's social power dynamics. In her article "Straddling the Cultural Divide: Second-Generation South Asian Identity and The Namesake" (2008), she explains:

The children of the post-1965 wave of immigrants are less visible in the media, and in academic literature. Although this group of second-generation Canadians have moved into adulthood and created their own social, personal, professional and familial spaces, their ethnic and national identity development has not been adequately researched. Exploration of second-generation Canadian identity is timely and significant in light of new research that questions the efficacy of official multiculturalism for the children of visible minority Canadians who exhibit "a more profound sense of exclusion than their parents" (2008, pp. 457–8).

According to Shariff's research, second generation Canadians, born around and after the adoption of the Canadian Multiculturalism policy, experienced racism and intolerance at both small and large scales, throughout their childhood and adolescence. Attempts at assimilation were part of a strategy of survival in an environment where normativity was greatly preferred over difference. I use "attempts" at assimilation to underscore the contention made by Homi K. Bhabha and others that for people of color, appearance inevitably excludes assimilation. Bhabha's famous formulation "almost the same, but not quite" from "Of Mimicry and Man: The ambivalence of colonial discourse" (1994), has also been paraphrased as "not quite/not white" to drive home how skin color is an immediately constant factor that precludes the completion of assimilation. These attempts at assimilation on a large scale have resulted in the loss of heritage language, the disappearance of any meaningful connection with the communities of one's ethnic backgrounds, and possibly a sense of betrayal by the "immigrant dream," where the idea of living in this land of plenty where all people would be equal has dissipated. Happily, however, my research also shows that children of immigrants born in Canada most often grow into their adulthood with confidence in their place in Canada, despite the ongoing "where are you from?" question. Furthermore, many have come to embrace their ethnic heritage(s) no matter the degree of its estrangement. With a cultural understanding of Canada firmly in place, empowered by the adversity of growing up "other" in their home country, there is now room for a desire to rediscover and re-connect with their eschewed ethnic heritages.

There are myriad ways to find communion with one's long lost ethnic origins. Food, music, dance, language lessons, and the observation of certain customs and holidays are among them. What I have discovered for myself is that wearing the cheongsam to experiment with the reclaiming of my Chinese heritage is highly significant. As mentioned earlier, my enthusiasm for the cheongsam was ignited by my grandmother, and is linked with a personal quest to locate and affirm my ethnicity while understanding more about the condition of my generation of Canadian-born women of Chinese heritage. As an artist, I wished to convey what I learned through the creation of an art installation that would express these findings through an abstract and poetic register while promoting dialogue and exchange.

Art of the cheongsam

The final manifestation of my research-based exploration of the cheongsam and its current wearing practices was the art installation *The Fitting Room* which was exhibited for one month in June of 2014. The cheongsam, which means "long dress" in Cantonese, has become internationally recognized as a symbol of Chinese cultural identity for women. Originating from a combination of Han and Manchu clothing styles, the ubiquitous cheongsam is an amalgamation of cultural, historical, and even political influences which shaped how it looks and what it symbolizes today. The characteristics of the ubiquitous cheongsam consist of a fitted dress, with a high collar, side slits and intricate fastenings called *huaniu*, commonly referred to as "frog" or "knot" buttons. Since childhood, my wardrobe has included a number of items of Chinese clothing. My mother would dress my sister and I in *hanfu*-style wraparound T-shirts and padded *ma gua* jackets. Throughout adolescence and into adulthood I have also worn a variety of cheongsam. Two of these dresses were custom made for my mother on her first trip to Hong Kong to meet my father's parents. Others were dresses that my grandmother had brought over from Hong Kong in the 1970s. I have also been partial to hybrid versions of the dress made by mainstream fashion retail brands, and more recently I became addicted to custom made cheongsam in wool and cotton that I have endeavored to wear on an everyday basis. I say *endeavored* because my wearing experiences combined with what I learned about the dress in the making of the exhibition and the writing of this book demonstrated that this is not as straightforward as I would like it to be. As I will explain, wearing the cheongsam is mired in a number of complex issues.

As mentioned earlier, I do not speak or read any Chinese language, nor do I "look" Chinese according to what I am told by Chinese people, when I tell them about my heritage. The expectations associated with a "typical" Chinese appearance can be linked with an essentialized notion of "Chineseness" perpetuated by China itself. While I will discuss this in more depth later, what I want to emphasize at this point is that the wearing of ethnic clothing such as the cheongsam has a way of declaring one's ethnicity to the outside world and can be employed, as I have done, to express one's affiliation with the community associated with that piece of ethnic clothing. At the same time, the wearing of ethnic clothing may pose a risk to those who do not wish to call attention to their ethnicity. As I have explained, the disavowal of my Chinese background was later displaced by a desire to be recognized as having Chinese roots. As I will show, the attraction/repulsion to the cheongsam is even more acute for women who feel their looks are undisputably Asian. With this and other tensions in mind, the garment offered a fascinating and vital site of exploration of the complicated meld of ethnicity, identity, and representation of Canadian-born women of Chinese heritage living in the Canadian context.

The employment of the art installation form, which in this case combined multi-channel video projection, sculptural objects, an audio montage, and site specificity, allowed for temporal and spatial freedom to present a complex, multi-sensory experience. As part of a research-based methodology I interviewed nineteen women of Chinese heritage born in Canada between 1968 and 1986, in order to gather current attitudes, impressions, and wearing practices of the dress. What aspects of this relationship might be static, while others are mutable or in flux? In terms of applying these findings to an art project, I wondered how these trans-cultural narratives presented in a specific place might reveal insights into the condition of second generation Canadians of Chinese heritage and resonate with recently arrived and long established members of the Chinese diaspora as well as non-Chinese people who have questions about their own link with ethnic heritage. What approaches might I employ that would support the multiplicity of opinions and experiences?

The making of *The Fitting Room* entailed a number of goals. First, I wanted to present the history of the cheongsam that would somehow suggest the inconsistencies of these accounts. I also wanted to illustrate its evolution as a result of historic, cultural, and political events in China. Another goal of the project was to trace the cheongsam's migration to Canada and to create object-based works that would relate the attitudes, ideas, and wearing practices shared by the women I interviewed. Furthermore, I wanted to propose how the selection and trying on of clothes is a unifying part of identity expression that is at once a vulnerable and affirmative act. As an overarching goal of this exhibition, I wanted this set of artworks, that pivot on a powerful cultural icon and artifact, to create a forum for a non-Chinese public, as well as the variegated Chinese community in Montreal, to reflect on and discuss the state of the Canadian-born Chinese diaspora. This latter experience exposed one of the most under-explored consequences of cross-cultural artforms: their potential to serve as community-based media for the open dissemination of advanced historical, socio-cultural research as well as working as forums for the exchange of ideas and opinions. The cheongsam, with its rich history that interweaves a diversity of narratives, provided an apt vehicle for the examination of ethnicity in flux, and the diaspora condition in an age of advanced globalization and the interrogation of national identity formation.

Cheongsam vs. qipao

The meaning of the word for this dress varies according to region and Chinese language. In mainland China and Taiwan, where the main language is Mandarin, this dress is referred to as *qipao*—*qi* which means "banner" or "flag" and *pao* which means "robe." *Qipao* is a direct reference to the clothing of the Manchu people. Also called *Qi* people or "Banner people," the Manchu ruled China during the Qing dynasty (1644—1911 CE), which would be the country's last. The term "banner" refers to the system of "Eight Banners" under which Manchu families were administratively organized.

In Hong Kong, where the predominant language of use has been Cantonese, the dress is most often referred to as *cheongsam* which means "long dress" or robe and refers to the one-piece garment first worn by Han men at the end of the Qing dynasty and later appropriated by women. The Chinese characters for this dress are the same whether it is for a man or a woman (旗袍).

Regarding this brief etymology of terms, it is clear that the term "qipao," contrary to many historians' explanations, is not merely the Mandarin word for cheongsam. The use of these terms unpacks the historical events and political struggles that shaped relations between Mainland China, Hong Kong, Singapore, and Taiwan, and in turn speaks to the importance of clothing and its use in carving out power relations. While knowledge of this garment and its subsequent influence came to me through my Cantonese-speaking grandmother and extended Chinese family, who lived in Hong Kong for many years, I have come to know this dress as the cheongsam and therefore privilege this term in my usage. In the interests of consistency of terminology throughout this book, I will use "cheongsam," even if *qipao* is used by a quoted author. I will maintain the word *qipao* only when it is used within a quote or employed in the title of a book or essay.

Laying out the pieces

The outcome of this book and *The Fitting Room* project reveal an unprecedented portrait of Canadian-born women of Chinese heritage through an exploration of the object and subject of the cheongsam. This garment raises social, cultural, and political questions that examine the meaning of clothing and the act of dressing, as it relates to the construction of identity, the representation of self, and the performance of the body.

In Chapter 2, I will provide an in-depth discussion on the concepts of identity, ethnic clothing, and art installation as they constitute the three threads that position and framework my treatment of the subject and object of the cheongsam. As the first thread, the concept of identity is informed by the seminal writings of Stuart Hall with more recent theorizations on identity politics formulated by Rosaura Sánchez and Alison Weir. An elaboration on the concept and uses of "hybridity" will follow to provide the basis for a discussion on identity in relation to Canadian-born women of Chinese heritage. The writings of Ien Ang and Peter S. Li provide a stimulating platform from which to consider the discourses of "Chineseness" and Otherness which impact on issues of identity formation for people of Chinese heritage. The consideration of theories of identity is also fundamental to my main research question, which aimed to engage with the power of the cheongsam to question notions of authenticity and representation, while examining how this dress shapes power dynamics connected with the expression of ethnicity. It is through these theoretical writings that I will further situate my critical perspectives, which will be illustrated through personal vignettes, and will also include an explanation of how I interpret the term "diaspora," in order to bring it more in line with the experience of being of Chinese heritage, born outside of China.

To explore the second thread, I will engage with the study and theorization of ethnic clothing through the writings of Margaret Maynard, Joanne B. Eicher and Sandra Niessen, Carla Jones and Ann Marie Leshcowicz. Each of them builds on the contention that ethnic dress is not simply a clear referent for a group with a common language, history, and culture. Instead, its meanings are mutable, changing, and have varied widely over time, a finding that challenges the notion that ethnic clothing is synonymous with tradition. These ideas, combined with Stuart Hall's foundational concept of the non-fixity of identity, allow us to consider the cheongsam as a tool of agency for Canadian women of Chinese heritage, to express and affirm their Chinese and Canadian heritages simultaneously, while finding empowerment through new modes of representation.

For the third thread, I will briefly discuss the birth and evolution of art installation as a form, to foreground the relevance of the application of the findings on the wearing of the cheongsam to the creation of *The Fitting Room*. What I will demonstrate is how art installation is an appropriate form for transmitting the complexity and richness of this investigation, as it is informed by a feminist and post-colonial critique that set out to challenge the status quo of the museum space and the way that art spaces have traditionally shaped how people view art.

I will end Chapter 2 with an outline of the methods I undertook for the interview process, as well as describing how ethnography, auto-ethnography, and historical research inform a holistic approach to this research and the transformation of these findings into an art project as a way of deeply engaging with a subject and object through a variety of sensory registers.

Chapter 3 is where I begin to set the stage for my own research material. In order to foreground this new information, I make use of the term "technology" informed by Ursula Franklin's book *The Real World of Technology*. In it she describes how technologies have the ability to discipline and impose certain practices which become normative and coercive over time, which I relate to the disciplining capabilities of the cheongsam. I will then sketch out an outline of the history and evolution of the dress in China up to the 1990s, through a synthesis of the historical work on the cheongsam by Hazel Clark, Wessie Ling (WESSIELING), Juanjuan Wu and Antonia Finnane. I will then provide an overview of the current status of the cheongsam in Mainland China, Hong Kong, and Taiwan from the early 2000s until 2017. Secondary sources including fashion websites and news articles will provide an update on the impressions, ideas, and wearing practices of the cheongsam by women in China and its territories through a discussion on the emergence of "cheongsam clubs" in urban centers such as Shanghai. I will also trace the cheongsam's current activity in the marketplace as reflected in the proliferation of cheongsam online clothing stores, fashion designers, and evidence of a new generation of cheongsam tailors. To close Chapter 3, I will chronicle the cheongsam's arrival and presence in Canada, sourcing the publication *Jin Guo: Voices of Chinese Canadian Women* in addition to the website database, *Chinese Canadian Women, 1923–1967: Inspiration—Innovation—Ingenuity* produced by the Multicultural History Society of Ontario. My analysis of this historical research will underscore my main argument that the cheongsam is a "complex" that consists of a set of established discourses that inform its status and quality as a "technology" shaped by historical, cultural, and political events in both China and Canada.

Chapter 4 presents the core of my original research, which I will undertake through an examination of the attitudes, ideas, and wearing practices of the dress gathered from interviews I carried out with nineteen Canadian-born women of Chinese heritage. These women were born in provinces across Canada between 1968 and 1986, the period just prior to and after the implementation of the Multiculturalism policy. They are the children of ethnic Chinese immigrants who arrived from Hong Kong, Taiwan, Mainland China, Malaysia, Viet Nam and Trinidad, mostly during the 1960s after Canadian immigration laws were relaxed. These women come from a variety of occupational backgrounds including student, elementary school teacher, cultural worker, marketing professional, university professor, animator, technical writer, graphic artist, and restaurant worker. This primary research reveals current wearing practices of the dress: whether women are wearing the dress or not, when and where it is worn, who can wear it, and what it means. What my analysis will show is that the dress inspires what I call the three "A"s ... a deep and complex ambivalence, an abiding interest in the concept of "authenticity," and an increasingly potent desire to wear the dress as a tool of agency. Long-term effects of xenophobia, the cheongsam's representation in mass media, and the very cut of the dress itself contribute to the garment's inspiration of ambivalence among all of the women I interviewed. The idea that the cheongsam must adhere to certain formal cues in order to be authentic is an apt analogy for the discourses on what consistutes authentic Chinese ethnicity. An exploration of this concept also reveals the struggle that women have on deciding who has the right to wear this dress. The third "A," agency, will be discussed with reference to Olivia Khoo's *The Chinese Exotic* in which she contends that changing power dynamics between China and the West have created emergent conditions of possibility for the expression of new, more empowering representations of Chinese identity. This "crack in the door" may permit Canadian-born women of Chinese heritage and other women of the Chinese diaspora around the world to embrace and assert an advanced expression of a mutable Chinese ethnicity in which cheongsam wearing can play a part. Ambivalence, authenticity, and agency will also constitute my main arguments about the current state of the cheongsam for Canadian women of Chinese heritage that will be summarized in the conclusion.

In Chapter 5, I will discuss the creation of *The Fitting Room* through a description of the three interrelated audio-visual and object based works as well as the thought process behind the selection of a specific, non-traditional site for the exhibition. I will also discuss the creative decisions behind each work that were further motivated by research into a range of topics including the history and applications of Chinese embroidery. To round out this chapter, a brief presentation and analysis of the reception of the exhibition will provide a sense of the discursive limits and possibilities for art that makes use of cultural specificity as a dialogic strategy. It will also present the state of receptivity to discussions about ethnicity and racialization in a contemporary Canadian, urban context such as Montreal.

In the final chapter I will lay out the conclusions that have come forth through the analysis of current wearing practices in relation to the historical, political, and cultural factors that bear on this garment. First, a number of mixed messages render the dress simultaneously intimidating and appealing for both women in China and Canadian-born women of Chinese heritage, whether they have worn the dress or not. These tensions ultimately underscore a relationship with the cheongsam that I qualify as ambivalent. Second, a number of entrenched discourses govern the perception of the dress and affect how, when, and where it can be worn which qualify the dress as a technology and show how the cheongsam inspires a preoccupation with the notion of authenticity. Third, I will discuss how the cheongsam is beginning to be worn as a tool of agency to express an evolved, mutable ethnic identity that takes diaspora and its contexts and experiences into consideration. In order for the cheongsam to survive into the future, I contend that it must evolve in a way that incorporates values and desires that are fueled by a feminist critique of the dress. Among my personal assertions, I contend that a more diverse range of cheongsam cuts would allow for more women to incorporate the garment into their everyday wardrobes, offering them a meaningful and progressive way to assert an empowered representation of Chinese ethnic identity, particularly in diaspora contexts as migration and globalization continue to increase.

The subject of ethnic identity for children of immigrants in Canada is complex and often brings forth emotions and memories that have long been suppressed. The consideration of ethnic clothing offers diaspora people of color a way to articulate the complexity of their own stories which include their family's chronicle of immigration and forced migration as well as experiences of racialization in a relatively young country such as Canada. These stories have a significant bearing on the construction of identity both inside and outside of the discourses of nationality. They are telling of the power dynamics that are embedded in history and enforced through culture, language, customs, and traditions. Wearing the cheongsam has been a way for me to channel women like my grandmother Charlotte who represents strength, beauty, courage, and intelligence. Putting on this garment has been a subversive gesture to disrupt expectations and conjecture formed by problematic characterizations of Chinese women in popular Western culture. Wearing this dress also affirms a connection to my Chinese heritage which I feel has been lost in a bid for assimilation into Canadian mainstream culture. But what I deeply feel has been gained is an understanding that these experiences are key to accessing the freedom to be something new.

CHAPTER 2
DETERMINING THE "FABRIC"

The creation of a garment begins with an understanding of its design, cut and desired fit. Next comes a deliberation over the material from which it will be made. How will it drape, envelope, or flow on the body? At what point does the design of the garment dictate what types of fabric and weave will work best? Establishing these decisions is analogous to the construction of the conceptual knit that informed this investigation and its eventual application to the art installation project, *The Fitting Room*. It consists of the interlocking of three major threads: identity, ethnic clothing, and the birth and evolution of installation art, a form that issues from critical feminist and post-colonial theoretical perspectives. Cheongsam wearing is bound up with identity formation that is both in flux, and influenced by a set of what I consider interior and exterior factors. Interior factors include class, education, language(s) spoken at home, customs and traditions practiced in the family, and early socialization. Culture, history, geography, and "official" language, customs, and traditions of the "new" country comprise exterior factors. An analysis of current explorations of the concept of identity provides context for the considerations that influence the wearing or not wearing of the cheongsam. Ethnic clothing and the circumstances of its wearing by people both in their home countries and as they move around the globe has been the subject of much study. The way that people negotiate the wearing of ethnic clothing in an era of advanced globalization and forced migration contributes to a contemporary understanding of the perception of the cheongsam and its wearability. I will also discuss the history of art installation as a form, to explain its relevance to the presentation of the sociological nature of the questions posed by this investigation. Historically, artists have taken up art installation for its capacity to engage with visitors beyond the dominant regime of the visual register. As a form that emerged from a need by artists to challenge these norms, installation art would be the most advantageous to this project for the purposes of calling attention to the power dynamics that have shaped thoughts, attitudes, and ideas about ethnicity, nationality, "race," and gender.

Identity, hybridity and the Banana Syndrome

Art historian Jennifer González describes Stuart Hall as having been the one "who has perhaps done the most to successfully articulate the progressive possibilities and pitfalls of the concept of identity and the complex histories of identification that work through it" (González, 2008, p. 11). Indeed Hall's seminal essay "Cultural Identity and Diaspora" (1994) had a profound and transformative effect on me. It was Hall who contributed the game-changing concept that identity is a 'production,' which is never complete, always in process, and always constituted within, not outside, representation" (1994, p. 222). Identity is a flexible and variable concept and therefore cannot be predetermined. It is informed by the external variables of place, history, culture, and class, as well as personal experiences that are always changing and evolving. In this way, the idea that identity is non-fixed can be a potent and empowering concept for second generation Canadians who are looking for ways to reconcile the multiple aspects of their cultural identities in a context that constantly endeavors to put people and things into neat categories. As briefly discussed in the Introduction, I am often asked in my own country of birth where I am from. Each of the women I interviewed for *The Fitting Room* had this same experience growing up, and this type of questioning persists today. Answers to this question vary, depending on the context and the person who is doing the asking. For each of these women, however, the question "where are you from?" continues to give pause, sending them into a frozen moment where they must at once consider their place of birth, their ethnic heritage, and their social and cultural conditioning, when forced to realize that assumptions have been prompted by their external appearance. In her chapter entitled "On a Critical Realist Theory of Identity" from *Identity Politics Reconsidered* (2006), Rosaura Sánchez affirms that "identities are necessarily also multiple" (p. 41) and argues for what she calls a "critical realist politics of identity" (p. 32) as a way to locate agency and self-determination for people of color systemically disenfranchised by "race" and class. What was most helpful to my project was her distinction between the terms "identity" and "identification," a differentiation which helps to articulate the potential for emancipation, through both a collective and an individual sense of identity. Sánchez writes that identification is:

> [. . .] a relational and discursive process that is always linked to a group or collectivity that is contained within a particular social space . . . it

can emerge from outside or from within a social group or space. (2006, pp. 39–40)

For Canadian-born people of Chinese heritage, experiences with racism and racialization at an early age were part of an externally generated "identification" formation process, whose visceral effects have mutated over time. For many of the women I interviewed, the effect was initially what Sánchez termed "non-identification" with their Chinese heritage. Later on in life, however, this distancing or rejection would transform into a vital re-identification with their Chinese heritage that would bring solace and empowerment through connection with a larger community of Canadian-born people of Chinese heritage. Sánchez's theory of identity takes individual subjectivity into consideration and connects it to a collective group sensibility that shares a similar experience. Identity is therefore defined as:

[…] always agential; it involves an awareness of identification as a containment process and entails a conscious acceptance of a designation, that is, of a discourse, whether it be imposed from the outside or generated within a group. (2006, p. 41)

In this way, identification imposed by external forces can be simultaneously limiting and emancipating, while impacting on one's sense of identity, which as Sánchez contends is, above all, "a discourse that serves to mediate between the individual and the world" (2006, p. 42). Many things inform this discourse, including the process and effects of identification, which together, according to Sánchez, can contribute to a sense of identity that is self-affirmed and ultimately liberating. She illustrates the relationship between identity and identification through the situation of Latinos who grew up in the predominantly white communities of the Midwest of the United States. She argues that once they migrated to bigger cities, they began to experience racialization, which made them "acutely aware of the identification process and of their designation as members of a particular group. At that point, their positionality is forced to undergo a major shift" (2006, p. 41). While they came to their own sense of identity through a process of individual evolution, they were also nurtured by factors such as family, school, and community. Once they came into contact with racialization, their sense of identity was forever altered, and choices were made—agency was enacted—that brought about either a process of incorporation (identification) or a process of disavowal (non-identification). What is clear in her argument is that identity and identification become linked through the realities of racialization and the perpetuation of discourses of ethnic "difference."

Alison Weir reinforces this idea in "Identities and Freedoms: Feminist Theory Between Power and Connection" (2013). Troubled by the critique of identity politics within academic circles, Weir attempted to take apart the notion of identity as "shackle" to show how identities are "sources of resistance" (2013, p. 2), that "... are better understood as complex, rather than paradoxical," and that can be "recognized as sources of important values: of connections to ourselves, to each other, and to ideals; and that these in turn constitute sources of freedom for individuals and collectives" (2013, p. 3). The heart of Weir's argument echoes Sánchez's distinction between identification and identity and takes it a step further with the contention that:

[...] understanding identities as sources of freedom requires that we differentiate identity as category from identity as connection to and identification with ideals, each other and defining communities. Thus it involves a shift from a metaphysical to an ethical, political conception of identities, and to a focus on practical, ethical, and political identifications as practices of freedom. (2013, p. 3)

For Canadian-born women of Chinese heritage, Weir's concept can help to get beyond the limitations of an essentialized notion of what it means to be Chinese or to be of Chinese heritage to allow for the inclusion and assertion of the multitude of complex and heterogeneous aspects of one's ethnic identity. For the women I interviewed, this can allow for the simultaneous embracing of a connection with Canadian-ness, with being of mixed heritage, reconciling these with a desire to feel a sense of belonging or acceptance within a larger culture, community, or country. Taken together, Stuart Hall's seminal writings, and Rosaura Sánchez and Alison Weir's more recent theorizations on identity provide a productive framework that can be used to advance the discussion on identity and, in particular, ethnic identity today.

Hall's declaration that identity is "constituted within, not outside, representation" (1993, p. 222) aptly gets inside of "race discourse" to unravel the effects of media on people of color in Canada. Jennifer A. González describes "race discourse" as "the politics of representation ... that insists on presenting people as 'racialized' subjects" (2008, p. 3). Race discourse is insidiously re-asserted in mass media as people of color have been either depicted stereotypically or are altogether absent from mainstream images. The under-representation and misrepresentation of people of color, including Asian women in Hollywood cinema, television, magazines, advertising, and other media, have had a profound impact on the women I interviewed. The dearth of people of color in mainstream media effectively delineated the margins from the center, contributing to self-esteem issues and in many cases, as mentioned earlier, an instilling of internalized racism which resulted in the disavowal of Chinese heritage for the women I interviewed. What few images there were of Asian women in mainstream entertainment media were often limited to colonialist fantasies, such as the "dragon lady" or "tragic prostitute." These limiting and even damaging characterizations were challenged by cultural workers in Canada and the US in two waves. The first was in the 1960s, when artists and academics were bolstered by the Civil Rights Movement to address issues of "race" and representation in Canadian society. In the early 1990s, a second wave of cultural workers, artists, and academics came together to raise awareness of the racialized depictions of people of color and indigenous people in mainstream media as well as the insitutionalized racism that kept their work outside of museums, galleries, and movie theaters.[1] This coincided with the upsurge of post-colonial theory and theories on identity politics and representation in academic discourse in the US, UK, and Australia. Slowly and painfully, more critical awareness emerged in Canadian institutions and resulted in concrete steps forward for the acknowledgement of the contribution of and participation in the creation of visual culture by people of color and indigenous people. As more of us managed to get behind the camera, the presence of non-racialized representations of people of color and indigenous people in mainstream media increased. I began to notice that more television news journalists and actors of Asian heritage started to appear more regularly on the big and small screens. Through that acknowledgement, it slowly started to seem possible for Canadians of Chinese heritage to not only re-claim but proclaim their Chinese ethnicity. In relation to my study, as the women I interviewed grew into adults who became fully confident in their ability to negotiate the Canadian terrain, it became increasingly important for them to re-connect with their estranged ethnic identities. This shift was crucial as it substantiated the power of images to feed the re-imagining of one's own identity, affecting a re-inscription of one's process of identification in external social structures.

In attempts to carve out my own sense of identity and how I wanted to represent myself, I have gone back and forth over the use of "hybridity" as a theoretical concept that might epitomize my experience as a mixed heritage woman of color. The idea of hybridity, as I understood it, independent of scholarly theory, was a positive one, allowing me to be all aspects of my ethnic heritages while acknowledging my upbringing in Canadian-Canadian culture. My aforementioned first video work, A Few Colourful Phrases (1995), dealt specifically with the reconciliation of my identity as "multiple," which I argued was the situation for most people in Canada. My eventual contact with hybridity in post-colonial theory seemed to articulate what I had been doing instinctively all along. In The Location of Culture (1994), Homi Bhabha states that a strategy of hybridity:

> ...unsettles the mimetic or narcissistic demands of colonial power but reimplicates its identifications in strategies of subversion that turn the gaze of the discriminated back upon the eye of power. (1994, pp. 159–60)

Bhabha's definition of hybridity appealed to me, as it affirmed the notion that my knowledge of the dominant culture could be employed for my own empowerment. While the need for assimilation had eclipsed the learning of my heritage languages, assimilation attempts informed me on how to gain fluency in the navigation of mainstream culture, or in Bhabha's sense, to use hybridity as a strategy of subversion. There are, however, conditions of possibility that distinguish my situation, such as my middle-class economic status which provided the means for the gaining of knowledge through travel (mobility) and post-secondary education. The issue of class points to some of the limitations of Bhabha's concept of hybridity which has been criticized for not fully considering the material and historical factors that put restrictions on a person or group's agency. Bhabha's concept has also been attacked for not constituting a truly subversive act that risks the re-inscription of a stereotyped ideal of a properly assimilated, "colorful," and visible post-colonial subject or "model minority." While these limitations have validity, what becomes crucial is not to throw out the concept of "hybridity" altogether, but to approach it with unflinching criticality, as Ien Ang does in her book On Not Speaking Chinese (2001).

> What we need to question, then, is not so much hybridity as such, which would be a futile enterprise, but the depoliticization involved in the reduction of hybridity to happy fusion and synthesis. I would argue that it is the *ambivalence* which is immanent to hybridity that

needs to be highlighted, as we also need to examine the *specific contexts and conditions* in which hybridity operates. (2001, p. 197)

Ang contends that for postcolonial and cultural theorists such as Stuart Hall, Paul Gilroy, Trinh Minh-ha, Homi Bhabha, and others, hybridity has "explicitly critical political purchase" (2001, p. 98). She describes how hybridity can find its political expression through Hall and Gilroy's enunciation of a "hybrid speaking position they call 'Black British'—a mode of self-representation designed to interrogate hegemonic 'white' definitions of British national identity by interjecting it with blackness" (2001, p. 98). Similarly, I can see how I have capitalized on the knowledge gained from my insider/outsider position, for the negotiation of all situations where I am marked Other. Bolstered by Ang's writings, hybridity therefore remains a vital strategy in my work and describes my artistic approach from both conceptual and political standpoints. The type of hybridity that appeals to me is in keeping with Ang's assertion that it "is a sign of challenge and altercation, not of congenial amalgamation or merger" (2001, p. 98). As an artistic approach, a strategy of hybridity reflects a conceptual desire to use forms and genres in various combinations to allow for an ongoing mutability and flexibility in creation. From a political standpoint, hybridity employs tactics of *combining* that can call attention to historically and culturally formed unequal relations of power. It is this *combining* strategy that has brought me to the subject of the cheongsam itself. Writer/historian Hazel Clark and artist/scholar WESSIELING contend that the cheongsam is a hybrid dress whose components can vary while maintaining a Chinese identity. As long as basic elements of the dress, such as the stiff, high collar and one piece base, are maintained it is possible to play with the fabric and other elements such as sleeve length or the addition of other adornments in order to make an unlimited number of combinations and statements. Even in the 1920s and 1930s, women were playing with these variables to express personal taste and style. In the case of *The Fitting Room* however, the kind of statement that I was interested in making, aimed at using—in Ang's words—the "interrogative effects" of hybridity to explore the experiences of Canadian-born women of Chinese heritage. In addition to making several cheongsams that would speak to the current condition of Canadian-born women of Chinese heritage, *The Fitting Room* examined critical strategies of hybridity that were reflected in current wearing practices. Likewise, these acts sought to question the dominant hegemonic "white" definitions of Canadian national identity by injecting "Chinese-ness" into them. But I would argue that they go even further, to question the dominant and essentialist ideas about what constitutes the concept of an ideal Chinese identity.

Taking into consideration Hall's description of identity as always in flux, writers and theorists have struggled with the impossible task of using words to name an identity in a way that considers nationality, ethnicity, and culture simultaneously. Chinese-Canadian, Asian-Canadian, Can-Asian, are all attempts to describe the multiplicity of identity of those of Chinese descent who immigrated to Canada or who were born in Canada. In "Bold Omissions and Minute Depictions" (1991), Trinh T. Minh-Ha discusses the use of the hyphen as it is applied in "Asian-American" as a way to acknowledge the "realm in-between, where predetermined rules cannot fully apply" (1991, p. 84). Bringing "Asian" into contact with "American" through the porous hyphen indicates a transitional condition as well as the tension of living in the interstices that is not limited to two or more cultures but extends into a deeper understanding of living in between and the knowledge that it can produce.

The "Chinese" in Chinese-Canadian is also fraught with its own set of power dynamics. When my parents would take me to Chinatown, I often heard Chinese people refer to me as *jook sing*, which means "hollow bamboo" in Cantonese. While I was not sure what it meant at the time, I got the feeling that it set me apart from other "real" Chinese. As an adult, I remember going into an herb shop in Montreal's Chinatown with two friends who are also Canadian-born of Chinese heritage. They, however, were able to speak a little bit of the Toisanese dialect. I had a very bad cold and they encouraged me to get a specific medicine. The shopkeeper addressed me in Toisanese and when I stared back at her, actually quite ashamed that I could not speak to her in "our" language, my friends stepped in. While I could not understand exactly what they were saying, I could recognize the conciliatory tone as they explained that I was born in Canada and did not speak Chinese, to which the shopkeeper replied, "Ah, *jook sing*." I was mortified. Experiences like these contributed to my insecurity about claiming and asserting my Chinese heritage. Not speaking or looking Chinese created a distance from a community and it nurtured a fear of losing connection with my own family. Being called *jook sing*, therefore, created a feeling of alienation for most of my adult life until I came upon "The Banana Blog: Echoes of the Jook Sing Generation."[2] The first topic of this new blog, launched on 30 June 2002, was about the term "banana" which is used mostly among Canadian-born people of Chinese heritage to describe our Westernization—or more bluntly—our "yellowness" on the outside and "whiteness" on the inside. The question posed was: "What is your definition of 'banana' as it relates to Chinese-Canadians?" As I began to read, my relationship to the term *jook sing* and the even more dreaded "banana" started to open and evolve. The first contributor to the blog wrote:

> To me, a banana is someone who is Chinese but "westernized" to the extent such that they cannot even speak or understand Chinese.
>
> A Chinese-Canadian is not automatically a banana. Most are "jook sing," while others are "westernized Chinese"; a "jook sing" being one who has some of both Chinese and Western values but not all of either culture, while a "westernized Chinese" is one who has mainly Chinese values with some Western ones so that they can adapt to this western society better.
>
> Then there are those who consider themselves "Chinese" and not Chinese-Canadians, regardless of the number of years they have lived here. Those are the ones who do not try to or wish to fit in and believe that they are "better" than everyone who is a "Chinese-Canadian." They also seem to be the ones that believe ALL CBC's (Canadian-Born-Chinese) are automatically bananas and make it seem like being a CBC makes one a social outcast. To them, anyone that is not "Chinese" is a banana.

Jook sing was not necessarily the ostracizing label I thought it was, and the term "banana" was also starting to lose its sting. Another contributor to the Banana Blog wrote:

> Other than a delicious fruit and phallic symbol the word banana has been used derogatively by others to describe a Chinese person (yellow on the outside) who thinks, acts, and talks like a white person (white on the inside). So if you can speak, read and write Chinese do you count as a banana?
>
> It is high time we reclaimed this word. We shouldn't be afraid to call ourselves Banana. It's not just used derisively by other people—but mostly by our own people.
>
> There is another alternative moniker, the CBC (Canadian Born Chinese). Though it is definitely more politically correct it still leaves a chasm in a description of the modern asian canadian. In theory it's a good label but in practice the CBCs who grew up in very Asian areas

such as Vancouver and parts of Toronto are closer to FOBs (fresh off the boat, new rich immigrants) on a scale.

...Truth is, what if you're neither a complete Banana and not technically a CBC, only you have a dash of FOB stirred in? What category do you belong to?

While offering a comprehensive inventory of the nuanced monikers that have been coined to describe being Chinese in Canada, this last entry also expresses how the existence of a fixed and reduced identity is virtually impossible. In the spirit of Stuart Hall, the writer then ends their entry with a call to "stop trying to label ourselves so definitively." The "Banana Blog" offers a first hand account of the complexity of identification and identity and does much to help confront feelings of shame and guilt about the loss of heritage language and culture. Likewise, Ien Ang (2001) casts a critical eye on the discourse formations around what constitutes "Chinese-ness," which, like the term "banana," circulates within Chinese communities. Drawing on Tu Wei-ming's collection *The Living Tree: The Changing Meaning of Being Chinese Today* (1995), she explores the source and construction of an essentialized Chinese identity that serves to haunt the Chinese diaspora, effectively limiting its ability to find comfort and stability in its inevitable evolution. She writes:

The notion of a single centre or cultural core, from which Chinese civilization has emanated—the so-called Central Country complex— has been so deeply entrenched in the Chinese historical imagination that it is difficult to disentangle our understandings of Chineseness from it. (Ang, 2001, p. 41)

In response to the Central Country complex, Tu Wei-ming contributes the notion of "cultural China," which Ang describes as a "symbolic universe" (Ang, 2001, p. 40) in order to de-center the Central Country complex. With "cultural China," Tu attempts to open up an essentialized "ideal" of Chineseness—one that is defined as "belonging to the Han race, being born in China proper, speaking Mandarin and observing the 'patriotic' code of ethics" (in Ang, 2001 p. 41) by challenging the claims made by Beijing, Taipei, Hong Kong, and even Singapore to be the "ultimate authority" in defining Chineseness. In issuing this challenge, Tu wishes to open up ideas of Chinese identity, and to "explore the fluidity of Chineseness as a layered and contexted discourse, to open new possibilities and avenues of inquiry" (Ang, 2001,

p. 41). Through this exploration taken up by Ang, the periphery, or Chinese outside of China, may gain the agency required to assert their realities, significance, and contribution to the freeing of a durable and reductive definition of "Chineseness." Combining forces, the Banana Blog, along with Ang and Tu's writings, helped me to consider how to articulate the situation of second generation Canadian-born people of Chinese heritage and the significance of the cheongsam.

The question of "Chineseness" is important because of what it contributes to the concept of diaspora and the limitations of this term. Returning to "monikers" for a moment, Sean Metzger proposes the term "Sino/American" in *Chinese Looks: Fashion, Performance, Race* (2014), and takes specific items of clothing as a lens through which to examine the changing relations between the United States and China over the last 150 years. Metzger's use of "Sino/American" is inspired by David Palumbo-Liu's (1999) "Asian/American." Metzger and Palumbo-Liu prefer the slash as a way to better indicate the "sliding over or 'transitivity' between two always undecided terms" (Metzger, 2014, p. 9). Metzger privileges the term Sino/American as a way to name the interface that facilitates his analysis of the changing power relations between the US and China. In this way, he clarifies his area of study so that it does not become confused with the substantive terms "Asian American" or "Chinese American." I have also been inspired to re-examine the terminology I use to describe the participants in *The Fitting Room* in order to articulate the specificities and significance of my particular target group. In the very early stages of research, I referred to the participants in this study as "diasporic Chinese women." Through further research on theories of diaspora, it became clear that while we are part of the Chinese diaspora in the literal sense, we are most often not so in the ideological sense. The etymology of the term diaspora refers to the dispersal of the Jews, but is now commonly used to refer to people who have left a "homeland" and are now scattered across the globe in a variety of places and nations. What marks the term diaspora, in an ideological sense, is that it refers to an intense longing for the homeland. For the women in the interviews, myself included, there can be no longing for a place that was never truly known. Again, I refer to Ien Ang who states that "(w)hat connects the diaspora to the 'homeland' is ultimately an emotional and almost visceral attachment" (2001, p. 32). While the participants are able to eloquently discuss their connection or lack thereof to their Chinese heritage, they do not speak about China in these ways. It is, therefore, not this aspect of the diasporic condition that interests me for this study. What is most pertinent to my exploration is the situation of women of Chinese heritage who were born in Canada at a particular time in history, a period which served to unsettle an understanding of the basic tenets of ethnicity. This is why I privilege the more precise use of "Canadian-born women of Chinese heritage" throughout this book.

Seen in this light, the cheongsam can be used to assess the ineffable quality of what it means to be of Chinese heritage in Canada today. In concert with my exploration of theories of identity, the research that I carried out reveals how the desire to foster a multiple and evolving expression of identity is of major importance to Canadian-born people of Chinese heritage. What I have attempted to convey here is that identity is a central conceptual thread that is integral to the complex and textured mesh that characterizes the relationship between the cheongsam and Canadian-born women of Chinese heritage.

Ethnic clothing

Before getting into a discussion of ethnic clothing, I would like to back up and address the term "ethnicity." In *Race and Ethnic Relations in Canada* (1990), Peter S. Li explains that ethnicity is "ascribed, or given at birth" and that the "important aspect of an ethnic group is that its members share a sense of peoplehood or identity based on descent, language, religion, tradition or other common experiences" (Li, 1990, p. 5). These common experiences also include the wearing of specific items of clothing designed and worn to distinguish one's ethnicity and belonging to this group. It will be revealed that ethnic clothing is not static, as globalization and migration inevitably reconfigure the modes of ethnicity.

The significance, meaning, and wearing practices of ethnic clothing have been undertaken in a number of studies. In *Dress and Ethnicity: Change Across Space and Time* (1995), Joanne B. Eicher examined the role of dress as a "sensory system of non-verbal communication" (1995, p. 5) and its link with and expression of ethnicity. Her research demonstrated that ethnic clothing is more than just a clear referent for a group of people who share the same language, history, and culture. Ethnic clothing takes many social and cultural factors into consideration that can be employed as a way for people to distinguish themselves and to "communicate their actual or desired autonomy" (1995, p. 305). Eicher also offered a clarification of terms and definitions for the words "clothing," "dress," and "fashion," which she felt were mistakenly used interchangeably. Not all clothing is fashionable dress, "fashion" is not limited only to dress, and "clothing" is only one aspect of dress. Yet, in order to examine these more distinct terms in relation to ethnic clothing, Eicher proposed the concept of "world fashion." "World fashion" refers to the dressing practices and garments of ordinary everyday people, set apart from "high fashion," which she described as "a dominant or monolithic fashion with exclusive, custom-made creations found in designer salons" (1995, p. 300). While "world fashion," like "high fashion," changes quickly over time, from year to year and season to season, Eicher argued that "ethnic dress," in contrast, implies "non-fashionable dress, dress that reflects the past with slow change and few modernizing influences," (1995, p. 301) and is "worn and displayed to signify cultural heritage"(1995, p. 299). While Eicher affirms that ethnic clothing is worn as a way to indicate connection with the group associated with that ethnicity, she was careful to qualify that this takes into consideration the understanding that the term "ethnicity" is also fluid and contingent as individuals move through space and time. In many ways, the cheongsam corresponds with aspects of this definition. The China-born garment was influenced by historical and cultural factors, and designated the representative garment of Chinese culture for women. As I will discuss in depth later, there exists an image of a ubiquitous cheongsam that has been nurtured and stays fixed in the popular imagination. At the same time, the versatility of the cheongsam has made it a fashion item par excellence since the 1930s. As the dress continues to capture the imagination of fashion designers around the world, the cheongsam lends itself well to modifications and hybridization to stay in step with contemporary trends and avant garde imaginings. As we will see later, the cheongsam became a staple garment for women up until the 1970s in places like Hong Kong, Singapore and Taipei. In these cities, the cheongsam transcended its role of national dress to become part of everyday dressing. In other words, the cheongsam could be considered at once both ethnic clothing and fashion. As I have emphasized previously, the paradoxical nature of the cheongsam and its ability to be both in and out of time make this garment a formidable analogy for the examination of identity and ethnicity.

In *Dress and Globalization* (2004), Margaret Maynard built on Eicher's work and employed a political economy perspective to examine the "ways in which cultures interact and engage with each other at the level of appearance" (2004, p. 13). What she found is that the dominant flow of Western clothing around the world has not had a homogenizing effect on dressing, but that, rather, "(in) non-western cultures, acceptance, rejection or a combination of western and traditional clothing is highly variable, complex and constantly changing" (2004, p. 27). To substantiate this contention Maynard brought the subject of ethnic clothing into dialogue with the process of globalization, which she traces back to the worldwide social and economic crises of 1968–71. The fall of the Eastern Bloc, economic reforms in China, the US real estate boom of the 1980s, the "social changes brought about by postcolonial rule and the changing, flexible rhythms of post Fordist production and outsources; the rise of multinational corporations; the globalization and finance systems and not least, the growth of world media networks and e-revolution" all contributed to an increasing flow of capital, culture, and ideas between countries and states. The growing interaction brought about cultural influence and exchange. Through globalization, the ethnic clothing of one country could have an influence on the style and dressing practices in another. How would this affect and alter the role and place that ethnic clothing has for people around the world? How does ethnic clothing retain relevance for diasporic people? How might an understanding of globalization and its effects on ethnic clothing inform an inquiry into the complex relationship between the cheongsam and Canadian-born women of Chinese heritage? The cheongsam is not an object of the past that has been cast aside. Rather, it continues to be a conduit through which to express the contemporary condition of complex identities in an advanced, globalized world. Not only can ethnic clothing be worn to demonstrate a connection, or desire for connection, with one's ethnic identity, it can be modified, embellished, or styled in a way that communicates multiple and even contradictory messages.

Also of interest to my study are Maynard's findings that demonstrate how "people use [clothing] tactically, to define, to present, to communicate, to deceive, to play with . . ." (2004, p. 5). Her work examines how people actively choose what they want to wear and how they would like to wear it, exercising agency through clothing. These choices can be influenced by a number of overlapping factors including socio-economic background, political viewpoints, as well as climate and geography. She cites a number of examples to demonstrate her claims, such as the case of "les sapeurs" from the Democratic Republic of the Congo. "La Sape" is a social movement that emerged in Brazzaville and is based on the acronym that stands for "*Société des Ambianceurs et des Personnes Élégantes*" (The Society of Ambiance Makers and Elegant Persons). Those engaged with the "*sapeurs*" movement are mostly men, who select and wear clothing that evokes the "dandyism" of the colonialist past as a form of resistance. According to the website dandy. org, "dandyism" emerged in England in the early 1800s. At that time, England had taken over the role of central cultural influence from France which reeled from its revolution. A figure by the name of George Bryan Brummel, also known as "Beau" Brummel, is credited with being the first dandy. He caused a sensation when he became friends with the Prince Regent and was considered "one of the most influential, and even powerful men in the nation, not by his birthright, or education, or military prowess, or scholastic accomplishment . . . but by being well dressed." Brummel launched a kind of new male representation that would be employed in literary texts such as Oscar Wilde's *The Picture of Dorian Gray*. Another important aspect of the figure of the dandy was his ability to dwell within the world of his "betters" as his insider/outsider status informed him of the upper classes and allowed him greater mobility. This tactical knowledge is similar for the *sapeurs* who employ Western clothing to express anti-colonial sentiments. *La Sape* offered a refuge from the difficulties of the experience of marginalization in Europe as many Congolese men were forced to immigrate to big cities such as London and Paris. *Les sapeurs* are a prime example of how clothing, in combination with performance and wearing practices, can become a vehicle of expression and agency in a context of uneven power dynamics.

Closer to home in North America, the Civil Rights Movement greatly inspired an increased sense of expression of affirmation of Black identity in the United States. The "afro" and the wearing of the West African *dashiki* are examples of popular hair and clothing styles that were adopted on a large scale as a way to reflect Black pride as well as the rejection of conformity to White American culture as cited by Walter Keenan in *Walking on Water: Black American Lives at the Turn of the Twenty-first Century* (1999). The wearing of the afro was also a symbol of Black self-esteem behind the "Black is beautiful" movement. These gestures were symbolic of resistance and agency for a large group of people connected through their shared history and struggle for emancipation.

Also significant to my research is Maynard's finding that ethnic clothing is not stagnant but rather evolves and changes while retaining its association with ethnicity, particularly when it comes to the migration of people.

As part of mutation within diasporic migrations and shifts, ethnic identities in new countries have been shown not to mirror precisely practices in the homeland, but rather, use a range of sources to shape new ways of doing things. (Maynard, 2004, p. 72)

To illustrate this point she presented a number of cases from around the world, including a study of Arab-speaking youth in south western areas of

Sydney, Australia, who employ a mix of Western clothing and ethnic clothing to exercise what Maynard termed "strategic hybridity" (2004, p. 72). This strategy brings together the clothing of mainstream culture with clothing that asserts ethnic heritage and allows people a way to negotiate their subject positions and to show the mainstream that while they understand the norms of society, they will excercise them on their own terms, using clothing to express a savvy navigation of cross-cultural spaces. Examples such as this support Maynard's main argument that ethnic clothing and its wearing practices are fluid and subject to evolution and change, contingent on the strategies of the wearer. As she explains:

> The term "ethnic" clothing becomes impossible to fix with any degree of certainty, however tempting. It is not exclusively hybrid clothing but attire chosen by the wearer for particular reasons and used in particular ways in different situations. Thus ethnic dress must be thought of as relational. It is attire in which the components are never absolutely static or "frozen," but in continual process. (2004, p. 73)

The women I interviewed aptly demonstrate Maynard's point. Those who choose to wear the cheongsam do so under a very specific set of circumstances. Many women only wear this dress to family occasions or special events that propose a context where they feel they will not be questioned or receive unwanted or inappropriate attention. Some have worn a semi-Western version or a store-bought version in combination with Western clothing to demonstrate a strategy of hybridity, while others are on the lookout for more casual-looking cheongsams to assert and affirm their connection with an ethnic identity on an everyday basis. In all of these cases, it is the wearers who determine how they want to wear the Chinese dress with an awareness of its dominant discourses. They may choose to modify it, to create combinations with it, or to re-invent it in ways that communicate a relationship with an ever-changing identity impacted by historical, social, cultural, and political factors.

The anthology, *Re-Orienting Fashion: The Globalization of Asian Dress* (2003) edited by Sandra Niessen, Ann Marie Leshkowich, and Carla Jones examines the tensions and complications that have arisen in dressing practices in Asia as a result of intensified globalization. Through the presentation of case studies that focus on the design, production and wearing of ethnic garments, such as the Vietnamese *ao dai*, the South Asian *salwaar-kameez* and the Korean *han bok*, the collected writings reveal how the processes of globalization which have given rise to "Asian chic" are simultaneously re-Orientalizing Asian countries and Asian people. They also discuss the strategies that Asian people have undertaken to take control of how and when they wear ethnic clothing in order to resist this process of re-Orientalization. Through a feminist and post-colonial lens, the writers concentrate on what they call the "mid-level actors": Asian designers, merchants, and consumers whose economic, political, and cultural positioning provide a reliable barometer for measuring the agency and limitations that affect the choices they make about dress and appearance. Useful to my own analysis is the concept of "performance practices," a theoretical tool developed by Niessen, Leshkowich and Jones that synthesizes Judith Butler's "performance theory" with Bourdieu and de Certeau's "practice theory." Niessen *et al.* (2003) contend that, on its own, practice theory "risks reducing people to the sum total of their socially and culturally defined roles" (p. 24), while performance theory "overemphasizes the notion of play in 'role-play'" (p. 24). Bringing these two theories together makes it possible to track:

> the constraints shaping and limiting identity creation and subversion. Even if we view the performance of self as stemming from conscious choice, we must recognize that our desire to be a certain way is not entirely self-generated, nor can we determine the outcome. (2003, p. 24)

While a desire to wear the cheongsam may arise out of an attraction to its formal traits and its representational link to Chinese ethnic identity, external racializing factors which include a linking of exoticization with eroticization have become entangled with the dress's image and impacted on a woman's actual wearing practices. "Performance practices" can therefore be employed as an analytical tool to examine agency for Canadian-born women of Chinese heritage, as they negotiate the wearing of the cheongsam today.

Another valuable contribution is Niessen *et al.*'s investigation of what they call "self-Orientalizing" gestures, which entail the "performance practices" of the wearing of ethnic clothing strategically, at the risk of re-inscribing Orientalist discourses. Rebecca N. Ruhlen's chapter in Niessen *et al.* (2003), "Korean Alterations: Nationalism, Social Consciousness and 'Traditional' Clothing," looks at feminist activists in South Korea who wear the *han bok* strategically at national and international women's events and fundraising activities. The editors' description of this case study explains how the wearing of Korean ethnic dress in these instances was carefully considered "precisely because it softened the potentially hard edges of feminism and insulated the wearers from accusations that feminism is a form of Western neo-imperalism" (2004, p. 33). In my research involving the cheongsam, I have termed these acts "auto-exoticization," in keeping with the critical examination of Orientalist and sexist discourses that have equated Asian with the exotic as well as the erotic. My use of "auto" implies a self-generated and determined action that underscores Niessen's, Leshkowich and Jones finding that women in Asia ". . . are strikingly aware of the stakes involved in their choices" (2003, p. 31). Ethnic clothing can be re-coded and re-appropriated as soft power for specific goals that can lead to increased empowerment and agency for the wearers.

The theoretical contributions of Eicher (1995), Maynard (2004), and Niessen *et al.* (2003) provided strong support for the analysis of the interviews I carried out with Canadian-born women of Chinese heritage. While a dominant discourse around the cheongsam exists, the meanings of the dress are multiple and have evolved over time, based on factors such as place, time, culture, mobility, and design innovations. There is evidence that women in Canada are starting to intervene with the cheongsam, wearing it in ways that challenge its established perceptions, meanings, and ways of wearing. There is a desire to address the constraints of the garment's cut and form that impose a narrow set of beauty ideals on the wearer. There is also a need to subvert the sexual stereotypes that have been associated with the dress, as women are looking for ways to wear it on an everyday basis instead of reserving it only for formal occasions. The dresses I made for *The Fitting Room* installation were an attempt to reflect this range of concerns, issues, experiences, and wishes.

Installation art

Given the complexity of the object/subject of the cheongsam, as well as the focus on Canadian-born women of Chinese heritage, I determined that the possibilities offered by installation art would appropriately convey the intricacy and multiplicity of historical narratives, theoretical ideas, and personal perspectives raised by the cheongsam. Furthermore, the immersive approach offered by installation art would allow for a deeper experience with the cheongsam and all it evokes. As installation art can include the potent combination of objects, photo, painting, moving image, sound, and performance as well as an engagement with a literal or figurative space, such a form would permit me to engage a diverse set of viewers through what would hopefully surpass an encounter, in order to become an experience. The theoretical work of art historians Claire Bishop (2005), Miwon Kwon (2000), and Jennifer González (2008) contribute to an understanding of installation art as a fundamentally critical approach that can expose the power dynamics that are enmeshed with an object and subject such as the cheongsam and foreground the confluence of issues that concern Canadian-born women of Chinese heritage. In order to appreciate the form of installation art as structurally suitable for the exploration of this garment, I will begin with a discussion of its origins and evolution.

In *Installation Art: A Critical History* (2005), Claire Bishop explains that installation art emerged from minimalism, conceptual art, and institutional critique, as artists were interested in challenging entrenched regimes of viewing, and a capitalist art market that emphasized a need for discrete, exchangeable objects. Installation art would also facilitate an artist's wish to explore the creation of works that established a meaningful relationship with a particular site or space. An installation would not simply consist of a space that one entered, but more specifically would be a strategy through which "the space, and the ensemble of elements within it are regarded in their entirety as a singular entity" (2005, p. 6). Mindful that approaches to installation are various and continue to proliferate, Bishop distinguished installation art from "traditional media (sculpture, painting, photography, video)" (2005, p. 6) by calling attention to the requirement of the literal presence of the viewer in order for the work to be complete. Unlike modernist discourses that bestow autonomy on a discrete work of art such as painting or sculpture, installation is dependent on the experience of the embodied visitor. Once dismantled, or removed from its particular site, place, or environment after the close of the exhibition, the work would no longer exist. Bishop further characterized the importance of experience for installation art by explaining the notions of "activation" and the "decentering" of the viewer. "Activated spectatorship" refers to a direct, multi-sensory experience presented by the work that offers the visitor a way to engage that is more akin to the way s/he engages with the world—as an active player functioning on a variety of registers, and not limited to visual contemplation alone. The concept of "decentering" is related to the subjectivity of the visitor and is based largely on post-structuralist theories that emerged in the 1970s that has also had great influence on art critics and historians who had been receptive to feminist and postcolonial theory. The concept of "decentering" posed a challenge to the "masculinist, racist and conservative ... dominant ideology" entrenched in the Renaissance perspective that positions the viewer as ". . . a rational, centred, coherent humanist subject" and purported that there is only one, ideal and "right" way of looking at the world (2005, p. 3). Bishop explained that post-structuralist theories served to undo these rigid conventions, contending that the way we "view our condition as human subjects [is] fragmented, multiple and *decentred*" (2005, p. 3). Rather than constraining the viewer to one position, the "decentering" effect, in essence, liberated the viewer and transformed her/him into a *visitor* as the multi-sensory and spatial aspects of installation would offer a multitude of viewing perspectives that subvert the Renaissance model of "centering." In her conclusion, Bishop identified a fundamental contradiction between "decentering" and "activation" which she reconciled by explaining how installation art is a simultaneous experience of both "centering" and "decentering" for the visitor. A tension is created between "the *literal* viewer who steps into the work, and an abstract, philosophical *model* of the subject that is postulated by the way in which the work structures this encounter" (2005, p. 30). In other words, the work requires the viewer's physical presence, which is centered in its subjectivity in order to be subjected to a decentering experience, which may enlighten, engage, or move the viewer. In Bishop's view, the "closer the ideal model to the literal viewer's experience, the more compelling the installation" (2005, p. 33). Where this idea is interesting to me is the extent to which the visitors through their own subjectivity can relate to the works that comprised *The Fitting Room* and their placement in a particular environment. What I take away from Bishop's theory is the importance of taking the visitor's subjectivity into consideration, and looking for ways to create a variety of entry points that would compel the visitor to engage with the works for a more meaningful experience. This resonated with my own intuitive approach to art making that is invested with the larger project of bringing people together through the sharing of stories and experiences that would bring about increased understanding and acknowledgement of the subjects at hand. With the realization that the experience of the Chinese in North American society would speak about a culturally specific group of people, I believed that the sharing of these stories through an installation strategy could open up a dialogue of transcultural exchange that would have some long-term positive effects on the dismantling of racializing discourses.

In the chapter "One Place After Another: Notes on Site Specificity" from the anthology *Space, Site Intervention: Situating Installation* (2000), Miwon

Kwon discussed the emergence of site specificity as a major element of installation art and offered a survey of its practices, which chronicle the changing meanings and uses of "site" in contemporary art. She concluded provisionally that the "definition of the site has been transformed from a physical location—grounded, fixed, actual—to a discursive vector—ungrounded, fluid, and virtual" (Kwon, 2000, p. 46). Like Bishop, she was careful to point out that the variety of approaches to site specificity do not emerge and phase out along a linear trajectory, but rather operate "simultaneously in various cultural practices today (or even within an artist's single project)" (2000, p. 46). The imperatives behind the interest in site specificity are linked with those that inform installation art in general (for instance, the emphasis on the embodied visitor, centering/decentering, and the subversion of the capitalist market economy), but also focus on the growing critique among artists and curators to challenge the established notion of the museum or gallery white cube as an "innocent" space. Again, informed by minimalism, conceptual art, and various forms of institutional critique, Kwon offered examples of artists who began to consider the context of spaces and to question the "*cultural* framework defined by the institutions of art" (2000, pp. 39–40). Following Kwon, the "white cube" style of gallery that can be described as a pristine, minimal space, that is meant to intensify the interaction between the work of art and the viewer, actually perpetuates its own ideology and discourse.

> The seemingly benign architectural features of a gallery/museum, in other words, were deemed to be coded mechanisms that *actively* disassociate the space of art from the outer world, furthering the institution's idealist imperative of rendering itself and its hierarchization of values "objective," "disinterested," and "true." (2000, p. 40)

As artists began to question the neutrality of the museum or gallery space, they also began to engage with the "outside world and everyday life—a critique of culture that is inclusive of non-art spaces, non-art institutions, and non-art issues" (Kwon, 2000, p. 43). This engagement reflected a desire to make work that would engage with social, political, economic, and cultural issues, concerns, and topics. Taking art outside of the physical site of the exclusive and even elitist context of the museum or gallery in favor of sites non-traditionally coded as art spaces was a critical and political act. Kwon argued that in addition to a concern with site, installation art was distinguished by its growing interdisciplinarity that included anthropology, sociology and cultural histories. She also explained that installation art became "sharply attuned to popular discourses (such as fashion, music, advertising, film and television)" (2000, p. 44). Furthermore, artists began to unmoor art from a fixed, physical space and to engage with spaces in a more itinerant way so that "unlike previous models [of installation art] the site is not defined as a *precondition*. Rather it is *generated* by the work (often as 'content'), then *verified* by its convergence with an existing discursive formation" (2000, p. 44).[3] With this, the idea of site specificity in art could offer a whole new set of practices. For instance, an area of inquiry or subject such as racism or colonialism could be considered a "site" as evidenced in the practices of artists such as Renée Green and Fred Wilson. Going further, Kwon described how artists could declare themselves the site, as they began to travel in order to create works in different places around the world. A further variation of site-specific art that gets away from the physical site itself is work that considers an *aspect* of site specificity so that:

> ... different cultural debates, a theoretical concept, a social issue, a political problem, an institutional framework (not necessarily an art institution), a community or season event, a historical condition, and even particular formations of desire are deemed to function as sites now. (2000, 45)

Site specificity has had a liberating effect on artistic practice. The conceptual play available to artists through this strategy can stimulate endless possibilities that can be critical, playful, and rigorous.

Jennifer A. González', in *Subject to Display: Reframing Race in Contemporary Installation Art* (2008), focused on the practices of specific artists as vital examples of those working primarily with the variables offered by installation art in order to engage with a "critical approach to material and visual culture that examines and ultimately attempts to undermine racist, colonialist and sexist discourses in a long tradition of *abolitionism*" (2008, p. 20). To do this she presented important examples of works by artists that employed various approaches to site-specificity in order to engage with a specific community but also to appeal to a wide audience. One of my favorite examples from her study is *En la Barberia No Se Llora* (1994) by Pepòn Osorio. For this work, the artist found an abandoned building located on a street accessible to foot traffic and transformed it into an installation work that looked like a typical neighborhood barbershop. Pepon's installation looked legitimate on the outside, as passers-by thought it was actually a new business in the community. But on the inside, it was a fantastical *gesamtkunstwerk* or total work of art. His barbershop worked with the conventional arrangement of barbershop chairs and mirrors, but intervened through the incorporation of art works throughout the environment. Images of male torsos, scissors, and razor blades were silk-screened onto the barber chair upholstery, television monitors were installed in place of the barber chair headrests and a floor-to-ceiling display of photographic portraits of historic and iconic Latin American and Caribbean men adorned the walls. The ambiguity between a "real" and a fabricated environment was intentional, and got people inside to experience Pepòn's work and to be exposed to the issues he wanted to raise and discuss. His strategy leads to a very key point about installation art and site specificity. The use of selected spaces makes it possible to bring projects into communities, places, and neighborhoods for the purpose of engagement with an intended target audience—in Pepòn's case, men of Latin American heritage. At the same time, this strategy posed a challenge to the institution of the gallery or musuem as the only valid place for art.

Also significant is how González situated the study of installation art as coming out of social movements such as student protests, civil rights, and feminist movements, all of which sought to challenge social and political norms and injustices. In terms of art practice, these inspirations also motivated productive ways of disrupting "the traditional semiotic and somatic boundaries assumed to exist among the audience, the work of art, the site of exhibition and the world beyond" (2008, p. 8). What installation art opened up for these artists was the appropriation of spaces and places that provided the terrain for serious play. Installation art offered an opportunity to transgress the social discourses that put limits on people's mobility, whether literal or figurative, due to racialization, gender, class, age, or occupation. González refers to Fred Wilson's 1992 work *My Life As a Dog* as a prime example. In this satirical performance offered to docents at the Whitney Museum of American Art in New York, Wilson's piece began with his greeting the group. He then asked the docents to meet with him in one of the upstairs galleries. Wilson then changed into a uniform worn by the museum security guards and placed himself in the gallery in which they agreed to meet. When the docents arrived they searched for the artist they had just met. When he finally revealed himself dressed as the security guard, they were surprised and embarrassed by the realization that he had been there all along. Wilson's piece demonstrated to the docents how the museum frames black bodies. They may be visible in works of art or within a predominantly "white" museum going public; however, when dressed as staff members, people of color become invisible. This work employed a site specific strategy, in this case the museum and its mechanisms, to create an experience that was immersive, visceral, and ultimately consciousness raising. Another ground-breaking aspect of this work was the use of the artist's own body as a mechanism of activation for the work's guiding questions and objectives. The site of the museum and its conventions of operation were engaged, as well as his own performativity within them, playing upon the assumptions that have become engrained within the museum environment. His role of security guard and artist had the final effect of bringing the docents in direct contact with their own conditioned perceptions. Wilson's use of performativity in this installation work was highly inspirational, further prompting me to work with all the possibilities that installation art could provide. Throughout this book, I will come back to the notion of "performativity" as it is a central aspect of cheongsam wearing practices, as well as a key strategic component of my final exhibition.

Art installation and its application by artists since the 1960s presents a range of possibilities for what installation art can "do." The concepts of activation, experience, centering/decentering, multiple ways of experiencing the work, the engagement of all the senses, and the interaction with a specific space and site, cohere with the kinds of questions and goals that were involved in *The Fitting Room*.

Selecting the tools: Ethnography, autoethnography, and historical research

In order to present an adequate portrayal of the complexity of the relationship between the cheongsam and Canadian-born women of Chinese heritage, I carried out in-depth interviews with nineteen women. The sample size is relatively small but the qualitative interviews reflect the diversity and range of experiences amongst this particular group of women. The information culled from these interviews also provided a pool of stories that would be utilized for the creation of *The Fitting Room*. Recruited through a process of snowballing, I focused on women born between 1968 and 1986 as they represent the first generation of children to be born in Canada as a result of significant changes to Canada's immigration laws which allowed unprecedented numbers of people from countries other than Europe to arrive. Another major aspect that guided the search for interview participants, was the need to include an equal representation of anglophone and francophone women as a way to address the variable links between language and its effect on culture and ethnicity in the Canadian context, to acknowledge Montreal, a bilingual city, as the location of the presentation of *The Fitting Room*, and to address certain expectations and assumptions about Chinese people in Quebec. It is important to point out that while I link dominant Canadian culture as being modeled on Anglo-Saxon settler origins, the situation is different in Quebec where the dominant culture is informed not only by francophone heritage but a Quebec-centric militantism that has fueled the desire for separation from Canada since the 1960s. As previously described, the Chinese in Canada have been historically affected by the perpetuation of Orientalist and xenophobic discourses, which I believe have cultivated an assumption, particularly in Quebec, that Chinese people or people of Chinese heritage find it difficult to assimilate and tend to learn to speak English before French. I therefore wished to subvert this assumption in the first place by making sure that francophone women of Chinese heritage were well represented. Taking all of this into consideration, it is important to point out that the participants were from British Columbia, Ontario, Quebec, and Alberta and that there is room to extend this investigation to include women from all provinces and territories whose unique experiences have been affected by the history and culture of those areas. The final group of participants came from a variety of Canadian locations, socio-economic backgrounds, and immigration situations that reflect the movement of Chinese people around the world.

Strategic methods and approaches consisting of ethnography, auto-ethnography, and historical research were applied to the research process that in turn fed the creative process to transform the gathered material into the works in the installation. A discussion of each of these methods will establish a foundation for the political and sociological standpoints that formed my anaylsis as well as the creation and presentation of the artworks.

Ethnography

Among the aims of *The Fitting Room* was the attempt to develop a multi-faceted portrait of the current condition of Canadian-born women of Chinese heritage through an analysis of their relationship to the cheongsam. Undertaking an ethnographic approach, which involved observation and meetings, I traveled to each woman's location, in order to engage in face-to-face interviews that were recorded in digital audio. I asked each woman about when, how, and under what circumstances her family arrived in Canada, where in Canada she spent her formative years of socialization (which province(s), what type of area—rural/suburban/urban), what her impressions of those formative years were, and how, if at all, her family practiced or still practices aspects of Chinese culture. The factors of class, language, geography, and key formative experiences revealed the diversity of the stories and also illustrated the impact of these factors on each woman's sense of ethnic identity.

My style and approach to the use of ethnographic study that is critical while respectful was influenced by documentary films made by the now defunct Studio D, the feminist studio at the National Film Board of Canada, where I got my start.[4] *Sisters in the Struggle* (1991) by Dionne Brand, *Women in the Shadows* (1993) by Christine Welsh, and *Return Home* (1992) by Michelle Wong are examples of classic Studio D films that shaped an approach to the exploration of a subject that is with and through people's stories. The major contribution of these films is their ability to give voice to a multitude of different women who have been historically silenced and essentialized in mainstream media. A strong characteristic of these films is the filmmakers' interest in the celebration of difference within communities of women that recognizes the mutability of identity while refusing to reaffirm the "center." Studio D films also demonstrated how the expression of contrasting ideas and opinions can open up opportunities for dialogue that can dismantle reductionist expectations of the "Other." It is in this spirit that I worked with an in-depth, face-to-face interview process that would garner a wide range of attitudes, ideas, and wearing practices in regards to the cheongsam.

Autoethnography

In "Autoethnography: Journeys of the Self" (1999), Catherine Russell explored the emergence and evolution of the term autoethnography and presented a number of examples of its employment in video and film. She acknowledged Michael Fischer's earlier use of the term "ethnic autobiography," as a precursor to "auto-ethnography," in his 1986 essay, "Ethnicity and the Post-Modern Arts of Memory". Russell quoted from Fischer's article to illustrate how "ethnic autobiography" in literary form, "partake[s] of a mood of metadiscourse, of drawing attention to their linguistic and fictive nature, of using the narrator as an inscribed figure within the text whose manipulation calls attention to authority structures" (Russell, 1999, para. 4). Russell built on this by contending that in terms of film and video making, autobiography becomes ethnographic when the maker positions their personal history within the larger context of social, cultural, and historical forces to reveal how identities are produced and performed. The insertion of the author into the video or filmic text, either as the first-person narrator, as an on-screen representation, or both, brings attention to the maker's (or artist's) deep understanding of what Russell terms a "staging of subjectivity—a representation of the self as a performance" (1999, para. 5). Russell goes on in her article to credit Mary Louise Pratt with introducing the term 'auto-ethnography' as an "oppositional term." In her book, *Imperial Eyes: Travel Writing and Transculturation* (1992), Pratt explains autoethnography as a term used:

> . . . to refer to instances in which colonized subjects undertake to represent themselves in ways that engage with the colonizer's own terms. If ethnographic texts are a means by which Europeans represent themselves to their (usually subjugated) others, auto-ethnographic texts are those the others construct in response to or in dialogue with those metropolitan representations. (1992, p. 7)

An autoethnographic approach is therefore a tool that artists can use to empower their representations in light of essentializing ethnographic practices that perpetuate discourses such as "Primitivism" and "Orientalism."[5] Those on the margins can harness the language and technology of powerful media, such as film and video, to tell their own stories from their own points of view. The timing of Pratt's writing on autoethnography coincided with feminist documentary and video art practices of the early 1990s when the discussion around identity politics took center stage in Canada, the US, and the UK. More and more, aboriginal artists and people of color were looking to take control over their representation across various media. One of the main approaches they took was to integrate themselves directly into the work, situating themselves within the content structure as a way to take ownership of the questions and objectives they wished to address. Another effect of an autoethnographic strategy was to call attention to how various media are carefully constructed in order to influence and perpetuate a particular viewpoint. If the power of the media is wielded by the person behind the camera, then it would be crucial for subjugated "Others" to take control of the means of production in order to frame themselves. The work of Yinka Shonibare CBE (RA), a British artist of Nigerian heritage, provides a prime example of the use of autoethnographic strategy that also links to an inquiry into the formation of identity and authenticity through clothing and style. His 2001 photo series *Dorian Gray* is based on the 1945 screen adaptation of Oscar Wilde's 1890 book *The Picture of Dorian Gray*. Shonibare created a revisionist version of this story of a handsome young man who gave up his soul for eternal youth while a hidden portrait depicted the effects of his aging, in concert with his growing moral corruption. The casting of himself as the title character raised questions about race and class in Britain. He took this reflection even further by incarnating the aforementioned "dandy" personified by Oscar Wilde, who was able to infiltrate the upper classes with his impeccable clothing, style and wit. Through the use of auto-ethnography as one of his strategies, Shonibare opened up the complex terrain of issues of representation. Similarly, I employed autoethnographic strategies in two ways for *The Fitting Room*. I recorded an interview with myself so that I might mix my voice and responses with those of the women I interviewed. I also incorporated new video content into two of the works in *The Fitting Room*. In one of these works, *(Chinese) Screen* I wore three different cheongsams made for the installation, and was filmed passing through three specific sites in and around the city of Montreal. I also incorporated clips of myself being fitted for and wearing a cheongsam taken from an earlier video work. These choices were aimed at exploring a critical reflection of the cheongsam that would subvert dominant expectations through the authoring of my own words and representation. In this way, autoethnography served as a tool for the expression of my subjectivity within the framework of the Canadian context and its impact on how my body as a Canadian-born (invisible) woman of color (visible) is seen and interpreted through dominant culture, as well as the culture of Montreal's Chinese community.

Historical research

Canadian artist Nina Levitt's 2004 installation *Little Breeze* exemplified an approach to art making that made direct use of historical data.[6] *Little Breeze* was an interactive installation that told the story of the often overlooked and misrepresented lives of European women who worked as spies during the Second World War. The work focused on Violette Szabo, a British officer, who bore the code name "Louise." By the age of 23 she had completed two missions in occupied France before being captured and executed a few months before the end of the war. In this installation, the viewer was confronted with a large-format projection of a sequence of spy portraits produced out of ASCII code. The projection screen was set within a wooden frame covered in dark stained wood laths which evoked the wall of an old house. About a dozen vintage suitcases were placed in front of the screen structure. By lifting a suitcase, an audio excerpt of dialogue from the film *Carve Her Name with Pride* (a film about the life of Violette Szabo) was emitted from the speaker embedded in the suitcase. When one opened the suitcase, an excerpt from the film appeared on the screen. The action of moving around the space and opening suitcases enabled the viewer to interact with physical elements in the space.

In a separate room, small photo portraits of nine female British officers who worked in the occupied zone of France were placed on a wall, along with a coded "teletype" text. A radio transmission of Morse Code was broadcast from speakers installed in the room. When the movements of the visitor were captured by a webcam, the Morse code sound transformed into the song "Louise" by Maurice Chevalier. Again, the movement of the visitor's body in the space triggered the change in audio and activated the visitor's experience.

Levitt worked with Second World War archives as well as a Hollywood film and a popular song as the basic components of her installation. This combination of historical information and popular media provided a useful reference for *The Fitting Room* as I brought archival images of Han and Manchu dress, photos of the "modern" cheongsams from my personal collection, and original video work into dialogue with clips from a well known film through a recombinant, nonlinear narrative that attempted to evoke the complicated story of the dress as well as a critical exploration of its historicity. I started by gathering data on its history from a variety of sources in order to map out the cheongsam's narrative. I then plotted out the many theories of its origins, the chronicles of its evolution, and the historical, socio-cultural, economic, and political events that affected the dress and its arrival in Canada. This charting allowed me to carry out a comparative analysis which confirmed my suspicion that rather than a clear, linear historical narrative, the story of the cheongsam's origins and evolution consists of a multiplicity of historical accounts.

Ethnography, autoethnography and historical research were integral to the range of tools used to elicit a sense of what the cheongsam means for partipants in this study. A critical examination of representation and identity as raised through the subject of the cheongsam required devices that had the ability to consider the dynamics of power that are historically, culturally and poltically formed. An ethnographic approach that was concerned with presenting a variety of voices, that are divergent and that do not let the discourse settle, contributed to a portrait that was not pre-determined by a particular interest or perspective. The incorporation of my own voice and image brought attention to the subject/object position that can confine or limit studies and artworks that explore an ethno-cultural text or artifact. The cheongsam is a point of entry through which to explore my insecure sense of identity as a woman of Chinese heritage, which when joined with the voices of the other women I interviewed, could contribute to what I hoped would be a portrait of ethnicity that aimed not to be the last word, but rather could underscore ethnicity's multi-vocality and fluidity. A thorough examination of the history of the cheongsam that traced its origins and evolution while registering the inconsistencies that emerged through an analysis of the cheongsam's various historical accounts was also crucial to a deeper appreciation of the many factors that contribute to the image of the cheongsam today. The conceptual threads of identity, ethnic clothing, and art installation fortified by the administration of ethnography, autoethnography, and historical research provided a framework for the study of the cheongsam and its complicated place in the lives of the women interviewed.

What I have attemped to do so far is to establish the structural components that make up the fabric of the study on the cheongsam as well as to name the primary tools that were applied to the interview gathering process and their eventual transformation into *The Fitting Room*. In the next chapter, a comparitive analysis of recent histories of the cheongsam in China and Canada will emphasize how the garment posesses mutable and fusionable qualities.

CHAPTER 3
THE CHEONGSAM: A COMPLEX GARMENT

A variety of political and cultural influences have shaped the evolution of the cheongsam, affecting its design and materiality, as well as how it is perceived today. Like the "military–industrial complex," which is comprised of a web-like system of relationships between legislators, armed forces, and the arms industry, I contend that the cheongsam is a complex itself, made up of a tight network of linked relationships that inform its quality as a "technology" shaped by cultural discourses, popular media, and the fashion industry, to affect the current perception and wearing practices of this garment by Canadian women of Chinese heritage. In this chapter, I will address the elements that make up the weave of this complex, through a sequential unraveling of its various strands. First, I will trace the emergence of the cheongsam through an additive comparison of accounts by Hazel Clark (2000), WESSIELING (2007), Juanjuan Wu (2009), and Antonia Finnane (2008). I will then map out the historic and cultural events that surround the cheongsam in China as explored by these authors. This mapping will expose how in addition to being taken up as a politicized fashion garment by women, the dress was co-opted by the nationalist interests of the Chinese government and later called upon for the needs of a growing economy. Following this I will then give an overview of the current status of cheongsam wearing practices and the cheongsam's market activity in mainland China as well as Hong Kong and Taiwan. With reference to the publications *Jin Guo: Voices of Chinese Canadian Women* (1992) and the website database *Chinese Canadian Women, 1923–1967: Inspiration—Innovation—Ingenuity,* produced by the Multicultural History Society of Ontario, I will close this chapter with a discussion on the migration of the cheongsam to Canada.

The "technology" of the cheongsam

Ursula Franklin's 1989 book entitled "The Real World of Technology," based on a series of lectures, advanced a compelling treatise on how technologies are systems "that entail far more than [their] individual material components" (Franklin, 1989, p. 12). In these lectures, Franklin was not referring to machines, gadgets, or the computer chips or gears that are inside them. Rather, she was interested in how technologies are constructed, owned, and controlled through "organization, procedures, symbols, new words, equations and most of all, a mindset" (1989, p.12). Through the analysis of a number of concrete examples, she revealed how technologies have permeated our everyday lives and claimed that over time we have become increasingly blind to the hegemonic quality of these systems, which have led to the deterioration of human relationships, quality of life, and the natural environment. She acknowledged her affinity to French philosopher Jacques Ellul's concern that technology may have a growing tyrannical hold on humanity. As a key to articulating her arguments, Franklin focused on technology as practice that imposes a certain way and how of doing of things in order to carry out the goals of a technology or system. She argued that practices as technologies in themselves "identify people and give them their own definition" (1989, p. 31) as well as "identif[y] and [limit] the content of what is permissible" (1989, p. 31). In other words, within a given technology or system, those who do not follow prescribed practices according to certain established norms may be considered deviant and subject to ostracization or some other penalty. For Franklin, what is ultimately at stake here is how practices have become ingrained into everyday culture to the point where we no longer see how we are complicit in supporting technologies which could have serious and harmful consequences on our social, political, and physical lives. Following Franklin, the cheongsam is indeed a technology in that it is governed by well-entrenched discourses that control and discipline the body, perpetuate a limited, idealized concept of Chinese femininity, further entrench essentialist definitions of Chinese ethnicity, and impose upon women a certain set of "correct" practices. I will explain how the dress changed over time, from being a loose-fitting garment that began as a symbol of Chinese women's emancipation during China's Republic Era, to become a thoroughly body conscious garment by the 1960s, as it came under the influence of the fashion industry and popular culture. The responses gathered from my interviews will reveal that these factors have not detracted from the overall high regard and desirability of the dress. Women are however aware of the unsettling issues attached to it, and are thinking critically about the garment and how to negotiate its wearing so that they might subvert general sexual and racialized stereotypes perpetuated in the Western context and affirm a link to Chinese ethnicity.

Tracing the emergence of the cheongsam

Scholarship on clothing in China reveals how the Chinese have always been acutely aware of the significance of dress. Specific customs, styles, and items have been instrumentalized to enforce political, cultural, and social agendas. For example, in *The Art of Oriental Embroidery* (1979), historian Young Yang Chung explains how during the Ming dynasty (1368–1644), the favored scholar class of the mandarins who attained high positions in the court and public life were awarded a special rank badge. This ranking system consisted of elaborately embroidered badges with carefully designed motifs that were stitched onto the chest area of the wearer's coat. Special attention was paid to color and symbol. Birds were allocated to the civil system while larger animal designs were given to those in military roles. In this way, rank badges worked to visually and symbolically structure Chinese society. According to Chung, these badges, commonly referred to as the "mandarin square," were "striking little masterpieces of handsome color, carefully organized design and skillful needlework" (1979, 34) that were either carried out by the wives or daughters of the officials, or by professional embroidery studios.

According to a number of accounts, the imposition of Manchu clothing and hairstyle on the majority Han people is another example of the importance of sartorial codes in Chinese culture.[1] When the invading northeastern Manchu took over rule of China to form the Qing dynasty (1644–1911), one of their first orders of business was to obscure the ethnic identity of the majority Han people. Han men were forced to abandon their ethnic clothing, to shave the front of their heads, and to wear the rest of their hair in a single braid down the back. Those who did not comply were summarily executed. In *Chinese Fashion from Mao to Now* (2009), Juanjuan Wu explained how:

> [i]n this brutal struggle between conqueror and conquered, clothes were weapons. The Manchu wielded this weapon as a means of imposing their authority while the Han clung to their own clothing styles as a means of resistance [...] (2009, p. 104)

In order to mitigate Han resentment, Manchu rulers eventually relaxed certain dressing rules which allowed Han women to continue to wear their own style of dress. This concession is a strong indication of gender inequality in Chinese society. Given an entrenched patriarchal system, women simply did not matter politically and the Manchu, therefore, saw no value in imposing any changes on their style of clothing. Women's struggle for emancipation and equality began shortly after the fall of the Qing dynasty and imperial rule, which is when the discussion of the birth of the modern cheongsam begins.

A comparative mapping of the birth of the cheongsam reveals a number of inconsistencies that point to disputes that are culturally and historically rooted, as I will explain. This is particularly revealing when applied to the responses from the women I interviewed in regards to their perceptions of the cheongsam. In what follows, I will attempt to provide a review of both the historical literature on the dress as well as a summary of the author(s) conclusions about its origins.

My review of literature revealed that English language writings on the history of the cheongsam began to emerge in the late 1980s, as part of larger studies on Chinese clothing. Valerie Garret has been one of the most prolific Western historians on this subject, starting with the publication of *Traditional Chinese Clothing in Hong Kong and South China 1840-1980* (1987). Given the scale of her research, she did not go into the history of the cheongsam in depth but she explained that it first appeared in the 1920s and "developed from the robes worn by Manchu women during the Qing dynasty" (Garret, 1987, p. 15) This assertion is one that is repeated and goes largely uncontested until later writings. It is on these later accounts that I focus my attention, as they provide some meaningful correlation with the divergent attitudes and ideas on authenticity and the dress that prevail today.

The Cheongsam (2000), by Hazel Clark was promoted as the first comprehensive account of the garment recorded in the English language. Through a feminist lens, Clark examined the origins, the historical and cultural influences on the cheongsam's evolution and perception, its production, its wearers and its influence on the Western fashion industry. According to many sources the birthplace of the cheongsam was Shanghai, and in terms of its origins, Clark is the first to begin to diverge from the prevailing discourse that the cheongsam was a descendant of Manchu dress. Her contention was that during the Qing dynasty (1644-1911) the two-piece skirt and tunic traditionally worn by Han women and the one-piece garment of the Manchu started to merge and "[a]s a result the styles between the two groups became somewhat blurred, increasingly so after 1800" (Clark, 2000, p. 4). Rather than evolving from the Manchu robe alone, Clark argued that the cheongsam was a hybrid style informed by two forms of dress and further influenced by American fashion and culture. Clark was also the first to call attention to the fusional nature of the dress that could combine fashion interests with a piece of clothing that could express national and ethnic affiliations as Chinese women encountered American fashion. The cheongsam proved a versatile garment that could sustain variations on the fabric, sleeve details, hem lines, and other decorative and practical details that greatly appealed to the fashion industry. Clark's statements about the origins and evolution of the dress served to complicate the cheongsam's story.

Fusionable Cheongsam, by artist and designer WESSIELING, is the publication that accompanied her exhibition of the same name, presented at the Hong Kong Arts Centre in 2007. The texts in the publication chronicle the cheongsam's rise and evolution, examine the image of the dress as seen through popular culture, and discuss the garment in relation to the hierarchies of the fashion industry. WESSIELING's main argument builds on Hazel Clark's assertion that the cheongsam is an inherently hybrid garment and explains that it is informed by the binary relationships of masculine/feminine, East/West, and traditional/modern, which established conditions of possibility for the wearer across a variety of symbolic and visual terrains. While WESSIELING asserts that the cheongsam had been associated with the Manchu robe, she argues that "its feminine image offers little suggestion of its affiliation with the men's attire of the Manchu" (2007, p. 10). Like Clark, WESSIELING located the political rise of the cheongsam in the 1920s, coinciding with the May Fourth Movement (1919–21) which she explained "was an intellectual revolution and sociopolitical reform movement led by students and directed toward national independence, emancipation of the individual and rebuilding of society and culture" (2007, p. 12). This movement marked the start of a new reform culture, driven by Western ideas in combination with Chinese patriotism, and included bids for women's emancipation after the fall of the Qing dynasty. It is against this backdrop that WESSIELING asserted that the cheongsam was able to become "the official formal dress during the Republican era" (2007, p. 12). Furthermore, she asserted that the dress descended not only from Manchu clothing, but also from the *changpao* worn by Han men, as described in Zhang Ailing's famous essay "A Chronicle of Changing Clothes," first published in January 1943. Both Clark and WESSIELING point out that until the Republican era, Han women had worn two-piece garments, while a one-piece robe was traditionally reserved for men. The appropriation of the one-piece garment by women was therefore an expression of their desire for equality during the Republic Era. The irony however, as pointed out by Clark, WESSIELING, and others, is that popular culture would eventually influence the cut of the dress, while increasing global trade would covertly transform the dress from a symbol of freedom into an instrument of constraint, both figuratively and literally.

Changing Clothes in China: Fashion, History, Nation (2008), by Antonia Finnane, examined connections between the modernization of China and its visibility to the rest of the world, from the viewpoint of the changes in the fashion industry and the Chinese dress. The chapter "Qipao China" looked at the roots and evolution of the garment in Beijing and Shanghai at the beginning of the twentieth century. Diverging from her colleagues, Finnane put forth that there are no clear links to the exact origins or precise dates of emergence for the dress and that the abandonment of the two-piece ensemble for the one-piece garment "is one of the great enigmas of Chinese fashion history in the twentieth century" (2008, p. 141). Like WESSIELING, she stated that while the dress may have been quoting Qing clothing, it should not be confused with the Manchu one-piece garment. Furthermore, she disputed the validity of Zhang Ailing's account of the emergence of the garment in 1921 as the writer would have been only a year old at the time and, therefore, could not have been speaking from first hand observation. Instead, Finnane looked to other writers and ethnographers at the time, such as Aoki Masaru, who studied Chinese dress. She also researched photos and accounts of prominent women who might have been seen wearing the cheongsam, in order to ascertain when it might have started to gain popularity. Although Finnane conceded that the cheongsam most likely appeared as student uniforms in the 1920s, at a time when there were a number of dress styles circulating among Chinese women (including Western clothing), she asserted that the modern cheongsam did not become truly fashionable until the 1930s. Furthermore, Finnane's research indicated that the high collar, which has become a major characteristic of the cheongsam, was scarcely seen on clothing in the 1920s. Finnane's analysis influenced my own understanding of the complex history of the cheongsam and further impacted on the strategy I would use to present this history in *The Fitting Room*.

In *Chinese Fashion from Mao to Now* (2009) Juanjuan Wu analyzed the ascendance of the Chinese dress through an examination of the rise of the Chinese fashion industry. In terms of the dress origins, Wu followed Clark and others who contend that the garment blurred together a combination of Han, Manchu, and Western clothing styles, but she stepped further towards an even more nuanced explanation of how the dress emerged.

[t]owards the mid-to-late Qing, upper-class Han and Manchu women started to imitate each other's styles, and a look that mixed both Han

and Manchu dress features became popular along with hybrid styles that mixed Chinese and Western features. By the Republican era, the ethnic demarcation of dress was obscured. As Han Chinese regained power in Republican China, the need to mark ethnic identity was overshadowed by the need for new symbols that would represent the new China as a national state. (2009, p. 107)

What makes Wu's explanation stand out is the idea that the cheongsam is a result of women *imitating* each other's styles of dress. The close proximity of women of different ethnicities such that they might influence each other in dress follows Maynard's contention about globalization's effect on culture, and is another clue to understanding the origins of the cheongsam. The other condition which Wu argued, gave rise to the cheongsam is how the assertion of ethnicities within China would take a back seat to the Republic's preoccupation with building national unity, personified by the projection of the Chinese as a singular people. The modern cheongsam worked well for this purpose as it represented a mode of dressing that was more "democratic in nature" (Wu, 2009, p. 108), while representing freedom in that "no restrictions were officially placed on its design and usage" (p. 108). In this way, the cheongsam was "embedded with modern meanings while still vested in a traditional frame" (p. 110) in keeping with the government's political interests at the time. In essence, the vocation of the dress evolved to become the symbol of a united country. Wu's contribution to the understanding of the complex nature of the origins of the cheongsam adds to the assertion that decisions around clothing and dress are not isolated. Instead, a diverse set of factors that include politics and culture play an important part in shaping how a garment and its wearing practices evolve.

The cumulative findings presented in the work of Clark, WESSIELING, Finnane, and Wu encouraged me to adopt a more nuanced and relative point of view concerning the origins of the cheongsam. A more productive approach would be to consider how a category of dress known as the cheongsam is a result of flows and exchanges, as well as the political and cultural factors that influenced its adoption by Chinese women. The story of the cheongsam is one of ethnicities and cultures coming into contact with one another to bring about a new representation for the dress and the women who desired to wear it. At the same time, the government seized upon an opportunity to bring a popular garment in line with its political aspirations.

The cheongsam's inconsistencies are analogous to the complexity of identity formation for Canadian women of Chinese heritage who are trying to bring their Canadian cultural upbringing into contact with an evolving sense of Chinese ethnicity. The cheongsam therefore can represent possibility, change, and an affirming and vital symbol for women in the pursuit of new sensibilities around identity that, as Hall states, are always "in a process of becoming" (Hall and Du Gay, 1996, p. 4).

Historical narrative of the cheongsam

While historians do not agree on the exact origins or date of birth of the cheongsam, the historical narrative of the dress follows the same general contours across all accounts studied, from the fall of the Qing dynasty into the late twentieth century. As mentioned above, the conditions of possibility for the rise of the cheongsam were born out of the fall of Imperial rule, China's desire to modernize during the Republic Era (1911–49), and the mixing and mingling of dress styles between Han and Manchu women which were further influenced by American fashion. As Clark put forth, Shanghai is often cited as the birthplace of the cheongsam during the 1920s as it was a dynamic port city in which "[i]ts trade connections and large population of foreigners, especially business people, made it increasingly subject to Western influence and the associated impact of modernity" (Clark, 2000, 9). During this period, the value of a woman's role in society grew in importance to the extent that the formal education of girls was encouraged among the middle and upper classes. According to Clark, the female student became a channel for the promoting of the "new woman of China" and represented, as such, the "potential for fundamental social change and self-liberation" (2000, p. 7). At the same time, women reformers began to speak out about women's rights and "respect for women's individuality" (2000, p. 5). Based again on the 1943 writings of Zhang Ailing, WESSIELING (2007) explains that the early 1920s cheongsam, with its loose cut based on the men's *changpao*, became the right garment to express the desire for gender equality, as it offered freedom from the heavy, restrictive Han and Manchu clothing, reflecting "the desire for women's rights and a respect for women's individuality" (2007, pp. 4–15). As WESSIELING explains further, the appropriation of the one-piece male garment by female reformers and activists became a meaningful expression of women's politics as:

> the "androgynous" cheongsam created the pleasure for women of being able to dream about being the opposite sex or having the

freedom to choose between sexes: one day a man in a cheongsam, the next day a woman in jacket and skirt. They could swap, or role-play, or sample "in between" gender roles through the significance of gender representation by the cheongsam. (2007, p. 15)

The concept of the modern Chinese woman in concert with the cheongsam's gender bending capabilities allowed for some play with tightly stipulated gender roles and allowed women to express their desire for more equality. In this way, the cheongsam grew in popularity as a politicized garment for women themselves, who employed it as a tool of agency. The history of the garment as a tool of assertion and affirmation continues with Canadian-born women of Chinese heritage a history that I will discuss in depth in Chapter 4.

WESSIELING drew on Finnane's 1996 article, "What Should Chinese Women Wear? A National Problem," to underscore how the popularity of the cheongsam partially also grew out of the May Thirtieth movement of 1925. This labor movement was characterized by anti-West demonstrations and a rise in nationalism which shouted out for the discarding of Western clothing, which at this time had entered vigorously into the sartorial vocabulary of Chinese people. As WESSIELING explained, "[g]iven that the cheongsam was already worn by some women who were seen as open-minded reformers, advocates of strengthening the nation, the cheongsam seemed to suggest the answer to the Nationalist cry" (2007, p. 7). By the late 1920s, the appeal of the dress was firmly in place and showed no signs of abating, and by 1929 the Nationalist government officially declared the cheongsam the national formal dress for women.

Juanjuan Wu explained that the cheongsam became the "most dominant urban female fashion of the 1930s and into the 1940s" (2009, p. 110) as it embodied the goals of modernity while signifying Chinese cultural tradition. She further explained that China's intense economic boom encouraged women to "act as modern consumers" (2009, p. 10) who would partake in the styles coming out of New York and Paris as a way to demonstrate their modernity. The popularity of cinema brought Chinese women in contact with Western customs and fashions. Early adopters of newer versions of the cheongsam were actresses and society women, and by the end of the 1920s "the cheongsam had emerged as an important part of the modern Chinese woman's life and representation" (Clark, 2000, 11). Into the 1930s, the cheongsam became more form fitting and Westernized. Hybrid styles that mixed Western and Chinese elements emerged with great creativity and fervor. Endless combinations and variations on necklines, sleeve shapes, lengths, fabrics, cuts, and trims abounded while the essence of the Chinese dress remained, as described by Clark:

> Unsurprisingly, the more unusual styles seem to have been worn in Shanghai. It appears the more affluent and internatonal the city became, the more daring the transformation of the cheongsam. International fashion details were incorporated to create unusual hybrid garments. . . . There were tartan *qipaos*, prairie *qipaos,* and even flamenco *qipaos* embellished with big black sashes and red satin frills. (Clark, 2000, pp. 17–19)

Even the quintessential collar was subject to fashion's whims and rose as high as the cheeks, only to shorten in the following season. WESSIELING (2007) argued that the wild fluctuations in the styles of the cheongsam were an indication of the importance of fashion in the lives of women at this time, as it offered them an opportunity to exercise control over something in their lives. The 1930s marked a time of great political and economic instability with the growing communist threat and conflicts with Japan that eventually led to the Sino–Japanese war of 1937–1945. Exercising decisions over one's cheongsam provided a way to react to the reigning anxieties and pressures of life, while providing some greatly needed pleasure and enjoyment.

China's push towards modernity in the image of the West exerted its influence on the cheongsam which exposed the Chinese woman's body like never before and made this image of femininity China's latest export. Hazel Clark (2000) describes how calendar posters contributed to this situation. Calendar posters were hand painted images that accompanied calendars that emerged in the late nineteenth century and were a popular art form, given as gifts and found in many Chinese households. As Clark explained, the development of lithographic printing made them more accessible and soon posters were "purchased and distributed by locally based companies" in Hong Kong and Shanghai "who added their names and products to mass-produced images" (2000, p. 4). While the circulation of these images may have contributed to the popularity of the cheongsam in China as well as the association of the dress with Chinese culture, Clark also contended that:

> [t]heir often very revealing portrayals of the female body not only drew attention to the product being advertised, but also covertly projected a notion of Chinese women as "exotic" and desirable

commodities. … The poster depicted women in a variety of roles, ranging from object of desire used to advertise popular brands of cigarettes, fabrics, or cosmetics, to the virtuous wife and devoted mother who appeared in the prints issued at Chinese New Year … both stereotypes were, in their own ways, sexually subordinate to their male counterparts. (2000, pp. 5–16)

As a popular and accessible item, the calendar posters greatly facilitated the wide dissemination of advertising images whose purpose was to suggest and influence consumption. The conflation of the cheongsam with Chinese female sexuality reinforced a subordinate subject position for women. In the West, the effect of Orientalist discourses further racialized the Chinese female cheongsam-clad body. These layered associations continue to haunt perceptions of the cheongsam in the minds of Canadian-born women of Chinese heritage today and greatly contribute to an attitude of ambivalence towards the dress, as I will explain in more depth.

By the 1940s, women of all classes in China had adopted the cheongsam as everyday wear. While part of the appeal was its connection to the urban fashion elite and leisure class, it had become more widely available as Shanghai-based tailors began to migrate to Hong Kong at the onset of the Japanese invasion in 1937. The popularity of the cheongsam remained high at this time, but the fluctuation of styles settled down. Wu explained that the Sino–Japanese wars and the insurgence of the Communist party during the 1940s greatly affected the fashion mood. Patriotism and frugality were called for in the media, while new tools and techniques from the West such as zippers, snaps, darts, set-in sleeves, and detachable linings for easy cleaning brought the cheongsam into step with a new set of practical needs.

The Republic Era ended in 1949 with the establishment of the Communist party and the founding of the People's Republic of China on the mainland. The values of austerity, hardship, and egalitarianism marked another shift in the history of China which was enforced through sartorial codes. As Wu described, "anything bourgeois was looked down upon, and the cheongsam accordingly fell out of fashion" (2009, p. 111). The dress that had initially represented freedom and modernity now signified extravagance in the eyes of the new ruling government. The cheongsam was discarded for a plain jacket and trousers, called the "people's suit," which exemplified the government's continued understanding of the power of clothing to shape ideas and attitudes.

In the 1950s the cheongsam mostly disappeared from daily life in Mainland China but was occasionally worn by certain elites such as the

Figure 2 Charlotte Sim in cheongsam circa 1940s (Courtesy Sim family collection)

wives of prominent politicians, actresses, and society women. In places such as Hong Kong, Singapore, and Taiwan, that functioned under a separate historical and political narrative, the dress continued to be a staple in women's wardrobes. For a number of the women interviewed for this project, including myself, the introduction to the cheongsam came through the mothers, grandmothers, and aunts who lived in these places during the 1950s and 1960s and later emigrated to Canada. The cheongsam was an everyday dress made from practical fabrics such as cotton, wool, tweed, and polyester. The women in our families brought their tailor-made and store-bought dresses with them to Canada and would have more made during visits back to Asia after emigration. As Mainland China became increasingly closed to outside influences, Hong Kong became the primary exporter of Chinese culture to the West. The cheongsam's popularity in Hong Kong, promoted through mainstream culture in the form of cinema, fashion, and beauty pageants, maintained its image in the West as a symbol of female Chinese cultural identity.[2]

While the cheongsam had arrived in North America via Chinese immigration, it became an international sensation through the musical *The World of Suzie Wong,* starring France Nguyen, which was later made into a

Figures 3 and 4 Women in cheongsam in Hong Kong circa 1950s (Courtesy Sim family collection)

Figure 5 The King family portrait circa 1960s featuring my great-grandmother seated at center and my grandmother Charlotte seated on the right (Courtesy Sim family collection)

movie in 1961 starring Nancy Kwan. Women of Chinese heritage born in North America in the 1950s and 1960s often cite the film version of this musical as an example of negative publicity for Asian women and the cheongsam. It tells the story of Hong Kong prostitute Suzie Wong and her romance with white British lover, Robert Lomax. Lomax is an architect who decides to move to Hong Kong for a year to try his hand at being a painter. He meets a woman named Mee Ling on the ferry to Hong Kong Island and, based on her clothing, he thinks she is a respectable young woman of good social standing. The next time he sees her is in a bar, in the company of a sailor and wearing a tight fitting, red cheongsam. He then realizes that she is a prostitute who goes by the name Suzie Wong. He asks her to model for one of his paintings and they begin to get to know each other. He finds out that she was forced into prostitution when she was ten years old. As they spend more time together, they start to fall in love, but Lomax attenuates their growing affair. Later, when Lomax's friend Ben Marlowe, a married white man, offers to make Suzie his mistress, she accepts to make Lomax jealous. But when Marlowe gets back together with his wife and asks Lomax to tell Suzie, the pain of rejection overwhelms her. A feeling of empathy overthrows Lomax's hurt pride, and he pledges his love to her. Their relationship starts off well and Suzie stops working as a prostitute, but faces difficulties when Lomax discovers that Suzie has been hiding a child. He accepts the child but their relationship is again put to the test when he starts to have financial problems. His pride prevents him from taking money from Suzie. When she pays his rent and offers to resume prostitution to help him, he casts her away in a fit of anger. After acknowledging his mistake he goes after Suzie. When he finds her, she has discovered that her baby was killed in the annual floods. They finally reconcile, committing themselves to each other forever. The "white knight" saving the tragic Asian woman is a narrative that is reiterated in other texts, including Puccini's opera *Madame Butterfly* (1898) and the hit Broadway musical *Miss Saigon* (1991). In relation to the dress, what women of Chinese heritage in North America remember best is how *The World of Suzie Wong* fueled the exotic/erotic appeal of the cheongsam. WESSIELING (2007) writes, "*The World of Suzie Wong* brought the cheongsam to Western audiences alongside the ascription of sexy-exoticism to the dress" (2007, p. 31). She goes on to explain that "[r]eflective of the plot, a love story that crosses racial, cultural and social boundaries, Suzie's beauty is contained through her appearance in the cheongsam which has been sexualised and exoticized ... feeding the desire of the gaze" (2007, p. 31). WESSIELING argued that the inter-cultural affiliations of the musical and film that bring the "Orient" into contact with the West through a hybrid setting (the film was shot in Hong Kong and London), hybrid plot (set in British Hong Kong), and a hybrid actress (France Nguyen, the star of the musical is of French and Vietnamese ancestry, while the star of the film version, Nancy Kwan, is of Chinese and British origin) increased the exotic appeal of the story in the West. Suddenly, white women wanted to wear this dress as way to access a fantasy-based mystique. The excitement over what became known as the "Suzie Wong dress" reverberated back to Hong Kong, Taiwan, and Singapore and the cheongsam became even more form-fitting, as evidenced in photographs.

As the cut came closer to the body, and the slits rose higher, American journalists started to take note. In a 1964 article in the *Saturday Evening Post*, Stanley Karnow observed that "the proper cheongsam is supposed to look as if it were painted on" and that "[t]raffic accidents in Taipei increase sharply at lunch hour, when girls in their slit skirts grace the city's boulevards" (Pepin Press, 85). The tightness of the cheongsam was a result of a feedback loop between fashion trends, media images, and the cultivation of a fantasy. In interviews, many of the women in this project felt that only slender women could look good in the dress, given its close cut. Even as late as 1996, advertisements for the "Suzie Wong" dress could be found in importer trade magazines in England and, as evidenced in my interviews, the cheongsam is still popular as a Halloween costume for those who wish to masquerade as a "sexy Chinese" type character.

The issue of cultural appropriation and the flattening of Asian culture, coupled with the association of the cheongsam with overt sexuality, continue to inform mainstream perceptions of the cheongsam today. The dress form that had emerged as a representation of emancipation and equality for women had now become one of constraint. With reference to Marcel Mauss's 1973 paper *Techniques of the Body*, the tightness of the modern cheongsam limited women's movement and forced them to adopt a whole other way of walking, sitting, standing, and bending down. The representation of the cheongsam in popular Western culture would also continue to associate the dress with sexual availability. While other pieces of Western clothing, such as the mini skirt of the 1960s and "skinny" jeans of the 2000s, expose the female body, it is the cheongsam's additional association with a colonialist fantasy that further marks the way it is perceived.

The onset of the Great Proletarian Cultural Revolution in China (1966–76) brought about a seek and destroy mission led by the Red Guard to rid society of any decadent, bourgeois clothing or accessories. Clark described a

Shanghai woman's account of how the "Red Guards burned all her cheongsam and ripped up photographs of her wearing them, using anti-imperialism as a justification" (2000, p. 23). Finnane also describes the story of Wang Guangmei, wife of President Liu Shaoqi, who had been filmed wearing a cheongsam during a tour to Southeast Asia in 1963. Her wearing of the cheongsam was noted by the zealous Jinggangshan Corps, which subjected her to a mock trial where she was charged with being "a member of the reactionary bourgeoisie" (2008, p. 227) and was "humiliated by being forced to put on a *qipao* too small for her, a necklace of ping-pong balls and high heeled shoes" (p. 228).

These coercive acts are reminiscent of those carried out by the Manchu during the Qing dynasty and are a continued testimony to the instrumentalization of clothing and the politics associated with what to wear and what not to wear. The cheongsam was out and replaced by the practical, androgynous, monochromatic clothing of the Cultural Revolution, which became the dress-image that China wished to present to the world. As Wu explained, "[in] the sea of monotonous blue and gray, outsiders divined a deeper meaning: uniformity in dress signified the desire for uniformity in thought and behavior" (2009, p. 112).

Hazel Clark (2000), Juanjuan Wu (2009), WESSIELING (2007) and others marked the late 1960s as the start of the decline of the cheongsam in places like Hong Kong, Singapore, and Taiwan where the garment survived after the founding of the People's Republic of China. As the ready-to-wear garment industry took off in Hong Kong, mass-produced Western-style clothing became more available and affordable. The desire for Western garments reflected the changing values and desires of a new generation which, as Clark notes, regarded the cheongsam as "old-fashioned and too obviously 'Chinese'" (Clark 2000, 28). This younger generation wished to incarnate, yet again, a Western style of modernity. Choosing to wear Western clothes at this time closely resembled the ideas of the Republic Era, which were linked with an image of social advancement and exemplified sophisticated taste and style knowledge. At the same time, the cheongsam sparked controversy for being worn too tight, with slits too high, prompting the Catholic Church and other community organizations to intervene. Clark described how the Kai Fong Association held a "Happy Family Life" campaign that urged women to wear cheongsam with knee length hemlines and only two-inch slits (2000, p. 30). By the 1970s, the hem of the cheongsam continued to rise in order to compete with the mini skirt. But this iteration of the cheongsam was considered vulgar and without the elegance appropriate for what was still considered the national dress. From this period onward, the cheongsam became outmoded as everyday wear for the new generation.

By the 1980s in Mainland China, Wu explained, "the political focus suddenly shifted from class struggle to economic development" (2009, p. 112). With this change of mindset yet again, people began to exercise more freedom in their choice of clothing, which brought about a revival of older ethnic garments including the cheongsam. The fashion industry got a major boost from the government to ignite the economic development of China. An attempt was made to resuscitate the cheongsam, whose appeal could be revived as a fashion garment for Chinese women and for women around the world. The cheongsam started to appear in magazines, advertisements and stores. In practice, however, with the Cultural Revolution and Red Guard tactics not so far in the distance, women still hesitated to wear the cheongsam. Wu explained that women's ambivalence was centered around the paradoxes now associated with the dress, which was "modish yet a fashion from a bygone era. It was feminine, yet backward looking. It was classic, yet looked out of place" (2009, p. 112). Wu cited the publishing of an article in July 1983 in the *Ximmin Evening News* titled "Women Like to Wear the Qipao: There is No Need to Fear" as an attempt by the government to mitigate women's concerns about the dress and stimulate its activity in the marketplace. The article told the story of a woman who wanted to buy a cheongsam but hesitated because she was afraid of what the leaders in her work unit would think. The formality and constraint of the cheongsam was also still out of step with the general desire for more casual and comfortable clothes. All of these factors worked against the government's attempt to revive the cheongsam for the sake of the growing fashion industry, and interest in the dress did not take off on a mass level. However, as Wu pointed out, "attempts to promote the [cheongsam] in the media did help to re-popularize it as ceremonial attire for traditional holidays and special occasions" (2009, p.113) and it still found an enthusiastic, if niche, audience in China, that as I will explain would increase into the 2000s.

The cheongsam as signifier of Chinese culture became part of the fashion vocabulary in the West, even if the mainstream public did not know its proper name. This message went back to China and, as Wu writes, "affected views of the [cheongsam] as serving as a symbol of Chinese identity" (2009, p. 116). To illustrate this point, Wu described how renowned Mainland Chinese actress Gong Li wore this dress for her debut at the Venice International Film Festival in 1992, and further explained how China experienced "its own China fad, marked by a revival of many traditional styles as street fashions along with a renewed and intensified interest in Chinese traditional culture" (Wu, 2000, pp. 117–18). As noted by Clark (2000), Hong Kong designer William Tang updated the cheongsam in his 1992 collection, which presented the dress in contemporary colors worn with eclectic accessories. At the same time a new crop of designers based in Beijing began to reference and re-invent the cheongsam. Shanghai Tang, a major retail chain launched in 1994, promoted home furnishings, gifts, and clothing including the cheongsam which drew on nostalgic images of 1930s Shanghai. Sun Jian and Guo Pei were noted as the first designers to arrive on the scene with their collections, which both featured pieces that evoked the cheongsam. Clark described their joint 1996 fashion show, called "Approaching 1997," as a reflection of "the eagerness with which Mainland designers awaited the return of Hong Kong to China, which would provide greater access to what was seen as a key fashion centre in East Asia" (2000, p. 58).

Clark, WESSIELING, and Wu described how the 1990s' attempt to revive the cheongsam triangulated a dialogue between Chinese designers, designers of Chinese heritage based in the West, and Western high fashion houses. In 1993, Anna Sui, an American-born designer of Chinese heritage, created cheongsams that merged contemporary popular culture with retro cheongsam styles. In Sui's 2010 biography, Andrew Bolton (2010) described how these dresses were inspired by her aunt Julia Fang, who had beautiful cheongsams with matching jewelry and shoes. But given the urban context of New York, Sui infused her cheongsam with a grunge feel by pairing them with tulle bell-bottom pants. These dresses were a riotous and exuberant take on a garment that directly referenced her Chinese heritage. By the late 1990s, the cheongsam had also infiltrated the most powerful couture houses of the Western fashion industry and designers such as Karl Lagerfeld, John Galliano, and Jean-Paul Gaultier had all included the cheongsam in their collections. The attention that the cheongsam received at this time brought the dress into every level of the fashion industry, from the suburban malls to the red carpet. Western actresses such as Nicole Kidman and Ginger Spice of 1990s girl group the Spice Girls were heavily photographed wearing the dress, the latter wearing a red mini-cheongsam version to meet former South African president, Nelson Mandela. The attempt in China to give new life to the cheongsam set off a maelstrom of new versions and visibility to the dress in Europe and North America. However, as described by Wu, despite its re-appearance in fashion shows, trade exhibitions, advertisements, and window displays, the cheongsam did not take off as a garment worn by the

Chinese masses into the 2000s. There were many factors that worked against its re-adoption. Younger people still saw it as old-fashioned, while the older generation continued to be haunted by a time when the dress was forbidden. Its use in the service industry as a uniform for workers, such as flight attendants, restaurant servers, and hostesses at commercial events also diminished the associations of the dress with perceptions of formal elegance and grace. As a new century dawned, the cheongsam was no longer officially considered the national dress of China.

The cheongsam in twenty-first-century China

Trying on the cheongsam again

To get a sense of the current status and relevance of the cheongsam in China I looked at activity in the urban centers of Beijing, Shanghai, Hong Kong, and Taipei, where it had been worn at the height of its popularity and where it proves readily available now. As discussed, the cheongsam lost momentum with the end of the Republic Era in 1949 and the rise of the People's Republic of China. When the Cultural Revolution (1966–76) took hold, the cheongsam was further condemned as the Red Guard were mandated to rid the country of clothing and accessories linked with bourgeois excess. With an entire decade of intense ideological shaping, it is understandable that the tarnished image of the cheongsam would stay present in the minds of Chinese society for years to come. But the garment's endless variability and versatility along with its past personification as the national dress of China made it an ideal item for the resuscitation of the country's economy through the fashion industry while nurturing the formation of a modern Chinese identity yet again. As discussed by Juanjuan Wu, the government attempted to encourage women to wear the cheongsam in the interest of stimulating the country's growing fashion industry in the 1990s. In practice, however, women did not readily re-adopt the cheongsam for a few reasons. While the reputation of the cheongsam was certainly sullied, there was also the question of comfort, cost, and practicality. After thirty years of loosely fitted pants, shirt, and jacket which shrouded the body, it would be daunting to wear such a figure hugging dress out in the everyday world. Wth the sharp decrease in the number of skilled tailors, the cost of a custom made cheongsam continued to make it inaccessible to most women. If a cheongsam were to be made, it would be reserved for formal occasions only. Despite the permission granted to wear the dress by the Chinese government, the dress remained largely "un"-ready to wear for women in China throughout the 1980s and 1990s. While it had been taken up by haute couture fashion designers and worn by celebrities in both China and the West, the dress had still been considered a *risqué* and intimidating item. There is, however, some evidence that a shift in attitude took place starting in the early 2000s, due to a combination of economic, political, and cultural stimuli.

It cannot be overstated just how much the film *In the Mood for Love* released in 2000 by Chinese director Wong Kar-wai has influenced the revival of the cheongsam in China, while boosting its appeal around the world. I will discuss the impact of this film on Canadian-born women of Chinese heritage in greater depth later, as it had a major influence on women's desire to claim ownership of the dress despite an ambivalent relationship with Chinese ethnicity. In Mainland China, however, where a sense of national identity is more firmly in place, this film stirred up intense feelings of nostalgia that ignited intense enthusiasm for the dress by a specific generation of women. An article in the online version of *The Telegraph* by Pascale Trouillard (2010) described the emergence of the Shanghai Cheongsam Salon founded in 2007 by retired teacher of Japanese Wang Weiyu. According to the article, Wang was inspired to open a "salon" or club that would be dedicated to the preservation of the tradition of the dress after seeing *In the Mood for Love*. Her passion for the cheongsam was initiated by her mother's practice of wearing the dress daily, and she considers it "one of the most distinctive symbols of Shanghainese culture." Wang then established the Shanghai Cheongsam Salon as a place for women to celebrate the dress through its wearing at meetings and events. The Salon would also function as a gatekeeper of cheongsam etiquette, instructing women on the how, when, and where of cheongsam culture. Members would learn the "body techniques" of its wearing, how to accessorize the dress, and even how to speak and eat when wearing the dress. Furthermore, the Salon would promote the *performance* of the dress through the teaching of songs and dances that Salon members would present at dances, charity balls, and receptions, often aimed at the promotion of tourism and cheongsam fashion. At the time of the article, extensive media coverage had contributed to a boost in the Salon's membership, which had grown to 370 women ranging in age from 22 to 70, with an average age of 55. Wang explained that the majority of members were older women who never had the opportunity to wear the dress in their youth because of its ban during the Cultural

Revolution. *In the Mood for Love* seemed to provide women like Wang the permission to at last step figuratively into their mothers' dress, as a way to live out a fantasy that embodied glamor, elegance, and refinement. The article described how "Zhou Fengying, in a pink frock with floral motifs, says she would not have dared to wear a qipao in her youth, but now enjoys sporting one when she goes to the teahouse with her old friends." Women who described their relationship with the garment reflected this desire in several quotes from the article:

"When I wear a qipao, I feel very beautiful. It puts me in a good mood," said 47-year-old Wei Jiali, sporting a vibrant blue dress with golden stitching.

"You need different colored dresses for different occasions," said the 53-year-old accountant, who gave a detailed rundown of how to wear the qipao—which can cost up to 5,000 yuan (£457)—and how not to wear it. "If you're going to a concert, you don't want to be too flashy. You want to be classy, so you'd need a dress in a darker color, with golden embroidery," she said. "If you're going to a tea house, wear a rather low-key dress in yellow or grey, perhaps with bamboo patterns," she added. "If you're going to a wedding, the qipao cannot be too bright or too extravagant—you don't want to upstage the bride! That would be too embarrassing!" (Trouillerd, 2010)

This last quote testifies to the importance of specific modalities that govern the "how to" of the cheongsam. What this indicates is how cheongsam wearing is a barometer for correct judgement that emphasizes the value of social capital through style savvy.

In an earlier 2009 CNN online article, (2009) Kellie Schmitt outlined the activities of the Shanghai Cheongsam Salon, describing their monthly meetings and excursions to Suzhou and Taiwan to take part in "cheongsam parades," which would consist of large gatherings of women displaying their best, most colorful cheongsams as they walked through the streets. This article also revealed that Wang's decision to start the club also came out of her volunteer work as a teacher of etiquette and culture. She explained that many of her students were older women who "... didn't have a high level of education, and felt like they were lower class," she says. "They wanted to learn manners and etiquette." Schmitt interviewed members of the salon who described what wearing the cheongsam meant to them:

"I always liked the Chinese qipao but there was never an opportunity for me to wear it," says member Chen Ling. "If I were to wear it alone on the street, it would be pretty strange." That all changed when Chen caught a glimpse of the Chinese qipao club strutting their stuff on Nanjing Lu. She joined the club, now holds a club leadership role, and has nearly two-dozen gowns of her own.

Schmitt's article also revealed another key factor of the Salon's popularity for this generation of women by noting that "[f]or member Zhang Jing Hua, the club is about confidence." When wearing the dress, "it makes you feel like a woman," she explained, as she showed off her black and white floral Chinese qipao—"Isn't it beautiful?" Schmitt's article described how the dress had a positive impact on the self-confidence of members, changing the way they felt about themselves. The popularity of the Salon lay in its ability to create a validating and safe space for women to wear the dress. The security of wearing the dress in large numbers established a sense of solidarity and fellowship that was freeing for women. Wang explained that some members even confided in her that the Salon had affected the way they were perceived by their husbands. At the time of the article, the Salon was planning to have an exhibition at the 2010 Shanghai Expo and planned to take its activities to Japan to promote Shanghai culture. This was all very exciting for Wang, as the Salon was now validated as a legitimate cultural entity. But it was the quieter achievement of recognizing the cheongsam's ability to help women discover their own beauty and grace that seemed to be of even greater satisfaction.

On 29 May 2012, another article about the Shanghai Cheongsam Salon was published in the *People's Daily*, the biggest newspaper in China. This article was then picked up by the travel website china.org.cn, which is aimed at an international audience. The article described the fifth annual gathering of the Shanghai Cheongsam Salon on May 26, 2012 during which approximately 400 members assembled on Shanghai's Century Avenue wearing their best cheongsams. The event attracted a reported 2,000 cheongsam "fans," consisting of tourists and local residents. Since its founding in 2007, the club had now visited Japan, South Korea, and several countries in Europe, spreading appreciation for the cheongsam while simultaneously promoting Chinese culture and its products. Wang Weiyu, now 65, wore a red cheongsam with pearl accessories, crediting the cheongsam for having a transformative effect on women, and stating that "[a]ll members of the salon are graceful and confident, and talk decently, thanks to the changes brought about by cheongsams." The article went on to report that as one of their orders of business at this gathering, the Salon wanted to establish 20 May as China Cheongsam Day, "[…] in hopes that every Chinese woman will wear a cheongsam on that day to show feminine gentleness and nobleness." While the average age of members still hovered around 55, the club was beginning to attract younger women born in the 1980s, like Chi Yiwei, who majored in flight attendance at the Zhonghua Vocational School in Shanghai. The article reported that she wore a cheongsam for the first time on that day, accompanied by eight of her colleagues as they walked "hand in hand with Wang in front of the sundial before the night fell to have a unique initiation rite." Another cheongsam convert, Chi excitedly said that she would "[…] wear a cheongsam in all future major ceremonies in my life." Wang was happy to see more women as young as eighteen, including many "overseas returnees," express their interest in wearing the dress, and explained that she would "focus on promoting cheongsams on [university] campuses in order to pass the culture on to the younger generation." She also set a goal to "recruit more women who like cheongsams in the second half of the year, and teach them cheongsam etiquette, so they will be beautiful both inside and outside."

The Shanghai Cheongsam Salon's presentations and exhibitions at fairs such as the Expo Shanghai in 2010 were strategic activities aimed at stimulating China's tourism and fashion industries. With its renaissance as a piece of clothing emblematic of Chinese culture, the cheongsam re-articulated the Chinese "brand," operating as a soft power. Bloggers have also been instrumental players in the popularization of the cheongsam, providing tourists with a comprehensive list of names, addresses, and detailed descriptions for what they consider the best cheongsam purveyors in a variety of cities. What I noted when browsing numerous online cheongsam stores and blog articles was how the terms "cheongsam" and "*qipao*" were now used interchangeably, which I presume is a move to ensure that potential customers would know that these terms referred to the same garment. All of this effort contributed greatly to growing the resurgence and popularity of the dress. On May 20, 2017, ChinaDaily.com reported that thousands of women from countries all over the world had descended upon Hangzhou, Zhejiang province, to attend cheongsam fashion shows and to gather in the streets wearing the cheongsam where they sang, read poetry, and posed for photographs.[6] Women wearing cheongsams were also offered special discounts in bookstores and coffee shops as well as admission to popular tourist sites such as the Xixi National Wetland Park. Mathilde Blaschyk, a French woman who had been living in China for the last six years, attended the festivities and was quoted as saying that "(w)omen in *qipao* are very beautiful and walk in a graceful way. I want to be more beautiful, and that's why I chose to attend the *qipao* fashion show today." The article also explained that twelve cheongsam fashion shows had taken place in Hamburg, Madrid, London, and Sydney during the month of May as part of the Global *Qipao* Festival "initiated by Hangzhou to promote the traditional dress, and the city, to the world." The instrumentalization of the cheongsam to attract tourism echoes its use in calendar advertisements of the 1920s and 1930s. These events show how the dress has been re-taken up as the object upon which the fantasy of an exotic trip to China could be projected. The endorsement of the cheongsam by industry players inside and outside China demonstrates the garment's ongoing relevance to social, economic, cultural, and political interests.

It is important to discuss in more depth the significance of Wang Weiyu's cheongsam project as an offshoot of her work as a lecturer in Shanghai's "A Million Families Learn Etiquette" project, which is a state sponsored "civility campaign." Thao Thi Phuong Nguyen's 2012 doctoral thesis, "The Discourse of *Wenming* ('Civilisation'): Moral Authority and Social Change in Contemporary Shanghai" (Nguyen, 2012) examined these campaigns and their part in the Chinese government's efforts to shape a new Chinese society. As Nguyen explained, civility is an approach to self-conduct "associated with all the idealised attributes that are embodied in a new citizenry: enterprising, self-determining, creative, prudent, law-abiding, nationalistic and above all, politically acquiescent to the CCP-led government" (2012, p. 22). Nguyen identified the "civilising campaigns," which began in the 1980s, as the primary approach used to carry out the formation of a new citizenry, as economic reforms were being introduced, shifting economic opportunity to urban areas. Not surprisingly, the campaigns suggested the superiority of city life over rural life, and that in order to aspire to living in an urban environment, one had to adhere to the norms of civilized conduct. With increased migration to cities there came a growing concern about the congestion of public spaces and general overcrowding. The campaigns were also used to impart basic instructional knowledge to make citizens "aware of basic ground rules governing everyday conduct" (2012, p. 23). These ground rules covered the execution of everyday tasks such as how to assist someone in need or how to choose a seat on the bus, to more personal self-conduct issues, such as to how to put on make-up when going out in public. Content for these campaigns was often culled from official publications produced by the Civilization Office and the Shanghai Municipal government and disseminated through etiquette booklets and courses like the "A Million Families Learn Etiquette" project. These initiatives accompanied the government's move towards a socialist market economy, which had enmeshed itself with global trade like never before. The civilizing mission was also attached to the government's rhetoric of "good governance," which yoked civility to the "goals of nation building, prosperity, harmony and stability" (2012, p. 22). Nguyen described an important change in approach to governance that was enunciated through two specific terms: "*jihua*" and "*guihua*." These terms were used to describe differences in approach to governing that put an emphasis on the concept of governance. While both terms mean "to plan," "*jihua*" emerged in the Maoist period and is associated with detailed planning and discipline by the state. "*Guihua*," on the other hand, was a reform-era term that was based on the same platform but introduced an aspect of latitude for cooperation and collaboration beyond state institutions. This would imply some degree of agency for citizens to have a say in how they would be governed. But what Nguyen pointed out is that while "*guihua*" implied space for consensus building between the state and civil society for the governing of the population, it covertly maintained control by shifting the task of civilizing from the political center to a "multitude of sites including communities, classrooms, workplaces and homes, that enforce the messages of national programs to influence conduct at a 'molecular' level without being identified with the party-state *per se*" (2012, p. 23). While Wang's impetus to start the Shanghai Cheongsam Salon was driven by her passion for the dress and its representation of the history and culture of Shanghai, it could also be seen as an extension of her work as a volunteer to instruct citizens further in the embodiment of civilized behavior. In other words, inside China, the cheongsam's ability to inspire nostalgia and fantasy, combined with its inherent seductive beauty, plays well into the government's desire to put into effect a set of normative codes of conduct. The cheongsam could be activated as a vehicle for the civilizing mission, which, for the state, is meant to serve the good of society. But as Nguyen points out,

we must be made aware that the call for civility, in whatever form, always has hidden socio-economic overtones. Manners, then and now, were as much about social distinction (for instance, in drawing class and gender divisions) as they were about a person's actual moral character. (2012, p. 26)

Many of the codes of conduct put forth in the state's etiquette guides provide practical information on how to politely negotiate a crowded city. However, the etiquette courses go further to teach one how to hone one's image and cultivate one's outer appearance. As the civilizing mission has taken hold, citizens have become increasingly concerned with their "dress, manner of speech and general demeanour" (2012, p. 209), instilling an understanding, as Nguyen explains, of the existence of "good taste," "good manners," and "good behavior." This ability to judge good from bad in this sense becomes a hegemonic force "whereby the ideas and ideals of the ruling class including their claim to social leadership become part of common-sense understanding and habitual practices of the general population" (2012, p. 27). In this way, the civility mission as it extends to manners may foster the authority of an elite who have mastered these skills, over those who have not. The fashion industry, cheongsam clubs, fashion shows, and festivals all contribute to elevating the dress to one of elite status. Like most status symbols, the cultivation of the desirability of the cheongsam resides in its high access barriers. *Savoir-faire* is inherent to wearing the cheongsam, as attested by Wang's etiquette lessons. One is concerned with having the correct body type, with discerning a "good" quality dress from a "bad" one, from knowing which cheongsam's combination of fabric and color are appropriate for a given situation, and from a mastery of the proper execution of the dress's body techniques. While the Shanghai Cheongsam Salon is driven by a genuine passion for the dress as well as the desire to encourage more women to wear it, it is difficult to deny that this drive could be bound up with the cultivation of exclusivity. A club after all has membership requirements, which would inevitable deny some. How might these clubs reproduce and re-assert socio-economic divisions in society as China has steadily established a strong *nouveau riche* and middle class over the last thirty years? At what point might the enforcement of proper cheongsam etiquette become an undeniably coercive quality of the dress as technology described by Ursula Franklin?[7] The glorious images of Maggie Cheung wearing a variety of exquisite cheongsam in *In the Mood for Love* add another layer to the combination of desire and dread that accompanies the dress, as the actress sets the bar for wearing the cheongsam incredibly high. While wearing the cheongsam is a very exciting prospect, it is mixed with a heavy dose of intimidation, which I argue further contributes to its appeal.

I am reluctant to fully cast cheongsam clubs as simply arms-length instruments of the state. These organizations offer women the occasion to indulge in fantasy and nostalgia, which I feel can be an empowering exercise.

The dress offers a kind of escapism, where women can live out an aspect of themselves that they were not permitted to enact in their youth. Furthermore, women find both communion in wearing the dress together and enjoyment through literally *performing* the cheongsam through the presentation of songs and dances organized for an audience or at an *ad hoc* gathering on the street. This mode of cheongsam wearing is a specified activity that draws strength in numbers and creates a safe space for engaging with the pleasurable performativity of the cheongsam. But the practice of wearing the dress in everyday life, such as to work or going out with friends, is still uneven. The United Arab Emirates online newspaper *The National* published a story by Daniel Bardsley on August 23, 2012 that described a woman's search for a cheongsam for her wedding to her Italian fiancé.[8] A 32-year-old Beijing local, Guo Bin planned to wear a Western style white dress for the ceremony, but wanted to wear a cheongsam for the reception, which had become a common custom for contemporary Chinese women. Guo explained that while the cheongsam was considered outmoded by her parent's generation, it was now considered fashionable by her generation, saying that "[t]he [cheongsam] can present beauty for a Chinese person that western clothes cannot present. The elegance, the traditional beauty—only the [cheongsam] can explain it." She bought her first cheongsam in 2003 and now has several in her wardrobe including a few that she occasionally wears to work. In the same article, Xu Qingbaio, a sales manager for Shanghai Xu, a Beijing-based clothing store chain that specializes in cheongsam, put forth his theory for the increase in women buying cheongsam, asserting that "... it's just that Chinese people are getting more confident about their identity. Chinese women think the [cheongsam] is more Chinese and they like to identify themselves as Chinese women." As a young professional, Chen Yuan, a 28-year-old accountant, is described in the article as being typical of the women currently buying cheongsam. She recently had a red and green dress made for a wedding reception, maintaining that "... [i]t's important, it's part of our cultural heritage. Chinese women have worn this for a very long time." An article by staff writer Nina Vickery posted on February 17, 2014 on Chinatoday.com added complexity to this viewpoint.[9] Entitled "Qipao Comeback," and illustrated with a still image from *In the Mood for Love*, Vickery described the cheongsam's renewed influence on Chinese designers as it was a central form seen on runways of the 2013 edition of Beijing Fashion Week. She also remarked the dress's growing popularity due to the efforts of the Shanghai Cheongsam Club. But what is more telling about the contemporary status of the cheongsam in Mainland China are the descriptions of wearing practices by two women in their early thirties who Vickery interviewed. As she describes in the article, Weiwei Ma and Sun Jian, both Chinese language teachers at an international school in Beijing, had very different experiences with the dress:

> Weiwei owns about five qipao, but she doesn't wear them very often. "I had one tailor-made for my wedding, and the others were bought ready-made. I bought them to wear at big events, including work-related events such as International Day, when students and teachers wear national dress to showcase the diversity within the school and to celebrate their cultural heritage. In fact, the last time I wore a qipao was International Day, and it did make me feel proud to be Chinese," Weiwei told me. When asked whether she would consider wearing a qipao every day to work, she said, "I prefer to keep my qipao for special occasions. Plus, I don't think wearing a qipao is suitable for everyone, as it needs to suit your character. While I do think the qipao can look elegant, I, personally, feel a bit uncomfortable in mine. But I have had colleagues who would wear qipao every day. That was their style."
>
> Sun Jian has never bought a qipao; the last time she wore one was when she was at school herself. "I remember I wore a qipao to school in the summer. It was a kind of everyday item for little girls then." These days, Sun doesn't think qipao suit her body shape. "I think qipao are very pretty and can look gorgeous on some people, but they are very demanding on women's figures. Models can get away with it." Sun recounted a humorous experience with the qipao: "Nowadays, it seems qipao are worn by receptionists at fancy restaurants or hotels rather than regular people going about their daily business. I remember one year, one of my colleagues wore her new, tailor-made qipao to work, and everyone joked that she looked like a waitress from Quanjude Roast Duck Restaurant!" (Vickery, 2014)

Vickery concluded from these testimonies that for the vast majority of women in Mainland China, the cheongsam had not made its way into everyday wearing practices. Captivated by the beauty of the dress, however, she expressed her desire for this to change with the hope that "by spring when Beijing warms up, so too will women warm up to the idea of reinventing the [cheongsam] as a wardrobe staple. By then, perhaps I will also be ready to go ahead and try one on, myself." From these accounts, it would seem the cheongsam was no longer vilified. But its general wearing would still come with a number of social, cultural, and market conditions.

The market

Into the 2000s, China became a major global economic player, in part due to the success of its manufacturing industry. While the cheongsam had not regained the popularity it had in the past, it did recover a remarkable degree of favor. This is due largely to the interlaced efforts of the state-supported fashion and tourism industries, which endeavored to change attitudes towards the dress which were further aided by cultural initiatives such as the Shanghai Cheongsam Club and, indirectly, by mass media and films like *In the Mood for Love*. Activity in Beijing and Shanghai as well as Hong Kong and Taipei demonstrates that the market for the dress is on a strong simmer. Offerings are slowly becoming more diverse and, thanks to the internet, versions of the cheongsam that consider more casual fabrics and easier to wear cuts are gradually becoming more available to women in China and around the world.

In Beijing and Shanghai, inexpensive but low quality mass-produced cheongsams can be found in shopping malls for around US$60. There are also more luxurious malls that offer a range of tailoring shops for custom made cheongsams. The client can choose their fabric and the model of the dress, which includes sleeve options, length of hem and other details, from a set of samples. After measurements are taken, the dress will take anywhere from twenty-four hours to ten days to complete, depending on the specifics of the dress and the number of fittings. On a trip to Shanghai in 2013, my mother went through this process, and said that upon the first fitting, each of the three dresses she ordered was perfect. The tailor shop she worked with only charged a very reasonable US$100 per dress for a basic model in house fabrics. But prices can easily move into the thousands depending on the choice of fabric and other details. The market for the cheongsam in Hong Kong and Taiwan is also active and showing signs of design and fabric innovation amongst higher end designer brands. However, more mainstream market offerings in these areas follow the contours of Mainland China's cheaply mass-produced dresses. The problem for the proliferation of the cheongsam lies in the fact that there is very little to be found in the mid-range that offers a well made dress, appropriate for work or school, at an accessible price point. This may be changing as new start-up companies which identified this gap have been given a chance to emerge. One of these is Pom & Co., which specializes in floral cheongsams, founded by Shi Minyue in April 2016 when she was just twenty years old. As reported in August 2016 by Rebecca Feng for *FORBES ASIA*, Shi was inspired to start the company while a sophomore art history student at Brown University.[10] She had always been fascinated by the cheongsam, and as part of a behavioral art project she decided to wear a cheongsam every day for one year starting in May 2014, while traveling to thirty cities on three continents. She wrote a book about her journey in which she said, "[t]he beauty of qipao is not that it makes you stunning on an important occasion. Rather, it reveals beauty in the ordinary everyday life with the fragrance of a cup of jasmine tea." During her journey, it occured to Shi that Chinese women were only wearing the cheongsam for special occasions because it was very difficult to find dresses that had quality design and fabrication for a reasonable price. In 2012, a custom made brocade, full length dress of fine silk could cost upwards of US$2500. A less formal, tailor made dress of good quality would cost around US$250. As the article explained, Shi thought there would be a good market for affordable dresses in classic floral prints that women could wear for everyday activities without feeling overdressed. She quit Brown after her sophomore year and attended one semester at Central Saint Martins College of Arts and Design in London. Two months after returning to her home city of Beijing, she launched her brand, Pom & Co. The article went on to explain that since 2013, the government had been nurturing the entrepreneurial spirit of college students through "building incubators for startups and providing stipends to students with start-up ventures." The company was described as doing comparatively well. While the average student startup received an average of RMB 500,000 (approximately US$80,000), Pom & Co. received two million (about US$300,000) in its first round of fundraising. At the time of the article, Shi already had seven full-time and two part-time employees. The main selling platforms were online marketplaces for independent designers like StyleWe and Wechat. With prices ranging from US$50 to 130 per dress, the company targeted middle and upper-middle class women in China. Its website, available in Chinese, presents the latest collection of ready to wear clothing for women that features about fifteen pieces including Western style tops, skirts, and dresses, and three cheongsams. The cheongsam all follow the classic sheath cut, are sleeveless, cut just above the knee with modest slits, and are otherwise minimal, without any *huaniu* or traditional flower buttons. On a different portal, I found more items, including knitwear, embroidered wool skirts, and velvet embellished sweatshirts. But when randomly clicking

Figure 6 My mother Rosalina Sim in one of her custom-made cheongsams purchased in Shanghai in 2013 (Courtesy Sim family collection)

through the Chinese-only website, I found more cheongsam dresses included in the Fall collection, in fresh and modern floral patterns but also in darker colors such as navy blue and gray. These dresses were also gently fitted, with long sleeves that hit above the wrist, a hem just below the knee, and one slit at the front-right side of the dress. The pretty and feminine prints, along with the tasteful cuts, were intended for a target market of women aged about 18–29. I also remarked that the Pom & Co online presence featured a mix of Chinese and white women as their models, which would indicate a branding strategy to be perceived as a company that is international in scope while in step with a modern Chinese sensibility.

Out of Hong Kong, there are two designer brands that stand out for their innovation in cheongsam design: *Yi-Ming* founded in 2011 by former model Grace Choi and *Classics Anew*, founded by designer Janko Lam. Clothing by *Yi-Ming* can be found at their bricks and mortar store and through their comprehensive website.[11] Grace Choi's label offers a full line of knitwear, dresses, tops, skirts, pants, jackets, capes, accessories, clothing for children, and formal cheongsams. In the "Dress" section of the website, there are several designs that bring the distinguishing features of the cheongsam together with Western style dresses, in a range of silhouettes. I was excited to see a straight, shift-cut, hot pink dress with high collar, long sleeves and black piping around the cuffs and collar. Another design was a silk wrap dress, with a pink and gray square chain print on white background, a V-neck finished with the high collar, three-quarter sleeves, a drawstring waist and gently draped skirt which would be perfect for an office environment. The "Qipao/ Cheongsam" section presented Choi's collection of cheongsam dresses in more formal fabrics such as lace, silk, and brocade. The shape adhered mostly to the fitted sheath cut, but there was some play with asymmetric hemlines and sleeve variations such as a cape affect. The price point is located on the higher side, with prices that hover around US$250 per dress. Yi-Ming's knitwear, which features a Victorian-style jacquard-loomed motif, includes capes and jackets with the characteristic high collar. While not available from Yi-Ming's online store, there were some images of cheongsams made from this same knit fabric. One image from a newspaper article featured Grace Choi's visibly pregnant body in one of these knit cheongsams. Its A-line cut and stretch fabric looked comfortable and easy to wear.

Janko Lam's *Classics Anew* is perfectly named for her line of clothing that re-works the cheongsam and other pieces of traditional Chinese clothing.[12] One of the signature aspects of her line is the use of leftover rough denim, a decision that won her the top prize at the Eco Chic competition in 2011. The use of denim gives her clothing a modern and casual feel, while the cuts and tailoring demonstrate a proclivity for the *avant-garde*. Her "QUE" collection features approximately fifty pieces that include dresses, trousers, tops, and jackets made from organic cotton, denim, linen, and silk. One of her more innovative cheongsams is made from black linen and features a trapeze cut, an asymmetrical hem that stops mid-thigh, and no slits. Three simple knotted buttons adorn the top of the right shoulder. The edgy and minimal effect is a far cry from the fitted silhouette and heavy brocade fabric of the traditional cheongsam. Another dress from the same collection is a loosely fitted mini sheath cut, made from distressed denim. A curved seam on the yoke of the dress is reminiscent of the diagonal opening across the top of cheongsam styles from the 1930s. The designer brand is aware that it is working in a hybrid mode of address, but is conscious of its customer's susceptibility to the garment's quixotic past. As stated on its website, the brand blends "Chinese traditional aesthetics with contemporary elements. With its unique, elegant and timeless design, it [keeps] the nostalgic Chinese romance alive."

At the other end of the cheongsam design spectrum are two Hong Kong tailors who for decades have been dedicated to bespoke dresses made in the traditional style with specialized techniques. These include Mei Hwa, the very first and oldest cheongsam shop, founded in the 1920s by the Kan family, and Linva Tailor, who opened in 1965 and were responsible for the creation of the dresses worn by Maggie Cheung in *In the Mood for Love*.[13] These tailors managed to stay open despite the dress's fall in popularity starting in the 1970s. Their longstanding reputation is built on highly skilled artisanship where the value of using a single needle and thread has been upheld against all odds. Both shops are committed to operating into the future, but the issue of survival depends on passing down their knowledge. Mei Hwa once had thirty tailors and now employs only two. As fewer and fewer people wore the cheongsam, these *sifus* or masters started to disappear. In Taiwan however, as reported on Hindu.com on September 28, 2017, Lin Chin-te, a seventy-four-year-old *sifu* with sixty years of experience, is currently training designers, three of whom are women.[14] The presence of more women in the traditionally male-dominated tailoring trade could also have a positive impact on design innovations based on real knowledge of women's current lifestyles and needs. Thirty-seven-year-old Hung Chu-Tsu plans on opening her own shop that will offer hand made cheongsams "adapted to modern life." The article also explains that the dress's appeal may have been hampered by the cheap, mass-produced dresses that flooded the marketplace, and some designers say that "recent growing anti-China sentiment has also put off young people, as they associate the dress with mainland culture." The challenge of addressing these political and design ramifications is motivation for these young designers, who are actively investing their time and energy into keeping the cheongsam alive and relevant. Lee Wei-Fan is a twenty-five-year-old designer who studied under a master for five years before launching his own business in early 2017. Under the name "Qipao Hunk," he built up a social media following and believes there is a viable cheongsam fanbase. Furthermore, he feels that as the market becomes more competitive, his training in hand-made dresses will give him an edge.

Into the late 2010s, it seems that the popularity of the cheongsam is linked to nostalgia and fantasy, an idea not lost on the marketing strategies of newer designers working with this garment. For the time being, the cheongsam has not been fully revived as an item of daily dressing for Chinese women, and continues mostly to punctuate a wardrobe as a formal garment. This could change, as opportunities for young designers looking to capitalize on the potential of the dress are on the rise. With the right combination of financial interest and innovative designs that take comfort, style, and price into consideration, the dress could be taken up more widely.

The migration of the cheongsam to Canada

The cheongsam's arrival in Canada can be traced thanks to two major contributions to the history of Chinese Canadian women in Canada. *Jin Guo: Voices of Chinese Canadian Women* (1992) is an oral history book project produced by The Women's Book Committee of the Chinese Canadian National Council. This groundbreaking collection of interviews offers an invaluable archive of stories and experiences of women who immigrated to Canada from China and Canadian-born women of Chinese heritage. It begins with an interview with Margaret Chan, one of the oldest living pioneer women, and ends with Sharon Lee, an artist and writer born in British Columbia. The second major contribution to the documentation of the history of Chinese women in Canada is the website project *Chinese Canadian Women, 1923-1967: Inspiration—Innovation—Ingenuity*, produced by the Multicultural History Society of Ontario (MHSO). This veritable goldmine of oral histories, photographs, pedagogical resources, and virtual exhibits was created in order to recognize and commemorate "Chinese Canadian women for the important roles they played during a challenging time in their community's history, the over four decades in which Canadian immigration policy was blatantly discriminatory."

Jin Guo: Voices of Chinese Canadian Women features a brief overview of the history of Chinese women in Canada and also features a fascinating selection of historically significant photos. In its historical overview, it is explained that most of the first Chinese women who arrived in Canada came from the Pearl River Delta region of Guangdong province in Southern China. People from this region had been moving around Southeast Asia for centuries, and as a result, "[w]omen from this area have traditionally demonstrated an exceptional independence" (Women's Book Committee, 1992, p. 8).

The website also chronicles the story of Mrs. Kwong Lee, wife of a well-to-do merchant based in San Francisco, who was the first Chinese woman to arrive in Canada when she landed in Victoria, British Columbia on March 1, 1860. Earlier migrant workers did not have the means to bring wives over or were unable to afford marriage. Edgar Wickberg's research for his 1982 book, *From China to Canada*, indicated that fifty-three Chinese women had arrived in Canada by 1885, as recorded in immigration records. From that year onward, more women arrived, predominantly wives of merchants, despite the new fifty dollar Head Tax legislated by the Canadian government to limit Chinese immigration. The *Jin Guo* publication explained that despite the fact that the merchant class were still able to pay the tax which contributed to their growing presence in Canada, "the new tax made any further immigration extremely difficult" (1992, p. 18).

While the Head Tax tended to restrict Chinese immigration to Canada, it did not stop it entirely. Families and friends continued to find the money to help pay the tax. However, as I briefly described in Chapter 1, the introduction of the second Chinese Immigration Act in 1923 effectively rendered any further immigration of the Chinese to Canada almost impossible until 1947. While Chinese women had already begun to arrive prior to the Act, they were subject to long decades of separation from their families back in China. But despite the rampant xenophobia of that time, Chinese women were active and engaged members of Canadian society, bringing their cultural heritage together with the customs and clothing of their adopted country.

An analysis of the images found on the *Chinese Canadian Women* database shows that Chinese women who first arrived in the late nineteenth century often wore Western clothing and were sometimes photographed in Han traditional clothing for formal portraits. The cheongsam arrived in Canada in the early 1930s, not too long after it became fully adopted in China. My hypothesis is that as the cheongsam took off in China at the end of the 1920s, the latest Chinese fashions from Shanghai and Hong Kong were seen in family photographs, magazines, and other advertising, prompting an influx of the cheongsam through regular importation and perhaps packages sent from relatives back in China. A 1934 group photo shows how traditional Han, Manchu, and Western clothing styles were combining and merging. One woman wears the Han style *ao qun* or two-piece jacket and skirt while another woman is wearing a Western style dress. A few of the other women are wearing the one-piece cheongsam or variations that work with all three styles. This fraternization of clothing forms lends visual support to an understanding of how Manchu, Han, and Western clothing co-existed, commingled, and enriched women's sartorial choices, allowing them a range of items to choose from in order to express complex temporal and cultural messages. Following Maynard (2004), we can again appreciate how Han, Manchu, and Western designs interacted stylistically, making space for the modern cheongsam, a fusion garment, to exist. Photos in the *Jin Guo* publication and the MHSO website reveal that the cheongsam continued to be worn by women in everyday situations from the 1940s until the 1960s. However, by the 1970s and 1980s it gradually became a dress worn only for formal or community oriented occasions, mirroring the decline of the dress's popularity as an everyday garment in Hong Kong, Taiwan, and Singapore.

Figure 7 Volunteer servers for the Women's Missionary Society's Chow mein tea, Calgary, Alberta, 1934 (Collection of Loretta Lee)

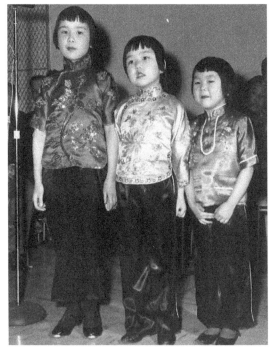

Figure 8 The Lumb sisters, Arlene, Pam, and Janet, wearing cheongsam tops *circa* early 1960s in Toronto, Ontario (Courtesy of Janet Lumb)

The cheongsam made its way to Canada despite the Exclusion Act that severely decreased Chinese immigration from 1923 to 1947. When immigration laws further changed in the mid-1960s, the cheongsam was seen on older women who arrived from Hong Kong, Taiwan, and other parts of Southeast Asia. With the promotion of the new Multiculturalism Act in 1971, the cheongsam came into mainstream view at multicultural festivals and Miss Chinese pageants organized by community organizations with the assistance of government funding initiatives. Many of these events endured into the 2000s, and the Miss Chinatown pageants continue to be held in Toronto, Montreal, and Vancouver. As a commodity, the cheongsam became an inexpensive mass produced item easily found in Chinatown stores and bought and worn primarily for weddings. In the 1990s and into the 2000s it appeared on Western actresses and pop singers. The cheongsam and elements of the cheongsam also continued to pop up in both couture and mainstream fashion retail collections in Canada, as I will describe in depth in the next chapter.

What I have attempted to demonstrate through this brief mapping of the history and evolution of the cheongsam is that this iconic garment has its

Figures 9 and 10 Family friends posing in cheongsam worn for a cheongsam fashion and beauty pageant presented at the Canton Pavilion of the now defunct *Caravan* festival held in Toronto. Taken by my father, Victor Sim, in 1976

roots in a deep and complex set of circumstances and influences that are shaped by political events that in turn affect its place in Chinese and North American culture. Furthermore, the cheongsam is a prime example of what Ursula Franklin (1989) describes as a "technology." It is surrounded by a tight set of discourses that shape, limit, and enforce ideas about who is permitted to wear it, how it should look, how it should be worn, when it should be worn, and what it means. As explained, cultural, political, and market forces have altered the dress's shape and its representations, transforming it from a symbol of freedom and progress for women to an instrument for the commodification and disciplining of the female body that also perpetuates an idealized image of Chinese femininity. Yet despite all of these paradoxical influences and currents, the cheongsam remains, even if perhaps secretly so, a desirable object. Pleasure can be taken in the enjoyment of the garment's fabrics, design elements, details, and even its form fitting shape. The appeal of the cheongsam also lies in its ability to be used as a performative tool for the expression of an evolving Chinese identity that is mutable and multiple, particularly in contexts outside of China. What I will present in the next chapter is how the wearing and non-wearing of the cheongsam by Canadian women of Chinese heritage is riddled with captivating contradictions.

CHAPTER 4
WEARING PRACTICES IN CANADA: AMBIVALENCE, AUTHENTICITY, AND AGENCY

Who's afraid of the cheongsam?

In my review of literature, I came across Chui Chu Yang's 2007 doctoral thesis, "The Meanings of Qipao as Traditional Dress: Chinese and Taiwanese perspectives," which explored the understanding and interpretation of the dress by women of Chinese and Taiwanese nationality attending Iowa State University. Her thesis also set out to question the influence of cultural contexts on wearing practices of the cheongsam at the time. In order to fully underline its historical significance, she focused on how the cheongsam became the national dress of China. Yang also conducted interviews with fourteen women between the ages of twenty-four and thirty, who had been living in the United States for less than three years at the time of the interviews. Yang's theoretical framework drew on Pierre Bourdieu's "practice theory," which "emphasizes a practical research method that can simultaneously investigate structural meanings and the meaning interpreted by social actors within the culture" (Yang, 2007, p. 10). Utilizing practice theory as an analytical tool, she concluded that the meanings and traditions associated with the cheongsam are fluid and unstable and that personal experience is the crucial factor to an understanding of how and when women wear the dress. Furthermore, while the meanings of the dress were similar for both Taiwanese and Chinese women, the political situation between China and Taiwan made it difficult for Taiwanese women to consider it their national dress. Western dress codes further influenced the meanings attributed to the cheongsam, and influenced ideas of the dress by the women interviewed, who were conscious of its perception as a hyper-feminized and sexualized object. While Chui's work focused on a limited scope of young Chinese and Taiwanese women living in Iowa for only a short time, what is useful to the present study is how her research offered further evidence of the significant bearing of external cultural and political forces on the perception of the cheongsam.

As part of the research I carried out for *The Fitting Room* art installation, I interviewed nineteen Canadian-born women of Chinese heritage. I adopted an autoethnographic approach in which I answered my own interview questions and combined these responses with those of the women I interviewed. The totality of these responses reveals how contemporary cheongsam wearing practices are informed by a multitude of factors including the garment's history, its representation in Western mass media, its physical implications on the body, history, and experiences of the Chinese in Canada, socialization, and family upbringing. What came forth in my analysis of the interviews was how the cheongsam continues to function as a "technology" that inspires great ambivalence amongst Canadian-born women of Chinese heritage. Similarly to women in China, the dress is bound up with fantasy and nostalgia but it also inspires a great deal of fear and apprehension. Where Canadian perceptions and concerns about the dress diverge from those of women in China, is when it comes to the issue of ethnic identity and the history of xenophobia and racialization in Canada. This combination of pleasure and pain makes the dress a veritable material-symbolic, cultural, and political complex.

I found women through a variety of methods that included a posting on social media, a group email, and direct telephone contact. These tactics helped connect me with women all over Canada through mutual friends and acquaintances. I traveled to each woman's city of residence and conducted interviews in one-on-one meetings in the place of her choosing. In the first part of the interview, I asked general questions about her background before talking specifically about the cheongsam. I asked about her ancestors: when they arrived in Canada, where they arrived from, and where in Canada they landed. I then inquired about when and where she was born, where she grew up, and what life was like for her growing up in her family within the Canadian context. Who were her friends and what were her experiences like at school and in her community? What religion, if any, did she grow up with? These basic questions allowed me to get a sharper sense of the context of a woman's formative years to offer more insight into her experiences and perceptions on the cheongsam in later life. One aspect that requires some clarification pertains to religion. In terms of my own trajectory, I was raised in a Protestant household. My mother's family was one of 17 percent of the Filipino population who declared Protestant Christianity as their main religion. While my father was also raised in the Protestant Christian tradition by his parents, he attended Lasalle College, a Catholic secondary boy's school in Hong Kong, as it had established a reputation for excellence in academics and an emphasis on the values of faith, service, and community. In this study, responses among the women varied from Christian Protestant to no religion. However, like my father, a few women were sent to Catholic schools (some of them private), regardless if their religious background. For these women's families, the desire for a quality education that would better ensure future success outweighed the issue of religion.

Building on these formative questions, I then asked each woman to attempt to describe her connection with her Chinese heritage. Did they practice any Chinese customs or traditions? Was Chinese spoken at home? Would she consider her family part of the Chinese community? With this foundation established, I then focused on a set of questions about the cheongsam. The first question was if she had ever worn a cheongsam. If she had not, I asked what factors contributed to her not having worn it, and I then asked if there might be any circumstances under which she might wear a cheongsam. If she had worn a cheongsam, I asked about the first time she wore it; the occasion, how old she was, what the dress looked like, where and how she acquired it, and how she styled it in terms of hair, make-up, and accessories. I then followed up with an inquiry into how she felt wearing it, both physically and in terms of her emotional and mental state. What reactions did she receive and how did they make her feel? Had she worn the dress since? If so, I asked her to describe these subsequent wearings: the occasion, how she felt, how she was received. Whether the woman being interviewed had worn the dress or not, I wanted to know about her impression of the cheongsam, what it might mean or symbolize for her. I also wanted her to explain whether the dress could be worn by anyone regardless of ethnic heritage, or if it should be reserved for women of Chinese heritage only.

It is also important to contextualize the Canadian fashion culture of the late 1960s–early 1990s, which is the timeframe in discussion. In the larger context, there has always been a keen market for fashion in Canada on the part of both production and consumption, with some marked variations from city to city. For example, Montreal, Quebec has long been considered a leader in personal style among Canadian metropoles, where the connection with a European sensibility has dovetailed with taking greater risks with fashion. I contend that in other cities across Canada, clothing styles have corresponded with lifestyle: a more conservative, professional approach would often be found in Toronto, while in Vancouver one would see more of a tendency towards casual, active wear.

For the women in this study growing up in Canada from the early 1970s up to the early 1990s, consumer culture and fast fashion had firmly taken hold. As I have mentioned earlier, Cougar boots and Roadrunner jeans were a standard for a style-conscious "tween" in the late 1970s. These generally inexpensive items were easy to find at the now defunct Sears department store chain. In the 1980s, depending on the subculture of choice, Canadian teenage tastes would range from Lacoste shirts and Vuarnet sunglasses to Ray-Ban Wayfarers and army surplus fatigues. By the early 1990s, multinational fashion retailers such as The Gap began to dominate the landscape while major street trends influenced by "grunge" and hip-hop music very much took hold. In this way, Canadian tastes have always been and continue to be impacted largely by the fashion market with the supplementary influence of American and British popular culture transmitted through music and film. The only limitation to fashion consumption in Canada has been choice and availability, which has somewhat improved since the arrival of internet shopping in very recent years.

The following section presents a synopsis of each woman's set of responses to these questions along with selected quotes that illustrate a particular, salient observation about the dress.

Have you ever worn the cheongsam? No.

Of the twenty women who participated in the interviews, seven women had never worn the one-piece cheongsam. Their reasons were multiple, ranging from not having had the right occasion to wear one, not feeling enough of a connection to it, not having a sufficiently developed knowledge of Chinese culture, not having the right body type, and not wanting to wear store-bought versions.

LC, who is of mixed Chinese and Trinidadian-Chinese heritage and grew up in suburban/urban Alberta during the 1980s, has never worn the cheongsam. She attended a middle-class elementary school, and then a middle-to-upper-class Catholic high school. She described the student population at both schools as predominantly white but explained that there were more Chinese students in her high school. What she remembered is that differences were more apparent across class than across "race." Her family was the only Chinese family in her neighborhood and they spoke English at home. LC explained that, in general, she does not identify herself as Chinese and feels closer to her mother's West Indian culture. If she does feel an affinity with her Chinese heritage, it is mainly through food. Her mother cooks Chinese and Chinese-Trinidadian meals, and LC chooses the most adventurous dishes on the menu whenever she goes out to a Chinese restaurant. In Alberta she never had to provide explanations about her ethnic background and it was only when she moved to Montreal that she truly became aware of her difference, and she is asked where she comes from on a regular basis. Furthermore, she has been exposed to racial slurs, and on one occasion during a job interview was shamed by one of her white interviewers for not having learned to speak Chinese. This combination of experiences led her to a current crisis of identity that has contributed to deep feelings of inadequacy due to her perceived lack of knowledge about Chinese culture. As a result, the cheongsam is a garment that she does not feel she would or should wear:

> I think my parents offered to buy me one in China and I think I turned [my mom] down. She probably thought it would be difficult to get anyways. I wouldn't know what to do with it. I wouldn't wear it to a white person's wedding because I wouldn't want to be the token person—exotic Chinese friend—at a white person's wedding. But I would wear it to a Chinese friend's wedding. But it's more because I don't know enough about it and would feel like a fraud—because I don't even know about the festivals and holidays. I think the dress is beautiful. I just don't think I would wear one. (LC)

ACV, who is of mixed heritage, also feels the fear of being an imposter. She was born in Hamilton, Ontario and grew up in the suburban town of Stoney Creek during the 1970s. She attended Catholic elementary and high schools that she described as 98 percent white, and became a little more aware of her ethnicity in high school when there was more diversity among the student population. Her parents divorced when she was a child and she lived with her Filipino mother, while staying with her Chinese father only occasionally. As a result, she felt that she had lost a connection to her Chinese heritage. She explained that even when her parents were together her father did not feel that teaching her Chinese was a priority, and that in Canada it was expected that one should speak English. She talked about how she hated Chinese food as a child, and that she didn't have any friends of Chinese heritage until she was in university. She also laughed about how her Black, Jamaican born, Canadian-raised husband uses chopsticks better than she does. She now lives in Markham, Ontario which is a suburb of Toronto that has become the new enclave for newly arrived immigrants from Mainland China. There are entire malls and shopping centers that cater to the Chinese community, offering activities and events during holidays such as Chinese

New Year and the Harvest Moon festival. She explained that she likes to bring her children to these events so that they might know a little bit more about their heritage. But because her appearance is more Chinese than Filipino, she is often worried that people will speak to her in Mandarin and that she will not be able to respond. These concerns are directly linked with why she has never worn the cheongsam:

> I think for me personally—I think it's the expectation of looking Chinese and wearing this dress ... people might come up to me and speak Chinese and I would feel foolish. And since I don't feel 100 percent [Chinese] I don't feel comfortable wearing the dress. ... I feel totally ignorant, through non-exposure—not educating myself. I can't speak to it. (ACV)

While ACV does not have a cheongsam, she does own a cheongsam-style blouse with gold embroidery and a red and black reversible Chinese jacket or *ma gua*, which she wears for special occasions. She styles these pieces with jeans and more casual Western accessories and feels that mixing Western clothing with these Chinese looking garments expresses her own style and also communicates that she is a mix of ethnic heritages as a way of mitigating any cultural expectations from white Canadians, recently arrived Mainland, Chinese, and other Canadian-born people of Chinese heritage.

Following Maynard (2004), this "strategic hybridity" is also employed by AL, who was born and raised in suburban Burnaby and urban Vancouver, British Columbia during the late 1970s and 1980s. Her father arrived from Hong Kong in 1968 and her mother arrived during the 1950s as a teenager. In elementary school, she remembers being bullied for being Chinese and wanted badly to integrate into mainstream society. At home, she only spoke English and says that her refusal to speak Chinese did not meet with much resistance as her father had stated that he knew what the values were in Canada when he arrived, and was ready to live by them. When AL reached high school, she started to feel more part of the mainstream as 80 percent of the student body was of Asian heritage. She now considers herself very Canadian, but "with a twist." Most of her close friends are of Asian heritage and she explained that they have created their own culture and community, given their shared experience of being of Asian heritage and growing up in Canada. Despite her interest in style and her studies in fashion, she has never worn the cheongsam. She explained that it was something she did not know how to access or make and that the ones she saw in the stores did not do justice to the beauty of the cheongsam, which she had seen in films such as *Joy Luck Club* and later *In the Mood for Love*. She said she would happily wear the dresses presented in those films, but still expressed a deep ambivalence similar to that of ACV:

> Without even intending I think I would feel very Chinese in it. There is some sort of significance. I do take clothing seriously and it is a way to express myself ... I do imagine that if I wore it, it would be a definitive expression of my Chineseness ... knowing at the same time that if I wore it my family would laugh, like, you look Chinese but you don't speak it! (AL)

ACV, LC, and AL's discomfort with wearing the cheongsam can be described as the "burden of representation," as articulated by Kobena Mercer (1994). Mercer's concept underscored the situation of Black artists in Britain who felt pressure from programming committees, arts councils, critics, curators, and art schools, to deal primarily with so-called Black issues in their work. This expectation limited the scope of what these artists could explore in their art and saddled them with the responsibility of speaking on behalf of a widely diverse community. In a similar way, for ACV and AL it is feared that, given their "very Chinese" looks, wearing the cheongsam would create the expectation that they were well versed in Chinese language and culture. For these women who are distanced from their Chinese heritage, the cheongsam is burdened with too much responsibility to comfortably withstand. But I maintain that the decision not to wear the dress is not a gesture of disavowal, but rather a move to defuse expectations and mitigate the disappointment of others while to some degree attenuating their own disappointment in having lost a connection with their heritage.

In a more insidious way, AL's hesitance to wear the cheongsam is linked with Western normative standards of beauty that had been transmitted to her mother and passed on to AL. Not wanting to be co-opted by these ideas, AL was motivated to wear components of Chinese clothing in her own way:

> I remember a white girl wore the [cheongsam] top and I asked my mom why it looked different and my mom said, "oh they look better on white people." So I wore the cheongsam top with baby barrettes, cat eye glasses, jeans, and combat boots. That was my interpretation. (AL)

AL's wearing of the cheongsam top in this manner expressed her desire and ability to explore and master the language of hybridity that echoes

ACV's strategy as well as Anna Sui's (Button, 2010) versions of the cheongsam. AL's ensemble is a reflection of the influence of grunge music on youth subculture and fashion trends, but also of her desire to express a playfully irreverent attitude to traditional Chinese clothing, re-appropriating it with her own style. Grunge music and the street trends of the early 1990s echoed the punk subculture of the 1970s, which was about transgressing social conventions, rebellion, and disenfranchisement due to class inequality. The combination of the heaviness and encoded masculinity of combat boots and jeans with the more delicate and highly codified top creates a dissonance that spoke to her feminist and identity politics. The cat eye glasses seem to evoke images of trendy Hong Kong girls from the 1950s and 1960s, while the baby barrettes worn in the hair were an accessory that emerged in 1990s rave subculture, along with other accessories of regression, such as baby T-shirts, backpacks, and soothers. With all of these elements together, AL played with Chinese clothing in order to resist the effects of internalized racism and to deftly shape and empower her own cultural and socio-political identity.

While ethnic clothing may be shunned because of its heavy charge of cultural responsibility, it can become an object of refuge when very little else is left to affirm one's heritage. AJ was born in Mississauga, Ontario in the mid-1980s to a Singaporean Chinese mother and a Czech father who both immigrated to Canada in the 1970s. AJ had also never worn the cheongsam. Growing up in suburban Ontario, she was made very aware of her mixed heritage and experienced racialized treatment. At the same time, she noticed how her parents did not give her much exposure to their own ethnic heritages. She hypothesized that this is linked with their embracing of Pierre Trudeau's discourse on multiculturalism. The possibility that the suppression of exposure to the culture of her ethnicities was, on her parents' part, due to an internalized colonialist mentality might have kept her from wearing the cheongsam. But there were other, more physical reasons that contributed to this:

They're shiny and overly bright and have hideous patterns that are often not well cut so the seams don't quite match up and the pattern is disjointed at the seams—oh my god they're so not attractive. But the idea of participating fully in my family and fully in my family's activities is what is appealing about it and what keeps bringing me back to these cheongsam stores despite the garishness of it all. I try them on and they wrinkle in certain places and they have extra material in others and the saleslady will reassure me that they can take it in and make it all fine. But it's not comfortable to be in and I feel self conscious about my body and the excesses of my body in some places, particularly my chest which are not intended to be there in the cheongsam, also my hips, which are not intended to be there and how the dress wrinkles whenever I sit down and . . . yeah, it's just not a look I can pull off. (AJ)

The availability of more formal looking cheongsam reflect how the dress is now worn almost exclusively for weddings and other special occasions that I will discuss further at the end of this chapter. Taking all of these factors together, subtlety and comfort are not characteristics of the contemporary, store-bought cheongsam. But AJ found other ways to bring Chinese ethnic clothing into her wardrobe none the less by incorporating the cheongsam tops that she inherited from her aunt and grandmother. She would wear these items as part of family gatherings, which would be met with positive feedback and encouragement. As another example of strategic hybridity AJ found a way to pay homage to her Chinese heritage and to instill in herself a sense of continuity.

I would love to wear [the cheongsam tops] to school and really own that history because I wasn't only in putting on those clothes, I wasn't only putting on those particular patterns that signify belonging to certain racial and ethnic groups. I was putting on my grandmother. I was wearing my family history. (AJ)

Paying respect to ancestors and carrying on tradition through wearing Chinese clothing was a comforting action for AJ, in an attempt to recover and make sense of heritages that had long been denied in the bid for assimilation. The garments she wore became conduits for remembrance and ensured that all had not been lost.

JY was born in Montreal, Quebec in 1982. Both her parents are ethnic Chinese who immigrated from Vietnam. She felt she had a fairly sheltered childhood, raised mostly by her grandmother, while both her parents worked outside the home. Cantonese was spoken in the family and she did not start to learn to speak French until pre-school. Her parents later enrolled her at a private francophone school with a mostly white student population. While there were very few Asian students, she did not feel marginalized by her ethnicity. Class differences emerged from time to time but she explained that the emphasis was primarily on academic achievement. It was not until she started university that she started to experience racialization more significantly in everyday life situations. She is close with her family and feels she has adopted a Chinese mentality as well as a set of Chinese values and customs. At the same time, she is aware of how both white and Chinese people have the ability to make racializing comments. When she was younger, she found the cheongsam to be too Chinese and would not want to wear it in public out of a fear of being seen as a newly arrived immigrant, rather than someone who was born in Canada. Now that she is older, she feels more confident about her place in Montreal and Canada and maintains a deep appreciation for her Chinese heritage. While she had seen photos of her grandmother in the dress and described her as looking elegant, regal, and chic, JY feels the cheongsam is not appropriate for everyday wear. Despite the fact that she has never worn the cheongsam, JY expressed that the dress is a symbol of respect for Chinese heritage and family:

It's a way of expressing and being in contact with one's heritage—it's the symbolism that is anchored in tradition—a sign of respect and community also, not only a garment but the fact that you wear it for other people. It's a good way to connect. (JY, translated from French)

While she does not feel that the cheongsam is associated with any negative stereotypes, JY does feel like AJ, that the cut of the dress is very limiting and that it is not accessible to women of different shapes and sizes.

. . . for me it idealizes a certain type of body. I hesitate to wear it as my body is not perfect. But I'm fine with that. For this dress, there aren't a lot of loose types to hide imperfections. It's also linked with the image that we have of Asian women too. We have a lot of pressure to be beautiful, thin, everything always in place. The dress is in this same chain of ideas—constraining. But if I found one that looked good on me, I would wear it. (JY, translated from French)

AH/1 and AH/2 are identical twin sisters, born in 1984 and raised in the small rural town of Chibougamou, Quebec. Their mother is a Chinese refugee from Vietnam and their father arrived from Hong Kong in the late 1970s. The population of Chibougamou is mostly white and francophone with very few visible minorities. The fact that AH/1 and AH/2 are identical twins, as well as being among the few Chinese people in town, made them very aware of their difference and visibility. They grew up speaking Cantonese at home and observed Chinese holidays, such as the New Year and Harvest Moon festival. While interviewed separately, one in English, the other in French, they both revealed how they feel equally close to their Chinese and Western cultural identities. While neither of them has yet worn the cheongsam, they each expressed the desire to wear one some day, for an important life event.

> There are moments in one's life, where it's the opportune moment and for me, the opportune moment would be for example, if I am being recognized for my accomplishments. It is then, maybe for a ceremony that I would wear something like a cheongsam. Because for me, what it represents are Chinese values like working hard, making sacrifices, having discipline, exercising modesty . . . so with just one gesture, I can represent these values. (AH/1, translated from French)

As explored in the dress designs of the 1930s, the cheongsam lends itself extremely well to hybrid styling that combines Chinese/Western elements. AH/2 explained that she would like to wear a cheongsam as a wedding dress one day, and described how she might use it to relay both aspects of her cultural identity:

> What I had in mind was to show that a big part of me will maintain and will want to express my Asian roots and to show that part of me is Westernized and North American. Not one or the other but a mesh of both. I want to take the Asian culture from my parent's generation and grandparent's generation and modernize it and make it relevant in modern society. I decided traditionally or culturally, cheongsam are usually for weddings and are red, while in Western culture, most brides wear white. I would go with an ivory or cream cheongsam rather than red. I also found different sites and people that make cheongsams and found one with a lace overlay, the Chinese collar and pearl buttons so there are combined elements of Asian and Western style. (AH/2)

For both AH/1 and AH/2, the dress is considered an elegant gown that must be treated with respect, as a way to honor family and heritage without eclipsing their Western cultural upbringing. They do not consider the cheongsam a dress that can be worn in an everyday context such as the workplace, however, due to its slim cut and fine fabrics.

For me, the cheongsam is more traditional and communicates elegance, and it's not in everyday life that we need this level of elegance. So for me, wearing the cheongsam everyday diminishes its value— what it represents, if we wear it anywhere and any how. (AH/1, translated from French)

There are very substantial reasons why women have said no to wearing the cheongsam. Those who slowly distanced themselves from Chinese language, values, and customs were concerned that wearing the dress would make them look like imposters, bringing upon them uneasy expectations about their knowledge of Chinese culture and further underscoring a sense of disappointment and even embarassment about not being able to deliver on those expectations. For some women, the cheongsam conjures up the idea of a shoddily made, uncomfortable garment made from cheap fabrics in showy colors. For others it is the epitome of elegance and beauty as well as an expression of reverence for Chinese values. As such it should only be worn for very special formal occasions and is inappropriate for everyday. The cheongsam's perceived insistence on being a close cut, form-fitting garment has also dissuaded women from wanting to try one on. What these responses all show is that the decision not to wear the cheongsam does not mean a denial of one's heritage but, rather, demonstrates the existence of nuanced reflections and strategies that are being undertaken to communicate the instability of ethnicity.

Have you ever worn the cheongsam? Yes.

Thirteen out of the twenty women had worn the cheongsam at least once in their lives. For some, wearing the dress was a delightfully pleasant experience, while for others it was a non-negotiable obligation.

AMJ first wore a cheongsam for her high school graduation ceremony. This would seem a bold move given the tumult of her younger years. Both of her parents arrived in Canada from Hong Kong and she was born in Montreal, Quebec in 1971. She was one of the few visible minority children in her downtown Montreal school and quickly became aware of her racialized difference. She was teased, bullied, and even experienced physical aggression, based purely on her Chinese appearance. While she did not fully reject her heritage, she grew up knowing that her visibility made her vulnerable to various types of attack, and that her best form of defense was to tread softly and attempt to assimilate into the dominant culture. In her final year in high school, she was named valedictorian of her class and was required to deliver a speech at her convocation ceremony. Her mother suggested that she wear a black brocade cheongsam along with a black beaded cardigan that she had been keeping in her closet for many years. Without any hesitation, AMJ proudly wore this ensemble and enjoyed how she looked and felt. She did not feel that the cheongsam would make her a target for ridicule, but rather saw this dress as beautiful and appropriate for a dignified and significant life event. Wearing this dress for such a public occasion was also an indication of AMJ's sense of agency, which was informed by her ability not only to successfully negotiate a cross-cultural context, but to fully grasp its dynamics of power.

> This dress is not about reminding me about my Chineseness. We don't live in a society that will let us forget that. So when we want to wear ethnically marked clothing, we have to do it out of our own choice. I'd be happy to wear the dress whenever I'd want to wear it. I would be unhappy to wear it when I would be expected to wear it. That would be feeding into assumptions that might not be well informed. (AMJ)

AMJ explained that her mother wore the cheongsam as an everyday dress back in Hong Kong, so in her perception the dress was considered quite ubiquitous and less charged with ethnic signification. At the same time, she was aware that in the Canadian environment, the cheongsam was a racialized and feminized garment that required certain consideration when deciding when and where it could be worn. Choosing to wear her mother's cheongsam for a public ceremony despite her earlier experiences was a show of confidence and empowerment.

Like AMJ, JW first wore the cheongsam as part of her high school graduation. She was born in Quebec City in 1980 and is third-generation Canadian. Her mother is Québecoise and her father, who is of Chinese heritage, was also born in Quebec City. She was raised mostly by her paternal grandmother and spoke Toisanese at home. Even though she was one of only a few visible minority children in her neighborhood and school, her father and grandmother established in her a confidence and pride in her Chinese ethnicity. As a child she had been dressed in various pieces of Chinese clothing, but her dream was to wear what she considered a proper cheongsam one day. When her high school graduation party finally came around, she and her father made the trip to Montreal's Chinatown to buy her dream dress. For JW it had to be full length, red, and made of satin brocade.

She had her hair and make-up done and said she felt incredibly elegant and beautiful.

> For me, there could be no other dress. I don't know if it was to identify myself as Chinese as much as it was because of the occasion. And from an early age, in my head, when you have a major event, you get to wear the beautiful Chinese dress … and it was my turn. (JW, translated from French)

Wearing the cheongsam was a rite of passage for JW as well as a long held fantasy. A high school prom celebrates the transition from childhood to adulthood, marking a major milestone and the start of a new phase in life, which comes with freedom and the ability to makes one's own decisions. JW and AMJ's choosing to wear the cheongsam for these special events demonstrated the taking of pure pleasure in wearing a garment that was not about calling attention to their Chinese heritage, but was rather a reflection of an appreciation for how the elegance of the dress resonated with a sense of occasion.

CW wore the cheongsam for the first time when she traveled to China. She was born in Montreal, Quebec in 1985 and both of her parents issue from the community of ethnic Chinese in Vietnam. They spoke only Cantonese at home and she was raised with very strict Chinese values. She attended a conservative, predominantly white private school for girls and, as a child, considered herself Chinese. All of her close friends were of Chinese heritage but as she got older, this changed. As a teenager and young adult, her awareness of racialization and issues of identity grew. This awakening attracted her to mainstream political activism. In the culturally homogenous environment of Québec, she felt she had to prove her *Québecois* identity to her peers. At the same time, she felt deeply constrained by her family and the pressure of the values that they strongly enforced. Feeling like a minority in both cultures, and with the feeling that Chinese people were just as racist as white *Québecois*, she began to reject her ethnic origins and to disconnect from her family. As an adult, she now feels fully integrated into Québec culture but still feels that her family's strict Chinese values are at odds with her own. In order to find more balance, she decided to go to China, where she bought her first cheongsam.

> It was the tourist thing to do. It was white, came to the knee and was subtle. I have worn it for many events since, but it was not to identify

myself as Chinese, it's because I found it beautiful. I wasn't seeking out this dress in particular. I just wear it because I feel I look good in it. I would even like to evacuate the whole "identity" part of the dress to escape all the questions and comments. I just want to wear it to please myself. (CW, translated from French)

Paradoxically, despite the dress's aesthetic appeal, CW also found its association with Chinese heritage to be more of a liability than a symbol of affirmation.

I find that the dress "folklorizes" me. That's not something I look for. I have always had difficulty with the Mexican that wears the "poncho," even if I recognize the pride that goes along with that. It brings about comments. The identity question is so present in my life, and I have so much to justify in regard to my politics which is why I am not very attached to the cheongsam. (CW, translated from French)

What is most fascinating is that CW actually has more than one cheongsam and wears the dress despite her reservations about how it marks her as Chinese and risks the attraction of uncomfortable questions and comments. This double discourse reveals a deep ambivalence that reflects her ongoing attempt to reconcile her Chinese heritage with her *Québecois* values. The attraction and repulsion of the cheongsam, therefore, seems to be analogous to the forced reconciliation of living within an East/West or Chinese/Canadian binary tension, a phenomenon also noted by each of the women interviewed.

Out of the thirteen women who replied yes to having worn a cheongsam, four women wore it for the first and only time to attend weddings, while three of the women wore a cheongsam for their own wedding. It is important to note that in China and the Chinese diasporas of Canada, the United States, Britain, and Australia, it has for a number years been popular for brides to wear a Western style white dress for the wedding ceremony and to change into a cheongsam for the reception. For Chinese women, this strategy offered the opportunity to wear a dress that they had come to see as desirable through exposure to Western culture, while also honoring their Chinese cultural heritage. I surmise this to be similar for women of Chinese heritage born in the West. However I feel that this gesture on the part of Western women of Chinese heritage carries additional weight as it declares to all present that her ethno-cultural background is a major part of her life and a way of representing herself. I feel an even deeper pronouncement of this conviction occurs when Western women of Chinese heritage forego the white wedding dress or hybrid white cheongsam altogether, and opt for the red wedding cheongsam. Interestingly, this was the case for the three women in this study.

Born in Toronto, Ontario in 1980, QL first wore the dress at her own wedding. Both Chinese parents arrived as refugees from Vietnam, and QL and her sisters were raised in the Jane and Finch neighborhood of Toronto, which was home to many low income and immigrant/refugee families. Growing up, she found it comforting to be surrounded by people who shared a similar story and background. As her parents began to prosper, they took QL and her siblings out of their comfort zone and into a more middle class neighborhood. With very few visible minority families and children around, she started to become acutely aware of her difference and recalled being teased by her classmates. While she says it was difficult to make friends, she did not reject her heritage and simply managed to completely disregard the insulting comments. QL described her parents as "very Chinese" in that they uphold strict and traditional values. She spoke only Cantonese at home and, when she was old enough to date, her parents made it clear that she could only date Chinese boys. As a result, QL considers herself 50 percent Chinese and 50 percent "accustomed to the Canadian way," but does not describe herself as Canadian. She also explained that because she no longer speaks Cantonese fluently, she is no longer considered fully Chinese by people in the community. But she remains close to her family and observes all Chinese holidays, rituals, and events with them. When she was planning her wedding, incidentally to a man of Thai heritage, she thought she would have to wear the ancient Chinese wedding garment based on Han clothing, which consists of a heavily brocaded jacket and skirt, along with an intricately decorated headpiece complete with a veil of pearls. She was incredibly relieved to find out that Chinese wedding garments had evolved into the form fitting, contemporary cheongsam that she saw when shopping for her own in Toronto's Chinatown. The dress she finally chose was full-length, sleeveless, and form fitting, but was not what she called the "authentic" red brocade cheongsam. Instead it featured hues of pink and, for her, appeared more modern. Despite being raised in a very strict Chinese household, she explained how the dress made her feel more Chinese. After appraising her cheongsam-clad self in the mirror, she exclaimed to herself, "Oh wow, I'm very Chinese now." Dressed in the cheongsam, QL came face to face with what she understood as a classic perception of Chinese femininity. Any trace of her Canadianness fell away, eliminating any ambiguity about her heritage. This sensation was not uncomfortable; however, in many ways she did not fully recognize herself. If I could interview her again, I would ask if wearing the dress made her feel as if she was playing a character or performing another version of herself.

FM was born in Edmonton, Alberta in 1978, and experienced the turmoil of this double bind in a very deep and intense way. Both of her parents arrived from Hong Kong in the late 1960s and she was raised in south Edmonton in a mostly white neighborhood. In school she was teased and ostracized for being Chinese, and wished that she had been born white, blond-haired, and blue-eyed. These experiences led her to reject her heritage, which included refusing to eat Chinese food and to stop speaking Chinese at home. She spoke only English with her siblings and eventually dropped out of weekend Chinese school. Living with a high degree of self loathing and internalized racism was untenable and, as a young adult, she worked very hard to overcome her anger. She now feels she has made peace with her family and her Chinese heritage, which she has come to deeply appreciate. The first cheongsam she wore belonged to her Hong Kong grandmother. Similarly to AMJ, she considered these dresses to denote more of a retro style than ethnic clothing. They were made from everyday fabrics such as wool and cotton and she styled them with belts to enhance their hybrid look. For her wedding, however, instead of wearing a Western style white dress or a hybrid style, she wore a red brocade cheongsam, which she considered more traditionally and authentically Chinese. Her decision to wear the Chinese dress for this occasion had a positive and healing effect.

> I found for the wedding that wearing the dress definitely brought me closer to my heritage—and [my family's] expectations and I was happy to do it. I like how it looks and how it feels—connecting with culture and with my family. They identify as Chinese not really as Canadian. So for me it was to please them and also to embrace that side of me that I never really embraced before. If not, my mother would have been upset and I didn't want to rebel anymore. I wanted to embrace my culture and be closer to my family. (FM)

SG offers another example of a desire to seek out and wear the cheongsam as a way to perform her Chinese heritage as an act of connection. Like FM, she also wore a cheongsam as the only dress for her wedding. Both of her parents are Malaysian Chinese who arrived in Edmonton, Alberta where she was born in 1978. Mandarin was spoken at home and she attended Chinese school on Saturdays. However, by adolescence, speaking Mandarin and going to Chinese school were gradually phased out. She attended a predominantly white Catholic school and recalled the racial taunts she received about being Chinese. In high school, she did not have any Chinese friends and was genuinely concerned about being perceived as an 'F.O.B.' (fresh-off-the-boat) or newly arrived immigrant. As a young adult, however, she felt very anchored and confident in her Canadian cultural upbringing, which is when she began to look for ways, as she states, "to stay Chinese." One of those ways was through experimenting with Chinese clothing. She recalled seeing Icelandic musician Björk wearing a modified cheongsam in a music video. The appropriation of the dress by a major European pop star gave it validation and moved SG to want to reclaim it for herself as a woman of Chinese heritage. In her early twenties, she found her first cheongsam in a junkshop in London, England. It was made from beige-colored cotton and had an appliqué pattern woven throughout the fabric. It was too small for her so she opened the side slits up to the waist and wore it with jeans. The second cheongsam, which she describes as "grandma style," is black with a big floral pattern that she also found in a vintage shop. Her mother altered it for her and she still wears it with jeans or leggings. Both of these dresses are styled in trendy and hybrid ways as part of her everyday wardrobe. The third cheongsam she acquired was made for her wedding. She only wore a cheongsam for her wedding, and did not have a Western white wedding dress. In order to find her dress, she went to a store in Edmonton, Alberta where a range of cheongsam styles could be selected from a book. She then selected her fabric and other details, and her measurements were taken. Her order was then relayed to a tailor in Hong Kong who sent the finished dress back to Edmonton for the final fitting. Her wedding cheongsam was made in a silky red brocade material, emblazoned with a phoenix and dragon motif, and it also had a wide, gold stripe down each side that connected with the side slits. While she would concur with MC, CW, and others that the dress can be uncomfortable and unforgiving, she continues to take great pleasure in wearing the cheongsam for its formal characteristics and its capacity to highlight her Chinese heritage.

While QL, FM, and SG felt good about wearing the cheongsam, other women wore it strictly out of obligation. TL, for instance, is a third-generation Canadian, born in Montreal, Quebec in 1968. Her paternal grandparents arrived in Quebec from the Toisan province and her father was born and raised in Montreal. Her mother arrived as a teenager from southern China.

Growing up in Montreal in the early 1970s, TL experienced racist taunts and marginalization due to her ethnic minority status. As a result, she worked very hard to integrate and to downplay her Chinese heritage.

> I wore a cheongsam only a handful of times and only for weddings and occasions where I would allow myself to wear a cheongsam. Since my mother came to Canada when she was 13, she had an idealized idea of what the cheongsam was all about and for her she took great pride in wearing the cheongsam. For me it was a completely different thing. As I got older it got more comfortable but as a young child it was like—ugh—why do you want to underline that Chineseness of yourself. For my mother it was very different because she was born in China. For her wearing the cheongsam was part of a nostalgic fantasy because she wasn't fully raised in China and she didn't stay there. So in retrospect now, it gave her the opportunity to live out the fantasy of being Chinese. (TL)

As a child and teenager, TL wore the cheongsam begrudgingly, and only under specific, negotiated circumstances such as for weddings as a way to minimize the focus on her difference in a society that was still tightly homogenous and ethnocentric. While she has now reconciled her childhood shame about being of Chinese heritage, she is still reluctant to wear the cheongsam. She may wear a Chinese inspired top occasionally, but explains that "they were not traditional clothes, they were sort of Western versions of . . . Chinese clothes." The appropriation of elements of Chinese clothing by the Western fashion industry gave her permission to wear clothing that she would otherwise do everything to avoid.

> [There] was sort of a Western "chinoiserie" phase that was becoming acceptable in popular culture. So I thought I could do it as well. But it was only when I got that sort of "ok" from popular culture that I was willing to explore my heritage. Prior to that there was no way. I just wanted to be like everybody else. And only as a young adult, when things changed and it became more fashionable, it was then that I was trying on tops and trying Chinese style clothes. But they were not traditional clothes, they were sort of western versions of what the fashion industry thought Chinese clothes were. I was more willing to explore that part and to use that sort of pop culture version of being Chinese . . . more than exploring my genuine Chinese heritage. (TL)

MC's parents arrived from Hong Kong and settled in the French-speaking region of Saguenay, Quebec, where she was born in 1977. She also wore a cheongsam for the first time out of a resigned sense of duty. She attended an English-speaking school that had some diversity due to the presence of aboriginal and international students, but otherwise had a predominantly white student body. She considered her upbringing to be more Chinese, and Cantonese was spoken at home. She too initially rejected her Chinese heritage as a way to survive the marginalization and xenophobia experienced as a child. This renunciation dissipated in adulthood and she now feels she knows how to negotiate Chinese and Western cultures. MC first wore a cheongsam for her brother's wedding. She had purchased it on a trip to Hong Kong and it was made from mint green brocade fabric, mid-calf length, featured flower buttons, and had cap sleeves. She had the dress altered to allow for more eating and breathing room, figuring that if she was going to be forced to wear a cheongsam, she could at least enjoy the banquet. For MC, the cheongsam is the kind of dress one wears for a special occasion and nothing more. She had no previous desire to wear this dress and wore it only out of respect for what she described as "the rules" and to follow through on her family's expectations. While she was happy that her family appreciated the effort, she has no plans to wear the cheongsam again, unless called upon for such an occasion.

JL also wore a cheongsam for the first time at her brother's wedding. What was initially seen as an obligation to endure, her experience turned out to be a positive one. Her parents arrived from Taiwan to do their Master's studies and first arrived in Toronto, where JL was born in 1978. She spent her childhood in the suburb of Burnaby, British Columbia and her high school years in the city of Calgary, Alberta. JL described her childhood as sheltered, and felt she was surrounded by a close-knit group of friends among whom most were Asian. Taiwanese was spoken at home and was gradually replaced by English. By junior high, she started to become conscious of her ethnic difference at the same time that she became aware of her lesbian sexuality. By this time she actively resisted feminized stereotypes by electing not to wear dresses. However, when it came to her brother's wedding, she felt it appropriate to make an exception and shopped for a cheongsam with her brother and mother in Toronto's Chinatown. The dress she decided to buy was a mid-calf, sleeveless dress with knotted "flower" buttons down the front, made from a deep blue brocade with a tiny cherry blossom flower motif. She remembered trying it on and having to come out of the fitting room in order to show it to her family:

Normally I would feel very self-conscious and I would have an emotional problem with that but with the cheongsam I remember I didn't have such a problem. I'll try this on and I don't mind people looking, and it was in a location where there weren't a lot of people. It was more pleasant than I thought it would be ... Because it was a more ceremonial and ritual dress ... but I don't wear dresses and I just tend to not wear clothes that are very feminine in general, but wearing the cheongsam ... I felt like this is MY dress. So it was ok to do and felt at the same time it didn't define me outside the family. This is for the formal setting of the wedding and for family. I perform for them anyways, so I thought that this was something I could do. (JL)

Wearing the dress was a way to be included in this special occasion, to honor her heritage and to please her family all at the same time. The pleasure in wearing the dress was linked with the positive comments that came from people at the wedding, and reinforced her place within her family. The wearing of the dress was also part of performing a role—partly her role as daughter, sister, and a member of the immediate family within the wedding party, and partly as a woman of Chinese heritage. The formal context of the wedding, therefore, provided her with a kind of protective membrane from the daily struggles of affirming herself in mainstream society and granted her permission to wear the dress. In *About Face: Performing Race in Fashion and Theater,* Dorinne Kondo (1997) contends that performances such as these are not hollow gestures. Kondo applies Judith Butler's "performance theory" to her focus on theater and fashion as modes or arenas for the performance of identity. She describes Butler's "performance theory" as describing the "notion of gender, sex, and sexuality as performatives that are constitutive—not merely attributes—of identity ... Performative citations are therefore never merely the voluntary choices of a humanist subject; rather they are the product of constitutive constraints that create identities" (Kondo, 1997, p. 7). She paraphrased Butler further, by contending that "repeated iterates of identity can both consolidate its force and provide the occasion for its subversion" (1997, p. 7). JL explained that she normally rejects the wearing of dresses as a way to undermine the tenets of hetero-normativity. Wearing the cheongsam was in this instance an indication of the complexity of identity that elicits compromises that are contingent and incongruous. JL explained that the wearing of the cheongsam did not compromise her identity, but rather articulated how her family and Chinese heritage are constitutive of that identity. She decided that wearing the dress and participating in the wedding's rituals were part of a performative act that brought a vital aspect of her identity into being, and that all of these aspects can exist harmoniously.

Also linked with the performance of identity, KT remembers wearing the cheongsam for the first time as a child. Born in Montreal, Quebec in 1976, she is a third-generation Canadian. Her grandparents arrived from Toisan and her father was born in Montreal. When it was time for him to marry, he traveled to the Toisan region to find a partner. As KT's parents worked during the day, she was taken care of by her grandmother and they spoke Toisanese at home. She attended private elementary and high schools in the affluent neighborhood of Westmount, where she was one of a small handful of visible minority children and felt in general that her childhood was free of trauma. When she was about eight years old, she was bought a cheongsam while on a family trip to Hong Kong. She described it as a "very cute, red, knee-length number," which she wore to school on two occasions, one of which was Halloween. For this event, she wore her cheongsam with white socks, black flat shoes, and pink glasses, and styled her hair in two "pigtails." She explained that she wanted to be a "Chinese girl" for Halloween and I asked her what she thought motivated that choice at such a young age.

> I don't know. but it must have been because, I've never worn one of these dresses before and I really wanted to kind of "play" my ethnicity. It's as if I wanted to say "This is how I'm different from you guys." I know what you mean about trying to fit in, but then sometimes you want to declare how individual you are, how you're different. (KT)

While CW expressed her discomfort with the dress's ability to "folklorize," and TL, JY, and others expressed the concern that the cheongsam might make them look too Chinese, KT wore the cheongsam to emphasize her Chinese heritage, secure in how her ethnic background made her special and distinctive within her school environment. In the spirit of Kondo's (1997) arguments, KT's gesture was one of joy and would seem demonstrative of a positive relationship with her ethnicity, which was exceptional among the women I interviewed.

Like SG and FM above, my sister LS and I have always had a strong attraction to the formal qualities of the cheongsam, as well as the dress's signification as a distinctly Chinese garment. We had also grown up seeing and admiring the dress on our parents' friends, aunts, and of course our grandmother Charlotte. For us, the cheongsam was familiar and we associated it with female strength and good taste. We were both born in Hamilton,

Ontario in the early 1970s and spent our early childhood in the suburbs of Ontario and then moved to the small town of Hudson, Quebec, an Anglophone enclave, in the early 1980s. Since our parents were of different ethnic backgrounds, English was our common language at home. Both my sister and I experienced teasing and bullying in our early years based on our Asian appearance, and worked hard to assimilate. Looking back I experienced more overt racialization in the suburbs of Ontario than in rural Quebec, and by the time I was in high school I felt less conspicuous and more comfortable with my ethnicities. LS, who is almost four years my junior, was an intrepid child and easily rebelled against authority as a teenager. In response to the reality of racialization, she looked for ways to assert her ethnic heritages that would fly in the face of beauty norms. In high school, she started to play with female Asian stereotypes by dyeing her very long hair extra black, wearing red lipstick, and emphasizing the almond shape of her eyes. As she says when interviewed, ". . . the whole stereotypes and the whole mythology behind the Asian thing . . . you know what? You have to flip it." For her that meant taking ownership of an essentialized Asian "look" and pushing it even further. In high school, I too was looking for ways to reclaim my ethnic heritages through appearance, and mostly exercised this through clothing. When I was fourteen, my family attended a huge Sim family reunion in Houston, Texas where much of my Chinese family was based. Being part of this gathering gave me a new appreciation of the reach and variety of the Chinese diaspora. My Texan cousins and mixed heritage second cousins made me feel like less of an anomaly, and gave me a sense of belonging and acceptance as well as permission to claim my Chinese heritage. This affirming experience opened doors to my understanding of identity as a process of becoming, well before I had read Stuart Hall's work. I was given a T-shirt with my first and last names on it. On the back, my first name was hand written in pink indelible ink. My family name, written in Chinese character, which loosely translates as "wise men by the water," was silk screened on the front. The proximity of my two names on the T-shirt established a link that would solidify my connection to my heritage and inspire one of the works in *The Fitting Room* art installation. Wearing the Sim name in Chinese had such an empowering impact that I had my mother create an appliqué of the character which she then sewed onto the back of my white jean jacket. I would wear both the T-shirt and the jacket for selected important moments as a gesture of pride and affirmation, just as KT had done when she dressed up as a "Chinese girl." My attempt to find entry points into exercising an affinity with my Chinese heritage brought me naturally to the wearing the cheongsam.

In concert with many of the women I interviewed, my sister LS first wore the cheongsam for a wedding in the early 1990s.

It was special because it was being made for me and I was getting fitted for it and getting it made in the style that I really wanted. And that's what I loved. I felt like a woman, like a whole other person wearing it. And when you put it on, your whole posture, the way you carry yourself, the movements that you make, they all have to be more conscious. When you respect the detail, the craftsmanship, the line, how it's supposed to make you feel . . . it makes you feel good. (LS)

The dress she had made was ankle-length, sleeveless, and made from satiny, black fabric. It had white piping, an intricate white appliqué on the front, and instead of side slits she opted for a single, off-center slit at the front of the dress. For the wedding whe wore the dress with black heels and put up her hair in a classic chignon. At the same time LS expressed how the dress "can be very oppressive and stuffy and that you have to have the right mental strength to wear it." Again, LS's comments echoed other women's observation that the cheongsam's proclivity to induce anxiety is equal to its ability to incite pleasure. She also expressed how, at that time, she believed one had to follow a specific set of protocols when wearing the dress.

You have to wear it in appropriate circumstances and in the right context. It's not for schlepping about. You have to respect the garment . . . You don't wear it with flip-flops, you don't wear it with flats, you really have to wear it with heels. You have to carry yourself in a different way. You can't be doing regular activities you would normally do because it's not forgiving in that way. You've got to do your hair, your make-up—everything has to be on point or else it just takes away from it, or belittles it. That's the disrespect. (LS)

This view is shared by other women in this study and would probably be part of the cheongsam etiquette described by members of the Shanghai Cheongsam Salon, but LS's attitude has changed over time. These days she feels the cheongsam can be worn to nightclubs and parties—events that are not connected with family or Chinese tradition—provided it is worn with respect. In this way she can enjoy wearing the dress in a way that brings her Chinese heritage in line with her contemporary Canadian lifestyle.

I'd love to have another cheongsam made but all in more modern fabrics and with newer techniques, but always keeping that traditional silhouette. So because I'm Canadian, because I'm half, because I'm living in the age I'm living in now versus old times, it makes me want to have something that takes the cheongsam to the next level, like Cheongsam 2.0! Now when I wear it, it's not about trying to look more Chinese, I find it's a dress that just has such a nice line to it. (LS)

LS's desire to wear a cheongsam that exhibits her cultural hybridity supports Sandra Niessen, Ann-Marie Leshkowicz, and Carla Jones's, argument that through migration, the feedback loops of the fashion industry, and the demands of wearers, ethnic clothing can change over time. While LS has no argument with the classic form-fitting cut of the ubiquitous cheongsam, she affirmed WESSIELING (2007) and Hazel Clark's (2000)contention that elements of the dress can be modified without denaturing its association with Chinese culture.

I admit without shame that my love affair with the cheongsam is based on a desire to emulate my grandmother, Charlotte. Her father had an important position in the national petroleum company and embraced the principles of modernity. Charlotte's feet were not bound and she started to learn English

Figure 11 Charlotte Sim in cheongsam with matching jacket circa 1970s (Courtesy Sim family collection)

in school at age five. Through an arranged marriage, she was wed to George Sim when they were both sixteen years old. She always joked that when my grandfather's family chose her, it was like selecting the president of a company. She became a savvy business-woman and had five children of her own. They spent a number of years running to escape the Japanese invasion, and later, the Communist government. During peaceful times, and in particular after the Second World War, Charlotte was in charge of running larger enterprises owned by my grandfather. Charlotte was a model of the Republic Era's projected image of the modern woman, as she was educated, had a career, traveled on occasion, and enjoyed both Western and Chinese fashion. Attuned to the tenets of Republic Era style, her socio-economic status allowed her to take up the cheongsam with fervor. She had cheongsams for work and formal occasions and had them made by a tailor in anticipation of every new season. Her dresses were made from a variety of fabrics including cotton, wool, silk, and velvet, often with short, three-quarter-sleeve matching jackets. In the late 1970s, my grandparents left their Hong Kong business to my uncle and immigrated to Canada. They lived with us for a few months every year, dividing their time amongst their children, who by then had all established lives in Canada and the United States. As I mentioned earlier, she kept a number of dresses in the room she stayed in when she visited us. Some of these dresses dated from before her arrival from Hong Kong. My sister and I slowly began to appropriate them and the first one I wore was a psychedelic paisley print of greens and yellows on a blue background of stretch polyester. It was the perfect garment to underscore my combined interest in 1960s mod style and Chinese clothing, and wearing it meant even more because the dress had belonged to her. The first cheongsam I had made for myself was for my wedding, to be worn as a second dress after the ceremony. It was made from a dusty rose colored raw silk, was tea length, had cap sleeves, and a burgundy appliqué of flowers on the front. The seamstress was not familiar with the fabrication of this type of dress, which I surmised from the rough seams, awkward fit, and the fact that it was not properly lined. While I did not enjoy wearing this cheongsam, my quest for finding good dresses continued.

When the cheongsam began to re-emerge as a fashion item in China, setting off a reaction in Western high fashion, I recall how clothing items that distinctly riffed on the cheongsam became available in mainstream retail clothing stores. Whether it was a top or a dress, each of these cheongsam-type pieces demonstrated the hybrid quality of the garment, that maintained a reference to Chinese clothing even when made from high-tech fabrics and/or designed with minimal details. I remember in 1993 when major Canadian fashion retail chain Le Chateau put out a number of cheongsam T-shirts made from a blend of cotton and lycra. I bought a red one with short- sleeves and a textured wave pattern knitted into the fabric. Metal snap-like buttons crossed diagonally from the center of the high collar to the edge of the shoulder. I wore it with black dress pants and black patent penny loafers. I parted my hair in the middle and pulled it back into a short ponytail. Later on in the late 1990s, at the height of rave culture that brought about club wear labels like Freshjive and Stüssy, I found a minimalist cheongsam with zippered slits and angular cap sleeves in a white, high-tech cotton/nylon blend fabric, and wore this dress for a very important concert in the year 2000. This sporty iteration of the dress and turn-of-the-century vigor gave me a Sino-futurist feel. I wore it with black platform sandals that had sports jersey mesh trim and velcro straps. My sister twisted my hair into an arrangement of buns that referenced European pop singer Björk's hairstyles. My growing collection of cheongsam started to include both vintage and what I considered contemporary garments.

Later, as word of my cheongsam obsession spread, I began to receive dresses from relatives and friends of my parents. Some of them I have had fitted for me, or modified just through shortening, and others I kept as

Figure 12 Author performing in high-tech, contemporary cheongsam in 2000 (From personal collection)

objects of appreciation. In 2009, I decided to finally have a tailor made cheongsam, as part of my video art project *Ode to the Cheongsam*. There happened to be one tailor in Montreal who had his own atelier and shop on the ground floor of the Holiday Inn hotel in Chinatown.[1] After finishing his studies in a fashion design program at Montreal's Lasalle College, he studied the market and saw that no one was offering tailor made cheongsam in the city. He studied under a *sifu* in Hong Kong for five years, and when he opened his shop he became the primary dressmaker for the Chinese beauty pageants in the city, and also made dresses for brides of a wide variety of ethnicities. The cheongsam I wanted to have made would be one I could wear to work. I had asked him to find a gray flannel suit fabric as I wanted to explore the female power of the cheongsam in relation to the men's traditional suit. I also wanted it to be sleeveless with simple *huaniu* buttons, have a gray lining, and a high collar, similar to the cheongsam in *In the Mood for Love*. While the tailor took my measurements we discussed the details of the dress. It would hit just below the knee and have a slit only high enough to facilitate walking. I was very excited about the first fitting, and when I tried it on, it already fit very well. In fact, I would have left it that way. However, in keeping with tradition, he pinned and tucked away and when I came back for the second fitting I noticed how the dress smoothed out my body in certain places and accentuated others. While I had worn cheongsam many times before, I had never had one that fit so closely. So the tailor gave me a crash course in the proper cheongsam comportment, showing me how to smooth the dress as I sat, to cross the ankles instead of the knees as the dress would ride up and expose too much leg. If I had to pick something up off the floor, I would have to slowly lower down at the knees, not bending at the waist, while keeping the legs together. I became aware of how these aforementioned "techniques of the body" exaggerated my embodiment of an internalized process of feminization. At the same time, I appreciated the quality construction and materials of the dress. It cost me C$250, which for me was definitely in the upper range but didn't stop me from becoming a little bit of an addict. The tailor made the same dress in black wool with a pale pink lining, and then a green one with white lining, white lace accents at the slits and a shorter collar. Later he found a green, black, and white print cotton/wool fabric that he finished with a bright yellow lining, yellow piping, and elaborately braided knot buttons. Each of these dresses was impeccably made but I started to realize that we never ever discussed a variation on the cut. My later request to have a mid-length dress made from royal blue crepe fabric with short sleeves and a loose cut, like those worn by female students in the 1920s, went unacknowledged. When I showed up for a fitting I was disappointed to find that the bodice had been fitted to the waist. The dress then jutted into an A-line with high slits on either side. When I mentioned this, the dressmaker explained that if he had made it the way I had asked, "it would have looked like a sack." I then remembered something he said in an interview I conducted with him for another video project:

> [M]ost of the time I will change a little bit according to what I think will look nice on your body. You know, if it doesn't look nice why bother coming to me? So I usually change things a little bit here and there. Other than that [the clients] know what they're getting so in the end result I don't usually have to change anything.

As he had been trained in the ways of a traditional cheongsam, rooted in a particular time and place, the tailor's cheongsam carried with it a basic set of assumptions that informed its general cut as well as how it should look on a woman's body. The tailor made a decision based on this training, guided by a set of strict guidelines. In the same interview he explained that the basic shape of the dress, with its s-curve silhouette, is not really negotiable. Changing it would mean the the that dress would no longer be a "true" cheongsam.

> Sometimes you have to be flexible about certain things so I do change once in a while, but not the pattern because the Chinese dress— cheongsam are always similar, same block. But you just fix a few things here and there, [but] it's always the same.

As briefly mentioned earlier, access to store-bought cheongsam in Canada is still limited to boutiques found in Chinatowns in major cities.[2] These dresses are imported from China and now show a little more variety in terms of fabric choice and decorative details than in the 1990s. While inexpensive, they are of mass produced quality, mostly unlined, and only come in small, medium, and large sizes. Finding a good fit is rare although some women have had some success by bringing their store bought dresses to a tailor for alterations. Floral prints and brightly colored garments in polyester and rayon continue to dominate the offerings but it is possible to find cheongsams that are made from more casual fabrics, such as cotton and cotton blends. Instead of a side opening with a diagonal closure from the center of the collar to just below the armpit, these contemporary cheongsams all have

Figure 13 1970s wedding reception in Toronto, Ontario (Courtesy Sim family collection)

zippers down the back. They also feature variations in decorative elements such as keyhole cutouts below the high collar and one slit at the back or on one side instead of two. Even though I did not see much change in the form-fitting sheath cut among the dresses available in Canadian stores, my hope is that the Chinese designers that have begun to innovate the cheongsam will influence larger manufacturers to relax the rules and perhaps once again these dresses will make their way over to Canada.

Suzie Wong vs. Maggie Cheung

Each of the women I interviewed was asked if they thought the dress was associated with any negative narratives, images, or stereotypes. For many women, it was difficult to separate the way they view the dress from the way it has been represented. As it is generally held in high regard, there was some hesitation around linking the cheongsam with negative images. However, after probing further, women were forthcoming about how the dress has been appropriated by popular media to present and fix a limited image of the Asian female:

> Outside of China the cheongsam can be sort of antiquated through media and cinema. You represent this docile, beautiful woman who is

going to serve whoever is in charge—who is usually male. And the darker side is that you are typically sexualized and licentious and available. "Asians look alike" so if you're wearing a cheongsam, you are automatically a geisha! Total Asian confusion. It's the hypersexualization of the Asian female that is signaled by the accoutrements. (AMJ)

AH/2 also described how she is conscious that the cheongsam's image has been sullied by pop culture which mirrors colonialist fantasies and maintains a set of expectations around the signification of the dress:

Another negative stereotype that would prohibit wearing the cheongsam on a day-to-day basis would be the "Asian beauty"—you're from another country, you're exotic and many North American men might exotize you. A lot of these movies are made by Western men and they portray the dress in a sexualized way and people accept these stereotypical ideas rather than looking into it themselves ... and the cheongsam is so recognizable. (AH/2)

As mentioned earlier, the form-fitting silhouette makes the cheongsam a garment that imposes a normative, idealized standard of beauty on women. The tight-fitting dress exposes the body, making it vulnerable to the "male gaze" as put forth by Laura Mulvey in her pioneering essay "Visual pleasure and narrative cinema" (1975).

So wearing the cheongsam is always fraught with weird sorts of conflicting feelings because you might think, ok this is pretty I want to wear this, but then you have to ask yourself "do I really want to do this"? Am I ready to face the world wearing this? Is some idiot going to drop a dumb comment? So beyond the idea that "this is a pretty top I want to wear this pretty top" there is the whole other "how do I deal with being Chinese" thing. (TL)

While there is a major concern for the misrepresentation of the cheongsam in popular culture, women were only able to cite examples that were symptomatic rather than causal. They were able to cite examples of what would be described as inappropriate or disrespectful uses of the cheongsam, such as its incorporation into a "sexy Asian" Halloween costume, or its association with prostitution in Hollywood movies. It can, therefore, be surmised that the way this dress has come to be associated with a submissive, sexually available, hyper-feminized, and racialized female is embedded within the history of patriarchy in China and the West, in combination with the racialization of the Chinese in North America as reflected in mass media. It was only when China gradually re-opened to the West in the 1980s that a larger repertoire of images of Chinese people entered into North America.

The emergence of the Hong Kong Second Wave (1980s–1990s) of filmmakers brought a major influx of never-before-seen images and stories about China and Chinese people to Western audiences. Wong Kar-wai is considered part of this wave with ground-breaking films such as *Chungking Express* (1994) and *Happy Together* (1998). The critical acclaim of these films brought Chinese images by Chinese directors to a global mainstream public and contributed to the changing perception of Asianness in the West. Alongside the Hong Kong Second Wave, feature films told from the Chinese-American and Chinese-Canadian perspectives started to emerge in the United States and Canada in the early 1990s. Examples of these are *Joy Luck Club* (1993) by Wayne Wang, based on the novel by Amy Tan, and *Double Happiness* (1994) by Canadian filmmaker Mina Shum. Regardless of their commercial success, these films were a source of social empowerment for Canadians and Americans of Chinese heritage.

The World of Suzie Wong has often been cited as a popular cultural reference that is responsible for propagating negative associations with the cheongsam. However, for the generation of women I interviewed, this film is considered too far in the past to be of relevance to their experience. The film that is more often referenced as having a significant impact on their impression of the cheongsam is the aforementioned *In the Mood for Love* by Wong Kar-wai.

In the Mood for Love—Maggie Cheung was definitely objectified but then I thought—I should have a cheongsam. (EYC)

The film *In the Mood for Love* gave me permission to wear it—it made me think of my grandmother and it also showed me that cheongsam can be worn everyday when it's the right material, like cotton or wool or something more practical. And because Maggie Cheung's character was not a dragon lady or any of those hackneyed Hollywood stereotypes it gave me permission to wear the dress with less fear about being questioned about my own heritage and without being hyper-sexualized. (CS)

In the Mood for Love? Maggie Cheung looked amazing. (AL)

When did *In the Mood for Love* come out? I loved that movie and she looked so amazing in that dress so it also that gave you permission to wear the dress. I would love to find the ones that Maggie Cheung wore—like in cotton. I would wear them all the time if I could. (SG)

As I have described, *In the Mood for Love* had a powerful effect on Chinese women, inspiring cheongsam fantasies and giving women the impetus to live them out. The same phenomenon occurred in Canada. While the dress loomed large in this film, its framework of representation operated differently than in *The World of Suzie Wong*. *In the Mood for Love* tells the story of unrequited love between Su Li-Zhen, played by Maggie Cheung, and Chow Mo-Wan, played by Tony Leung. Both are married and find out that their respective partners are having an affair together. They turn to each other for comfort, and while there is attraction and longing, their relationship is never realized. The film is set in Hong Kong in 1962 and Maggie Cheung's character wears the cheongsam exclusively, as was the custom at that time. Her elegant and graceful movements are enhanced by the use of slow motion and a recurring musical theme. Apart from looking incredible, the dress also served as a metaphor for the constraints of Su Li-Zhen's situation as a woman trapped in an unhappy marriage and unable to emancipate herself. But what comes forth more readily for the women interviewed for this project is how the dress incited desire—a desire to wear the cheongsam in order to embody the image of stylish, Chinese femininity that Cheung so magnificently presented. Furthermore, Cheung's character was an average woman who worked in an office. She was not a prostitute or a "dragon lady." While her cheongsam-clad image was undeniably stunning, it was not hyper-sexualized. All interaction between the two main characters was chaste, even frustratingly so. Furthermore, many of the women in the film wore the cheongsam, reinforcing the notion that this dress was part of everyday life in Hong Kong, worn by women of all ages, effectively de-rarifying the garment. Given that many of the women I interviewed talked about feeling unattractive and outside of the norms of beauty while growing up, this film also affirmed the beauty of Asian women and showcased the cheongsam as a dress that is truly owned by Chinese women and women of Chinese heritage. The need for validation on the level of beauty and aesthetics is forever problematic. The question of what constitutes beauty across ethnic backgrounds is a double-edged sword. How do you pull apart standards of beauty that have been put into place by patriarchal interests from one's own desire to be beautiful? While this discussion is beyond the focus of this book, it is none the less entangled with the narratives that surround the cheongsam and how it functions as a technology. What is important to emphasize here is that, for the women interviewed for this project, Wong's film was highly impactful in its depiction of Chinese women on the big screen, going about their daily lives, wearing exquisite cheongsam.

Forbidden cheongsam

The question of who should be allowed to wear the cheongsam makes it clear that ethnic clothing is contested terrain. The majority of women interviewed strongly felt that non-Chinese women should not wear the dress:

> When I was younger there was a certain urgency and reaction when you see white people wearing [the cheongsam]. You're appropriating our culture and you think it's just fashion. It means nothing to you. Now it's not the same dogmatic reaction . . . I just silently judge. (AL)

> It would just be one of those moments where I would get angry and I would just desperately want to ask, why are you wearing this piece of clothing. I would wonder where it comes from whether it's some form of cultural appropriation from someone who is in a privileged racial position to give herself an air of exoticness or to buy into certain fetishes. That would be an automatic suspicion for me. (AJ)

> It's a question of context. What's the goal, the intention, or the occasion to wear it? I've said in the past that appropriating other cultures is insulting. White people wearing Chinese characters is a fashion trend. We see people appropriating symbols or aspects of a minority culture most of all in Western cultures just for fashion—and it's not only Chinese culture that is being appropriated. We still have a lot of work to do to educate people that mutual cultural respect is an exchange and not an appropriation. (MC, translated from French)

Cultural appropriation is one of the main issues expressed by women to support the contention that the cheongsam should only be worn by women of Chinese heritage. This argument underscored a deeper concern about how the cheongsam stands in for assertions of cultural ownership. TL is reluctant to wear the cheongsam herself, yet she is genuinely shocked by her insistence that only Chinese women should wear the cheongsam:

I don't want to uphold Chinese culture. I shouldn't be the one doing that just because I wear a cheongsam. But mind you in the same breath, if a white chick was wearing a cheongsam I'd say "No, what the hell is she doing in a cheongsam!" So I'm stuck between a rock and a hard place. I can't believe that this is how I feel. They don't compute. It doesn't make sense but this is how I feel. (TL)

Questions are that TL's comment raises for me are, how do we buy into these ideas and how do they rob us of our power to transcend racialization? I have given this issue a lot of thought, as I fall into the category of women who intellectually and morally feel that anyone should have the right to wear the cheongsam, and yet I instinctively feel that the wearing of this dress is a privilege that comes with many caveats and conditions.

It took me a long time to feel I could wear the dress and because we have so little as women of Chinese heritage I feel protective of it. It's paradoxical. The more Chinese culture proliferates in the West, the less division we have. On the other hand when you think about unequal power relations that exist—and people of color in general have had to resist and struggle to retain a sense of their ethnicity in spite of the pressures to assimilate, it feels like a kind of little victory to say "this is ours" and it is something that cannot be appropriated easily in good conscience. It comes at a price. So maybe everyone can wear it if they acknowledge the power, the history, the understanding that it issues from Chinese culture, that it is worn with a certain amount of dignity and that it means something really important to people. I think then I would be ok with non-Chinese people wearing the dress. (CS)

Responses such as these are evidence that for Canadian women of Chinese heritage, the cheongsam is a contentious and jealously guarded object. Linked with power, privilege, and one's own inquiries, this garment is a site of profound and often hidden insecurity. On the one hand, its beauty is seductive and brings about the desire to lay claim to wearing it, while excluding it from others. On the other hand, a democratized attitude to cheongsam wearing could reinforce its appreciation in a larger, cross-cultural context. The women I interviewed are still divided on who has permission to wear the cheongsam. But what these statements reveal at this point in time is that wearing the cheongsam lies somewhere between a right and a privilege, depending on a variety of factors that include context, knowledge, and intention.

Unraveling the three As

An analysis of the interview responses reveales three intermingled concerns: ambivalence, authenticity, and agency. These threads contribute further intricacy to the wonder and consternation that surrounds the cheongsam and describe if, how, where, and when the dress will be worn. Selected excerpts from the interviews will illustrate my brief discussion of each one.

Ambivalence

All of the women I spoke to conceded to the beauty of the cheongsam and the desire to wear it, but only under specific circumstances. For a few, there was an insistence on wearing the dress simply for its formal qualities. But as it has become associated with an array of historically and culturally formed expectations, this garment is anything but neutral. Instead it emanates a number of binary oppositions that complicate its meaning. Indeed wearing the cheongsam can elicit great pleasure through an appreciation of its fabric, construction, and details. As a piece of ethnic clothing, pleasure can also be taken in wearing the dress to honor one's family and ancestors, to affirm and identify with one's ethnic heritage, and to represent the culture and values of one's ethnicity. But when faced with the decision to wear the cheongsam in public, or outside the safer bounds of one's family environment, women expressed the fear of having to deal with awkward questions that would have them justify or explain their heritages. Wearing the cheongsam might also make them vulnerable to sexist and/or racist comments. As most women became estranged from Chinese culture and language due to attempts at assimilation into the dominant order, there was also the concern that they might be perceived as imposters when wearing the cheongsam, saddled with the burden of representing a cultural history that they know little about. Furthermore, wearing the cheongsam may have the effect of re-asserting colonialist fantasies and solicit unwanted sexual attention.

> I have a problem with being objectified in this dress as hyper feminine or Asian. People think of the dress as visually beautiful so I assume that it's a compliment but then there is the fear that all the "yellow

fever" people might crawl out of the woodwork. So it is about this thing of assumptions and expectations of what a person who wears this dress is like that concerns me. (JL)

AH/2 describes her issue with wearing the cheongsam within an everyday, office setting:

[. . .] many North American men might exoticize you if you're wearing a cheongsam instead of a suit. It's harder to be taken seriously. I would wear it for Asian events because we understand the context. (AH/2)

The exotic/erotic synthesis is one of the core ambivalences that surround the cheongsam which continues to make its wearing a delicate and tricky negotiation for Canadian-born women of Chinese heritage. As a result, wearing the dress takes a particular degree of courage and strength, which is perhaps why the Shanghai Cheongsam Salon has become so popular. Given the cheongsam's tumultuous history in China, the act of coming together in droves to wear this dress can be perceived as a political gesture. But rather than having to negotiate the wearing of the cheongsam in isolation, these women can assert their right to pleasure and play in the safety of numbers.

Many of the women in this study also expressed the desire to wear the cheongsam if it were made from casual fabrics and in more comfortable dress shapes. The emerging presence of female tailors in China may bring this exciting prospect to fruition one day. But for the cheongsam to be a truly progressive dress that can represent new, empowering modes of representation for both Chinese women and Canadian-born women of Chinese heritage, it remains vital to acknowledge how popular culture, fashion, politics, and an undercurrent of patriarchal discourse have brought about the dominant aesthetics of the garment that persist today. Despite the more dignified image of the cheongsam in films like *In the Mood for Love*, the dress and the woman in it are none the less fetishized. Long-standing archetypal representations of Chinese femininity will need to be dislodged as new models of the cheongsam emerge in order for more women to wear this garment on their own terms. For now, ambivalence continues to shroud the cheongsam.

Authenticity

I was further convinced of the existence of a cheongsam "authenticity" discourse when I encountered two high school-aged women at *The Fitting*

Room exhibition. Both born in Montreal and of Chinese heritage, one of the women had worn a cheongsam before, while the other had not. When I asked one of the woman to tell me why she had never worn the dress she explained that the material was too stiff and the dress itself too tight and uncomfortable. I asked her whether she would wear a cheongsam if the cut were altered to make it easier to wear. She wrinkled her nose at this idea and said, "but then it wouldn't be elegant." For this woman the form-fitting cut of the dress was a non-negotiable, defining characteristic. After this, I recalled how throughout the interview process, time and time again women described the "authentic" cheongsam in very certain terms. This affirmation of the existence of an exemplary image of the cheongsam revealed a deeper pre-occupation with the slippery notion of authenticity. For all of the women interviewed, the quintessentially "authentic" cheongsam is a long, form fitting dress made from brocade fabric, most often red, with high collar and

Figure 14 Woman in tight fitting cheongsam circa 1960s, Hong Kong (Courtesy Sim family collection)

side slits. Furthermore, apart from the necessary characteristic of the high collar, it is the dress's cut and shape that seems to be a major defining feature. In other words, a cheongsam without the s-curve silhouette is not considered authentic. I also noted that in many of the interviews, the terms "traditional," "classic," and "authentic" were often used interchangeably, so it is important to pull apart the nuances between these terms, as they reveal an added layer of complicated power dynamics.

The term "traditional" when applied to the cheongsam evokes labor processes, an established practice, a developed skillset and an adherence to a set of guiding principles. Hong Kong cheongsam shops such as Mei Hwa and Linva Tailor describe their cheongsam as "made in the traditional way," and base their longevity in the business on the skilled quality of their work. The employment of the term "classic" is intertwined with "traditional" in that it refers to a dress made according to a certain set of techniques and standards of quality, that may vary in nuance as it seems to connote a dress design that has stayed consistent over time to the degree that it becomes distinct and unmistakable. While the denotation of "classic" indicates that the dress's creation should follow strict guidelines, it does seem not to deny the legitimacy of cheongsam that have variations on style details. In this way, a dress that has a variation on sleeve length or decorative details would still be "classic" as long as it follows the same basic block and level of tailorship. The concept of "authenticity," however, contends that the cheongsam's legitimacy is dependent on its adherence to a specific and essential combination of form, fabric, and finishings, as described above. This attitude finds concert with the propagation of a singular definition of Chinese identity that is destabilizing for people of the Chinese diaspora in Canada and around the world. The insecurity of non-compliance with the tenets of what makes one "authentically" Chinese is allegorically infused into ideas about the cheongsam, further complicating a discussion of the dress. What makes one dress more authentic than another? Does it matter who makes it or where it is made? How is one dress more legitimate than another and how are these ideas perpetuated? In order to acknowledge how the term "authentic" infers its own unequal power dynamic, I have preferred to use the term "ubiquitous" to refer to the most commonly held image of the cheongsam as expressed by the women I interviewed.

There are a number of factors that have shaped the dominant perception that an authentic cheongsam must have a form-fitting silhouette and be made from rigid brocade fabric. When the decline of the cheongsam as an everyday dress met with the rise of more affordable and comfortable ready-to-wear Western clothing, only the brocade cheongsam remained in use as a garment assigned to formal occasions in Canada and China. The larger garment industry recognized the changing status of the cheongsam, and rather than innovate the garment, the characteristics of the dress seemed to freeze in time from the 1960s to the 1990s to cater to the changing role of the cheongsam. For a new generation of Canadian-born women of Chinese heritage, the ubiquitous cheongsam would be for many women the only one they had ever seen. This is where perceptions of the cheongsam diverge among the women I interviewed. For some women, myself included, the cheongsam was the dress our grandmothers, aunts, and mothers wore the in everyday life *and* for special occasions. This type of exposure to the dress contradicts the authenticity discourse. Whether it is worn for the first time at

Figure 15 Billboard poster of the "Salon de l'Asie" featuring "La Chine" in Lyon, France. Photo taken by the author in fall of 2017

a wedding or worn with a wool cardigan for school, the dress became the conduit through which we could connect with our families and by extension our Chinese heritage. Notions of authenticity for the cheongsam are therefore varied and uneven, problematizing the very definition of the word as it applies to ethnic clothing. My argument is that both the tweed cheongsam with the A-line skirt that I picked up at a flea market, the gray wool cheongsam I had made by the Montreal based tailor, and the silk brocade dress with the s-curve can all be considered authentic as, in a world of advanced globalization, authenticity becomes almost impossible to define and trace.

The power dynamics that play out when fashion and ethnicity collide become even more complex in a discussion about authenticity. The clothing items that appropriate cheongsam elements for the mainstream and haute couture markets are considered inauthentic by all of the women I interviewed. While they do not feel the same level of posessiveness towards these hybrid styles, these garments do gain another type of cultural capital. TL described how cheongsam-inspired Western clothing had a leveling effect when it came to reconciling her Chinese heritage with her Canadian cultural upbringing, as "things changed [in Canadian society] and it became more fashionable [to be Chinese]." Her experiences with racialization brought about a need for acceptance in mainstream Canadian society. Distancing herself from "traditional" clothes and her "genuine" Chinese heritage in favor of hybrid Western/Chinese clothing designs reflected her need to display her Canadian upbringing and mastery of the dominant cultural language in spite of her Chinese appearance. As I described earlier in this chapter, I adopted similar strategies in my choice of how to wear the cheongsam and other pieces of cheongsam-inspired clothing offered by the mainstream market. These practices were ways of negotiating the terrain as a racialized person in Canadian society, ways that were no doubt exacerbated by the unflattering media narratives that had become deeply internalized. In another interview, AL presented a number of examples of how her mother's experience as a teenager growing up in Canada impressed upon her that white, blond, and blue-eyed were the beauty ideals upon which all else would be judged. These messages were overturned when cheongsam-inspired clothing offered by the mainstream fashion industry promoted the Chinese "look" as attractive and desirable. Canadian-born women of Chinese heritage played with these items, and took ownership of what signified them as Chinese in order to play with and experiment with a new type of representation. In other words, cheongsam hybrid clothing items brought Chinese ethnic clothing into the Western dressing vocabulary, rendering pieces like the cheongsam more familiar to mainstream Canadian culture. As Chinese culture gained further appeal in popular culture and society at large, mixing components of Chinese clothing into daily dressing became a way for some women to proudly accentuate their ethnicity.

This point brings me back to the question of who has the right to wear the cheongsam. The fashion industry, that includes traditional cheongsam tailors, is disinterested in a garment's ethnic ownership, history, or meaning. Its stakeholders are ultimately interested in business, and the more people who want to wear cheongsam the better. As Chinatowns around the world have opened up to diverse publics for their own survival, mainly as areas of interest to tourism and leisure, cheongsam are all the more accessible to all kinds of buyers. For the few remaining bespoke cheongsam tailors around the world, ethnic background is not a prerequisite for wearing the cheongsam. While the interviews show that the democratization of the cheongsam does not sit well with everyone, perhaps the time has come to take the discussion of the politics of the cheongsam forward, as it may be a crucial step towards real agency for women of Chinese heritage in Canada and around the world. Part of this agency comes from the changing power dynamics between China and the West. What I will show with the support of recent theories is how these dynamics, while unstable, may offer possibilities for the creation of new modes of representation and an increased degree of freedom from the limiting perceptions of the Asian female in Canada and other countries in the West.

What, therefore, constitutes an authentic cheongsam? Ingrained concepts of authenticity as "pure and therefore superior" are a reflection of Ien Ang's (2001) description of the "Central Country" complex, and an "authentic" cheongsam re-asserts the optics of a singular definition of Chinese identity. When fear of the loss of ethnicity emerges, rules about what constitutes ethnic authenticity become stronger. In short, we are confronted by the old adage that "the Chinese in Canada are more Chinese than those in China," with the exception of the second generation, for whom the anxiety persists that we will never be Chinese enough. When the women I interviewed began to contemplate the complexity of their own ethnic identities, they also began to question the meanings of "authenticity" and, by extension, to consider how they might like to see the dress evolve in ways that could better reflect their values and ideas with a recognition of the role that the fashion industry plays in that evolution:

There is the classic model, a red dress, fitted, with two slits on the sides. But there are lots of variations, colors and cuts. Even in China I had never seen ones like that. With time, fashion changes. (JW, translated from French)

As described earlier, there is every indication that cheongsam designers in cities such as Beijing, Shanghai, Hong Kong, and Taipei are interested in serving the demands of potential buyers. In Canada, Hong Kong born, Toronto-based fashion designer Alice Ko has been making formal versions of the dress since 1991. Ko is the principal cheongsam designer for the Miss Chinese Toronto and Miss Chinese Vancouver pageants, in addition to making cheongsam gowns for gala events and weddings. In an online article by Erica Ng (2014: thefashionglobe. com), Ko explained that she brings together the "cheongsam's traditional eastern aesthetics with western techniques of dressmaking," in order to make the dress "more practical and suitable for the current society of women." While her business model does not currently include casual cheongsams, this might be encouraged if more women came forward with the demand. Echoed again is Margaret Maynard's contention that the evolution of ethnic clothing is relational and in continual process despite its discourse. Maynord states, "[t]here is no habitual way of defining ethnic dress nor can it be expressed in terms of its stasis" (2004, p. 71). The way that ethnic clothing is made and worn will continue to evolve as a result of the variety of forces, including but not limited to technical innovation, economics, and the fashion market in symbiosis with everyday practices experienced and exercised by diasporic people as shaped by history and culture. In this way, the definition of authenticity loses its rigidity, and ethnic clothing is able to have multiple meanings and iterations.

Agency

In my explorations with cheongsam wearing, I have attempted to subvert the concern of self-Orientalization by wearing cheongsams in everyday life as my grandmother did, in an attempt to render it "familiar" rather than reserving it for culturally specific occasions. As mentioned earlier, I mixed them with Western-identified pieces of clothing, much like they were worn in the 1930s. What these experiments have shown me is that the wearing of a dress that has come to symbolize the "exotic" can, in this current globalized context, create agency. My ability to wear the dress as a demonstration of a cosmopolitan fluency is a direct result of my experience as a Canadian-born women of Chinese heritage.

The increase of positive images of Asian women in Western media and popular culture finds correlation with the changing global economic landscape, as China and other places such as South Korea, Singapore and Hong Kong have gained economic power, as expressed by TL:

> Men would drop stupid comments whether I wore a cheongsam or not. It was about being an Asian woman, period. But I get that less and less today … It's really a different world we live in and the world powers are very different. So that was before China was a super power. This was before, "oh my god we all have to do business in China" (TL)

In tandem with my hypothesis that the dress can be employed as a tool of empowerment is the recent theory put forth by Olivia Khoo in her book *The Chinese Exotic: Modern Diasporic Femininity* (2007) in which she explains that:

> The Chinese exotic is also differentiated from colonialist or imperialist exoticism in that it conceives of women and femininity, not as the oppressed, but as forming part of the new visibility of Asia, connected with the region's economic rise and emergent modernities. What is exotic now is no longer the old (primitive) China within Asia, but the idea of a new Asia (Asia the cosmopolitan, the rich, the modern, and the technological) … the Chinese exotic consists of both subject and object positions, whereas the old exoticism consisted only of object positions. (2007, p. 12)

At the heart of Khoo's argument is the contention that "exchanges within diasporic cross-cultural contexts have produced new images and representations of Chinese femininity" that "can also be negotiated so as to create the possibility of positive agency for its subjects" (2007, p. 170). In relation to the focus of this study, the concept of the "Chinese exotic" generates possibilities for Canadian-born women of Chinese heritage to replace old representations with more progressive ones given their ability to successfully negotiate a cross-cultural and intercultural environment such as Canada.

As more people of Asian heritage have risen to prominence in areas such as law, journalism, medicine, politics, television, and especially Chinese cinema, being of Asian heritage in North America has become less stigmatized. The narratives that supported efforts to vilify the Chinese during times of political upheaval and war are becoming unmoored. At a certain point, as expressed by LS, "it was cool to be Asian." I echo Ien Ang's (2001) assertion that in a world where globalization and rapidly growing transnational regional economies are the new reality, being an Asian "other" still exists. However, "the status of that otherness has changed" (2001, p. 140). As a result, I see Khoo's "Chinese exotic" as a concept that combines the baggage of imperialist exoticization that can be used as source of information, with newer, empowered representations to be capitalized upon by women of Chinese heritage in order to more fully determine themselves. Within the theory of the "Chinese exotic" lies the strategy of wearing the cheongsam and cheongsam-inspired clothing produced by the mainstream fashion industry. The way that Canadian-born women of Chinese heritage have been wearing these garments and mixing Western and Chinese garments demonstrates that they have been exercising elements of Khoo's "Chinese exotic" all along. My wearing of the cheongsam has been informed in major part by the desire to transcend the discourses around the cheongsam that limit when, where, and how it can be worn. I argue that it is important to take the dress out of the confines of protected environments and contexts, bringing the fabric and cut into the realm of the everyday, in order to evacuate notions inside and outside the Chinese community that the dress is a strange and rarified object. The conservative views which keep the cheongsam inside the community have been shaped by a long history of the racialization of the Chinese in Canada, which has in turn been internalized by second-generation Canadians of Chinese heritage. I argue that the time to redress the effects of these historic experiences is now, and that making the cheongsam part of the vocabulary of modern dressing is an act that can be both political and pleasurable, which is another vital concept put forth by Dorinne Kondo (1997). Her contribution of the productive expression "politics of pleasure" focuses on how the enjoyment of fashion is both a life-giving force and a political act that has the serious power to challenge and celebrate. Applying the "politics of pleasure" to the cheongsam underscores how its wearing mixes pleasure and assertion that is ultimately a gesture of empowerment, resistance, and experimentation. Kondo writes that:

> ... the world of representation and of aesthetics is a site of struggle, where identities are created, where subjects interpellated, where hegemonies can be challenged. And taking seriously that pleasure, that life-giving capacity of aesthetics, performance, bodies, and the sensuous is, within our regime of power and truth, an indisputably political act. (1997, p. 4)

Wearing the cheongsam is a gesture that carries with it the courage to question hegemonies, to define one's identity, and to exercise empowerment. It is a tactic to affirm the productivity of difference when put forth on one's own terms. Putting an end to self-effacement, women use the cheongsam to present a set of ideas that are complex, multi-faceted, and ultimately unapologetic, as is so eloquently expressed by AJ:

> In terms of identity I do feel much more conscious of myself as a racialized person when I put these pieces of clothing on. It's almost as though racialization and that whole process of realizing that I was a racial other was beyond my control whereas when I put on certain pieces of clothing that connotes "otherness" I am regaining control of that entire process and taking ownership of this identity that has kind of been thrust upon me. (AJ)

Presently, the cheongsam may be able to transcend its perception by Canadian-born women of Chinese heritage as being old-fashioned and "too Chinese." While signs of a media backlash against China and the increased presence of Chinese people in North America continues, Canadian-born women of Chinese heritage need to acknowledge that they have developed a polyvalence that allows them to deftly move between Canadian culture and their own sense of a Chinese identity, making more space to experiment with the wearing of the cheongsam that is strategic and opens up entry points towards further empowerment and freedom. AMJ, who wore the cheongsam to give her high school valedictory address, underscores this idea:

> If you elect to accentuate your visible difference with very obvious ethnically charged items of clothing you are making a statement. What kind of statement are you making . . . what do you want to make? What is the context? How are people receiving you? Are you speaking to an informed crowd or are you catering to their expectations? In spite of it all, you will do that anyways. I think there's a kind of empowerment in that. (AMJ)

During the Republic Era, the cheongsam was the right dress to express a woman's modernity. In twenty-first-century Canada, women are finding that it is still the right dress for the expression of a diaspora experience by the grace of its mutability, dexterity, and adaptability. It is modern now, as it is able to convey a current, living reality.

There is much to investigate in the contemporary wearing practices of ethnic clothing in Canada, some of which have been explored in depth here. What these interviews reveal is that a connection to one's heritage can be expressed through the wearing and non-wearing of ethnic clothing. It is an overwhelmingly hesitant practice that is contingent, negotiated on an ongoing basis, a strategy of contestation, as well as a tool for experimentation with one's identity. These days, despite the reigning discourses that govern the image of an authentic cheongsam, there is an increasing desire to see this dress in different cuts and types of fabric.

As Canadian-born women of Chinese heritage continue to discover and claim this dress for themselves, they are finding ways to access a heritage that exists beyond a singular, essentialized concept of Chineseness. The women who spoke to me have a relationship with the cheongsam that is informed by their varied experiences as children of immigrants, finding ways to survive and thrive in the Canadian context. While this dress can be desirable for its formal qualities, its link with tradition and family make it a way to show pride in one's Chinese heritage. At the same time, the cheongsam can produce anxiety in a situation when its display on the body may further underscore Otherness and concerns about the reinforcement of stereotypes that cater to the male gaze. It is a dress that effects a performative posture that can be a reproduction of colonized fantasies of Chinese femininity, while simultaneously presenting the potential for an empowered image of the diasporic Chinese female. The cheongsam can therefore be defined as a site of ambivalence governed by discourses of authenticity. In this section, I attempted to outline how cheongsam-wearing practices that transcend these discourses may provide agency for women of Chinese heritage. It is this set of paradoxes that makes the cheongsam a technology that is part of a larger "cultural–political complex" constituted by historical, political, economic and cultural forces.

CHAPTER 5
GETTING INSIDE "THE FITTING ROOM"

The collection of attitudes, ideas and wearing practices generously offered by the women I interviewed provided a rich pool of material from which to develop *The Fitting Room*. I was interested in presenting the history of the cheongsam in a way that might reflect its enigmatic origins not only through content but also through structure. I was struck by the diversity and divergent experiences and opinons about the cheongsam and how the range of views might be correlated with a woman's sense of connection with her ethnic heritage. The massive influence of media images and popular culture on shaping these views was also important to present and I wished to incorporate the multiplicity of voices with aspects of my personal experience into the creation of three cheongsams. As another goal for this installation, I wanted to underscore how the "trying on" of the cheongsam is a gesture of feeling out aspects of one's identity that have not fully been explored. In the interest of an intercultural dialogue, I thought it important to demonstrate how the choosing and wearing of clothing to represent oneself in everyday life is an action that transcends ethnicity, gender, and generation. My hope was therefore to make this exhibition an inclusive experience despite the focus on culturally specific subject matter.

In order to situate my work within the context of recent contemporary art, I will begin with a discussion on the artistic practices of a few selected artists who have significantly engaged with clothing and fashion as a way to explore issues of "race," gender, and ethnicity, as well as the diaspora and post-colonial condition. The one quality that seems to unite them is what I term "politicized sensuousness," an aesthetic strategy of using formal beauty to relay a critical message. This approach can be productive for artists as a way to open up audience receptivity to a potentially confrontational idea. In this way, a stylistically sumptuous proposal may disarm the viewer while baring subversive teeth.

Situating *The Fitting Room* in recent contemporary art

Sara Rahbar

Born in Iran in 1976, Sara Rahbar's family left for the US during the Islamic revolution and the Iran – Iraq war when she was five years old. Raised in the

United States, Rahbar's artistic practice is informed by the emotional tug-of-war between her adopted country and her country of birth. Rahbar works at the intersection of textile art, photography, sculpture, and installation. Her multi-pronged approach includes autoethnography, history and the semiotics of cultural and national signifiers to operate, as Catherine Grenier writes, "at the intersection of two traditions that art has often brought together ... a feat she achieves by basing her work on her personal history, creating an aesthetic of mixing."[1] Through a hybridized approach to materials and treatment she effectively brings about an aesthetics of the diaspora experience. Among Rahbar's works that resonate most profoundly with my concerns is her series of photographs *You are Here, Safe with Me* (2008). These images depict the artist wearing a variety of textiles, including the flags of Iran and the United States as a hijab and burka. The wearing of these flags as clothing marks the body as gendered and contested by national allegiances. With this strategy, we are confronted with a variety of personal and political statements that are engaged with conflicting concepts of nationalism, national identity formation, religious, and ethnic clothing. Saheen Merali describes this oscillation as "an apocalyptic memory (that) has been revised in her reworking of traditional materials into proto-contemporary textiles and textures of national belonging."[2] The auto-ethnographic strategy of inserting herself into the image is also a powerful gesture that is reinforced by the use of the tradition of portraiture, through which she offers a challenging gaze. Rahbar's artistic and personal pre-occupations are very close to my own questions about identity, the fluctuating meanings of ethnic clothing, and the relationship between the two. The conceptually layered and formally captivating nature of her work provides me with a sense of communion and aspiration.

Yinka Shonibare CBE (RA)

Yinka Shonibare CBE (RA) is a British artist of Nigerian heritage born in London. At the age of three, he moved with his family to Lagos, Nigeria where he spent his childhood and adolescence. He returned to London to attend art school in the late 1980s with an interest in global political issues. When he created a work about Russian *perestroika* one of his tutors remarked, "Well you're African, aren't you? Why aren't you producing authentic African art?" Bemused by the assumption that his ethnic origins should dictate and limit the scope of his artistic terrain following Mercer's (1994) theory of the "burden of representation," he countered by engaging fully with the concept of "authenticity" in his work. What constitutes "authenticity"? What are the signifiers of Africanness and what do they look like? A reply to some of these questions came to Shonibare in the form and style of Dutch wax fabric, which would become the main conceptual and formal device in almost all of his work. While this fabric has become an established marker of an essentialized pan-African culture, it is actually Indonesian in origin, based on *batik* techniques, which were appropriated and industrialized by Dutch colonizers. With its mixed and mistaken provenances, Dutch wax fabric provides a sumptuous yet probing vehicle to evoke the complexity of concepts such as identity and its links with class and race, and further complicated by notions of authenticity, ethnicity, and hybridity. His critical reflection on power relations between Africa and Europe is delivered through a formal treatment that is both lavish and decadent. In a related area of investigation, he reveals his affection and respect for British culture and institutions while simultaneously questioning class and privilege. For example, his 1998 work *Mr. and Mrs. Andrews without their heads* presents a sculptural version of a painting by Thomas Gainsborough created circa 1750. Presented in this portrait are a young couple indicative of the emerging merchant class who wished to immortalize themselves and their vast estate in painting. Shonibare took this image and made a sculptural rendition of the couple. In his version, their Victorian finery is made entirely from Dutch wax fabric as a wink towards the imperialist actions that brought about Mr. and Mrs. Andrews's fortune. The artist also presents the couple headless, in reference to the fate of the aristocracy during the French Revolution. Shonibare is one of the few artists to employ interdisciplinarity to underscore a strategy of hybridity. As Rachel Kent explains, "working across cultures, and seamlessly integrating the language of contemporary art with that of popular culture, fashion, literature and cinema, he suggests a range of grey areas rather than simple 'categories' for the framing of ideas."[3] Shonibare's work underscores an ambivalence that most productively unsettles simple binaries and reveals the intricacies involved in the conceptual use of a fabric so bound up with an erroneous historical narrative and the loaded concept of authenticity. Furthermore, he actively engages his work with "politicized sensuousness," as Kent further contends. "Shonibare has frequently cited his use of beauty as a device to draw viewers in and gain their attention before confronting them—ever so gently—with less palatable truths about the world in which we live."[4]

Mary Sui Yee Wong

Mary Sui Yee Wong is a Montreal-based multidisciplinary artist who immigrated to Canada as a child from Hong Kong in 1963. Her work refers to issues of identity and cultural diversity that are implicated in her various roles as a Chinese-Canadian artist, mother, teacher, and community activist. Wong's practice is inspired by personal memories, histories, and legacies as it attempts to examine the mutability of personal and national identity formation, especially in light of advanced globalization. Her multidisciplinary installations operate at the intersection of Western theory and Chinese philosophy. The works of most relevance to my project are *Yellow Apparel* (2004–8) and *Mei Ren* (2008). *Yellow Apparel* features a collection of outfits of different styles made from a bolt of fabric the artist found in a local shop. The fabric is printed with a graphic design of what seems to be stereotypical images of "ethnic" children who all have the same peachy-brown skin color. Wong used this material to make a series of outfits that re-appropriate the stereotypical clothing styles represented in the fabric motif. As Alice Jim explains, "[a]s it unfolded into a global economics of desire through the designs of a single rolled bolt of fabric, *Yellow Apparel* unraveled other constructions of difference at the same time."[5] These outfits were displayed on a rack in the middle of the gallery space, swathed in plastic, as if they were soon going to be shipped off to a fashion show or boutique. The installation also featured large-scale photographs of people of color wearing these garments, thus employing the language of fashion photography, ethnography, advertising, and contemporary art. More of Wong's "designs" were presented in the gallery's street level vitrine and she staged a fashion show for the opening. In her artist statement, Wong explained that *Yellow Apparel* was meant to engage with her concern for the current Western fascination with all things Asian, from fashion to home decor. She linked these trends to her own passion for textiles and patterns and used them to explore questions of representation, cultural consumption, and racialization. In this way, the installation engaged with the workings of the fashion industry, in order "to re-appropriate the appropriated and play with notions of acculturation as part of the everyday."[6]

Mary Wong's other work of particular resonance for me is *Mei Ren* (2008) which means "beautiful person" in Cantonese. This participatory sculptural work consisted of a lifesize paper doll and various paper doll outfits. The paper doll is a cutout from a black and white photo of the artist as a toddler in which she is wearing Western clothing. She then created a wardrobe of paper doll outfits that quote both Western and Asian period dress. Visitors were invited to choose outfits and to "dress" the doll as a gesture to explore how post-colonial Orientalism is marketed, disseminated, consumed, and perpetuated. As Rebecca Duclos explains in the exhibition catalogue essay, "the historically correct outfits [are] key in this regard as their delicacy ultimately confirms that our fantasy about Wong's 'Chinese-ness' is just that—a fantasy that is as two-dimensional as a cut-out dress and as disposable as a drawer full of paper dolls."[7] In the spirit of Duclos's observation, I had a supplementary interpretation when I carried out the action of dressing the doll. In addition to sensing Wong's statement on the commodification of Chinese culture in the West, my own feelings of inadequacy surfaced about never measuring up to the idea of embodying true Chinese-ness. In this moment, which was a very powerful result of Wong's decision to make this work participatory, I was struck by the fear that I may also be seen as an imposter when wearing the cheongsam.

Wong's body of work is informed by questions that resonate with my own about the cultural functions of identity, post-colonial discourse, and representation. Furthermore, her conceptual use of fabric and clothing offers a critique of the Western fashion industry and its appropriation of Asian culture while addressing material issues of labor, production and consumption. Her deftness at conveying this multitude of aspects through the use of tactics such as participation and humor are among those I hoped to incorporate into *The Fitting Room*.

WESSIELING

Of all the artists I researched, only one had engaged directly with the formal, conceptual, cultural, and political aspects of the cheongsam. With her exhibition *Fusionable Cheongsam*, Hong Kong-born artist and fashion designer WESSIELING investigated the cheongsam's hybrid nature, that blends East/West, modern/ancient and male/female binary relationships. In a series of installations, WESSIELING presented the constantly evolving and multiple identities of the cheongsam that have emerged through popular culture, history, fashion production, global circulation, and consumption. *Authentic Dress* (2007) consisted of the ubiquitous red-brocade cheongsam, which as discussed previously is the most commonly held image of the Chinese dress. In WESSIELING's piece, the dress looked as if it was being lifted out of a Chinese wok by a pair of floating chopsticks, making reference to cultural expectations and how they are readily consumed. *One Dollar*

Dress (2007) was a cheongsam made out of fabric printed with the American one-dollar bill. Hanging on a wire hanger, as if being packed or unpacked from a well-traveled suitcase, this work provoked a reading on the current state of Chinese migration in pursuit of the American dream, while simultaneously commenting on the economic reforms that have rapidly transformed China. *Red Guard Dress* (2007) is a cheongsam fashioned from a Red Guard uniform that strikes an ironic chord given the fact that the dress was banned during the Cultural Revolution. *National Dress* (2007), made from a Chinese flag, played on ideas of a national identity formation. This work inspired reflection on the tensions that have erupted in Hong Kong over the last few years due to Mainland China's intervention into its political system. WESSIELING's media piece *Nam Kok Staircase* (2007) consisted of a torso of a female mannequin onto which clips from a variety of Hollywood films that feature the cheongsam were projected. This piece offered the viewer insight into the cultural construction of the dress's identity, its link with popular culture, and underscored the power of images to inhabit the imagination and influence perceptions. With rigor, beauty, and a high level of virtuosity in their execution, each of these works contributes to a cohesive matrix of ideas that are embedded in the semiotics of the cheongsam. WESSIELING's work adopted a Hong Kong perspective that extended beyond the fashion industry to engage with the influences of identity, history, migration, globalization, and capitalism. Her work also articulated the cheongsam's hybrid evolutive nature in a direct and tactile way. The artist's use of "politicized sensuousness" revealed historically formed inequalities of power through an experience of precise beauty and conceptual rigor. As Christian Huck writes in the publication that accompanied the exhibition, "[i]t is this double connotation, the colorful mix of fashion on the one hand, and the struggle over the meaning of particular dresses, that Wessieling's work on the cheongsam brings to the fore."

The exhibition context

Chinatown & The Swatow Plaza

When I began to think about the exhibition, I imagined that it would take place, as if by default, in a typical gallery setting. However, as the project began to take shape, and as I started to imagine the works in a space, I became absorbed with how the use of place would contribute deeper meaning to the subject of the cheongsam and its significance as an object to discuss the situation of second-generation Canadians of Chinese heritage. Also, given the level of engagement with social, cultural, and political issues within the theoretical foundations of the work, it became appropriate to carefully consider the question of whether an art gallery would be the best place to activate its dialogical aspirations. Over time, the use of a non-art space provided the appropriate frame of reference for the work's engagement with ideas of belonging, representation, meeting, and dialogue. Since the exhibition was conceived as an investigation of the cheongsam and its relationship with Canadian-born women of Chinese heritage it seemed clear that it should directly bring members of the variegated Chinese community in Montreal, second-generation Canadians of Chinese heritage and non-Chinese people in contact with one another. It was therefore crucial to take that investigation and its multi-faceted conversation to a place where these communities were likely to intersect. As mentioned in Chapter 2, Miwon Kwon (2000, p. 40) asserted that the art historical movements of Minimalism and institutional critique of the 1970s helped to challenge the "innocence" of the gallery or museum space, working to reveal its hidden agenda, which she described as "furthering" the institution's idealist imperative of rendering itself and its hierarchization of values "objective," "disinterested," and "true". Taking the art experience out of a space marked and coded as "gallery" into a space outside could allow an artist to address a different set of power relations and to bring communities together in order to consider the dynamics of culture, history, and migration. My choice of a particular site was informed by three interrelated considerations: the actuality of the location, the social conditions of the framework of the site, as well as what the site offered discursively, in terms of "a field of knowledge, intellectual exchange, or cultural debate" (Kwon, 2000, p. 44). Montreal's Chinatown is a site of comfort and discomfort as well as security and insecurity for me and other Canadians of Chinese heritage, who feel a certain connection to the place while experiencing a sense of alienation and non-acceptance within the Chinese community. This tension provides another important reason for the exhibition to take place in the potentially unpredictable context of Chinatown, rather than the more familiar and branded space of a gallery. The presentation of *The Fitting Room* in Chinatown represented a gesture of affirmation as well as a risk of rejection. I felt that a gallery would be too safe and could undermine the fundamental goals of the exhibition. By taking these works outside the comfort zone of the white cube, I aimed to upset the established power dynamics of the gallery, exposing my work and, by extension, myself, to the rigors of a non-art space frequented by potentially unsuspecting art visitors. Montreal's Chinatown also offered an opportunity to address the notions of "ghetto" that are still relevant issues in Quebec society. Chinatowns were established as safe places for immigrant and migrant Chinese who were subject to the ebb and flow of xenophobia that accompanied state sanctioned efforts to curb Chinese immigration. These neighborhoods are places for people to run businesses and offer services to the community as well as to nurture social bonds and kinship through family associations. Montreal's Chinatown has been historically constrained to only two city blocks and is no longer Chinese-centric. The businesses on the lower end of Saint Laurent Boulevard, which used to be the heart of Chinatown, now share the strip with a hipster tiki bar and a Mexican taco restaurant. The choice of the historic site of Chinatown was therefore rooted in a transcultural strategy that aimed to engage with a neighborhood that has survived despite a turbulent history and is now frequented by a wide diversity of people.

Given the subject matter of my exhibition, the use of a storefront or boutique space seemed an obvious choice. During my location search, the Swatow Plaza quickly came to mind. At the time it was Chinatown's newest building, spanning half a city block and bordered by Clark street, Saint Laurent Boulevard, De la Gauchetière street and Viger street. In an amazing coincidence, Swatow is also the city of my father's birth and the place I have heard the most about from my grandmother as significant to her life. This six-story, multi-purpose building has a large supermarket in the basement, retail kiosks and services on the ground and first floors, a travel agency and administrative offices on the fifth floor, and a luxury Chinese restaurant on the top floor. During the time of the exhibition, the third and fourth floors were being converted into retail furniture showrooms. I visited the building a few times and upon noting the existence of a number of empty retail kiosks I contacted their leasing department. To my delight and surprise, they were willing to rent spaces to me for the one month I required, even though they did not fully understand the project nor why I was not using these spaces for commercial ends. I rented three commercial stalls on the first floor with the idea of placing each of the inter-related works in its own space. By chance they were situated remarkably well in relation to one another as well as blending thematically well with what the other stalls were selling. My closest neighbor happened to sell clothing and accessories of both Western and Chinese styles, all imported from China. Another stall featured knick-knacks such as clocks, vases, fake flowers, and figurines, and a few of the other adjacent kiosk spaces showcased Chinese furniture. In order to access my installation you had to find your way up the main escalators or elevator and then wind through the initial labyrinth of stalls offering all kinds of goods, from teaware to watches, men's suits, women's undergarments, and other household goods. Some visitors who came specifically to see the exhibition said they had some difficulty finding it, as it seemed to blend into the mix of the other kiosks. For me, this was an excellent indication that the chosen context would deepen the questions and significations raised by the exhibition. The immersive retail environment also evoked additional layers of consideration around commerce, labor, and exchange. What also occurred to me is that the infiltration of a non-commercial art exhibition into the context of a shopping mall could be analogous to my insider/outsider status within Chinatown. How might my physical presence and my work in this mall be received?

(Chinese) Screen

As mentioned briefly, *The Fitting Room* exhibition consisted of three inter-related works, each of which can be considered as smaller installations within the whole. The first work that the viewer encountered upon entering the general area of the exhibition was *(Chinese) Screen.* This work was based on a type of multi-paneled screen which consists of a folding structure and functions as a piece of furniture. As a cultural form, it emerged during the second century CE. Used to decorate palaces and grand manors in China, these screens were a luxury item, often decorated with lavish carvings or fabrics and inlaid with precious materials, such as jade or mother-of-pearl. The concept of these screens therefore embodied decorative and practical characteristics. They were used to delineate and articulate space, as well as provide privacy while dressing or undressing. In this way, the screens created spaces that can be hidden or revealed. I chose to make my screens out of simple, 2 × 2" pine frames, with rear-projection screen material stretched on one side, which gave the screens a sense of front (to be seen) and back (not to be seen). The frames were sprayed with a clear, matte lacquer in order to give them a protected and finished look. I used wood, as it is the material typically used in the fabrication of these screen objects. But instead of the rosewood or mahogany favored for this type of piece, I used easy-to-find Canadian pine to incorporate a hybrid strategy that would bring a Chinese object into contact with Canadian materials. The panels were joined by simple nickel-colored metal hinges found at a local hardware store. The overall minimalist aesthetic of the screen object itself, in contrast to a traditional ornate screen, created a framework that would heighten the appreciation of the rich and colorful video content. I decided to go with a 4:3 aspect ratio with screens that each measured four feet by three feet in order to evoke a retrospective feel since the content would explore the origins, history, and evolution of the cheongsam. The relatively low height undermined the idea and function of privacy yet the object was still able to delineate space. As a projection surface the screen opened up a new space, inviting the viewer into another realm. The human scale of the screen allowed me to work with the screen's ability simultaneous to conceal and reveal.

In addition to the screen's cultural references, I chose rear projection over flatscreen television monitors for the multiple references that the concept of projection offers in relation to identity, representation, and the influence of cinema. We project ideas and images onto ourselves while others project their own ideas and images onto us. From where are these ideas and images derived and and how are they perpetuated? Projecting images onto screens, rather than having them emanate from inside monitors, allowed me to evoke and explore these questions in a polysemic sociocultural space-time.

The fact that the screen normally consists of multiple panels further allowed me to explore the possibilities of multiple images and interrelationships between time, narrativity, and historicity. For example, I used archival images of the Chinese dress, personal photos, documentation photos of cheongsam tailors in Hong Kong, and calendar illustrations from the 1920s to illustrate the early history of the dress, to suggest its origins, and to show how it was represented. These images are part of the dress's past as well as China's history. I brought these older images into conversation with contemporary references, specifically excerpts from the film *In the Mood for Love*, to reflect the significance of this filmic text for the Canadian-born women of Chinese heritage and Chinese women discussed throughout this book. I also incorporated clips of myself being fitted for a cheongsam from my previous work *Ode to the Cheongsam*, and added new video footage of myself clothed in each of the three dresses fabricated for the *Hybrid Dresses* component of the exhibition. For these sequences I worked with a cameraperson who, according to my direction, recorded me in long shot, walking through different locations and landscapes in Montreal. Each dress was worn in a specific, corresponding location. I wore the *Banana Dress* while walking across a recognizable downtown intersection, as a reference to my attempt to assimilate into dominant Canadian culture. In Chinatown, I wore the *DNA Dress* in order to address my invisibility as a person of

Chinese heritage within the Chinese community. In a local park, I walked amongst the trees and falling leaves wearing the *Sim Dynasty Dress* which was made from red brocade fabric, richly infused with Chinese symbols and my Chinese name, hand embroidered into any available space within the motif. To add to the fantasy and performance aspect of these images, I reduced the playback speed of the images to slow motion in the editing process, mimicking the rhythm of Maggie Cheung's walk as she moved through scenes in *In the Mood for Love*. My aim was to bring the past and the present together, where Chinese origins echoed through my presence in Canada. I also aimed to explore an autoethnographic approach to my subject matter as my presence on screen allowed me to reference the performance of my identity in everyday life in terms of the "transgression" of specific places and environments in Montreal. Moreover, the empowerment of my own image was also a way to exercise agency and to bring attention to the precarious power dynamics of image-making and representation. On the one hand, by directing all aspects of the shooting, editing, and presentation, I aimed to take control of the mechanisms through which women of color are continuously misrepresented and underrepresented in mainstream media. On the other hand, I worked with some of the language and techniques of conventional filmmaking such as speed and shot composition, to convey a tension that exists between the seductive image of the cheongsam and the fear and vulnerability that its wearing entails. Use of the moving image from an existing text and from original material allowed me to impart the multiple layers involved in the performativity of the dress. There is Maggie Cheung, who represented a "model" cheongsam-clad body in contrast to my own, which through an incongruous combination of dress and contexts, I hoped, would raise questions for the viewer. I did not give any obvious prompts to the viewer that I was the artist, in order to work with the ambiguity of my appearance and how the general public might read it. While a limitation of an autoethnographic strategy may be defined by the strategy of making it clear to the viewer that it is the artist who is putting him or herself in the work in order to ensure a preferred reading, I felt that the cultivation of an authorial ambiguity could be more evocative of my inquiry around identity and its relationship with the construction of appearances.

The multi-screen strategy also gave me the opportunity to play with narrativity and historicity. My research into the birth and evolution of the cheongsam revealed divergent narratives confirming that cultural items, such as clothing, are in ongoing flux in terms of design, symbolism, and use. I thought I might be able to relay this cultural fluidity by employing a strategy of recombinant film techniques for the four-channel work. Instead of synchronizing each channel so that the same images would come up together each time the loop repeated, every day I started each player manually. At times a single player would start from the beginning of the loop, while others would continue to play back from where they stopped the day before. This meant that the images would come together across the four screens in different combinations continuously, never offering the same combination twice during the run of the exhibition. This constant reshuffling of the combination of images echoed the complexity of historical events that gave rise to a garment such as the cheongsam, as well as the complexity of identity and its ongoing re-formation.

The throw distance of the projectors obliged me to bring the screen further out from the back wall of its designated kiosk space. This meant that viewers could easily see the whole technical apparatus of projectors, media players, cables, and wires. The off-wall placement of the screen also created enough space for people to circulate around the installation, thereby creating situations where attendees' shadows were periodically cast on the screens. This shadow play extended the discourse on the construction of identities and performativity through the direct interaction of the spectator in the construction and reception of meaning. It was also the inspiration for a performance presented at the opening of the exhibition. Canadian-born actor and theater director of Chinese heritage Sophie Gee, who happened to be visibly pregnant at the time, wore a black cheongsam and engaged in a play of postures behind the screen, casting her shadow onto them in a way that directly interacted with their unfolding content. Watching her shadow move across the screen and seeing her actual body at the same time conflated reality and illusion. I was struck by how her posture, gait, and movements were altered by her donning of the cheongsam. Within the liminal context of the Swatow Plaza, her gestures seemed completely natural and yet somehow affected.

Hybrid Dresses

Hybrid Dresses was a smaller installation of works within the whole of the *The Fitting Room* exhibition and consisted of three dresses and an audio piece. This set of works evolved dialogically through a reflection on the constitutive elements of the cheongsam that would also reflect the complex and multi-faceted meanings of the garment for the women interviewed. It entailed an in-depth investigation of personal and cultural symbols and images, the symbolic use of color in Chinese history and cosmology, the history of embroidery and its significance to China, and an exploration of discourses that influenced the design, fabric choice, and cut of the garments.

As previously discussed, color is of major symbolic significance in Chinese culture and offered another conceptual layer to play with in the creation of the three cheongsam. In *Chinese Clothing* (2011) Hua Mei explains that Chinese color symbolism is based on the Five Elements Theory of Taoism and Yin and Yang, which was drawn on for sumptuary laws from the Qin dynasty (221 BCE) onwards. Certain colors were favored in different dynasties. Red was regarded as the most important color during the Zhou Dynasty (1046–256 BCE), symbolizing happiness and good fortune. During the Qin Dynasty (221–206 BCE), the principle color became black, symbolizing stability, knowledge, and power, influencing all officials to wear black as often as possible. When the Han Dynasty (206 BCE–220 CE) took over from the Qin, yellow, which symbolizes earth, the dragon, and the center, became the color of the highest status. As a result, yellow was attributed to the Emperor alone, a rule that remained in place until the end of the Qing Dynasty in 1911. Colors were assigned to other members of the courts and its subjects as well. The primary colors blue and red were reserved for the royal family and high-ranking officials, while members of general society were permitted to wear complementary colors as a way to be represented figuratively as children of the royal family. It is in reference to this color code, which is also part of the basic color code for Western art, that I chose yellow, red, and blue as the basis for my the three cheongsams in the exhibition.

When thinking about how to apply motifs to these works, I carried out a study of the various techniques used to apply image to textile in Chinese history to determine that embroidery would be the most useful technique, conceptually and formally. Young Yang Chung's three books, *The Art of Oriental Embroidery* (1979), *Painting with a Needle* (2003), and *Silken Threads: A History of Embroidery in China, Korea, Japan and Vietnam* (2005) provide a comprehensive overview and analysis of the history, techniques, and cultural history of Asian embroidery. Above all, her writings underscore and examine the significance of embroidery as a major traditional art form in East Asia (China, Japan, Korea, and Vietnam), influenced and nourished by cultural, political, philosophical, religious, and commercial factors. In addition to being a world-renowned textile historian, Dr. Chung is also an accomplished embroiderer and teacher herself. Many institutions have collected her embroidery work, and in 2004 she founded the Chung Young Yang Embroidery Museum (C.E.M.), an exhibition, educational, and research facility at Sookmyung Women's University in Seoul, South Korea. Her detailed and practical explanation of techniques and stitchery enlivened her historical and theoretical discussion of the form. Chung's research supports the claim that embroidery is the oldest method of applying image to cloth and is linked directly to the discovery of silk in China. While printing and forms of tie-dyeing also occurred in China, they arrived later and did not have the same global impact. In *The Art of Oriental Embroidery,* Chung describes proto-embroidery as dating back to the Paleolithic era:

> The north Asian prehistoric tradition of self-adornment, shamanistic symbolism, and magical rituals connected with the hunt expressed in the proto-embroidery and embroidery decoration of costume was carried over many millennia by the nomadic Mesolithic steppe and taiga peoples into China, where it became incorporated into the Neolithic development that resulted in their settlement there. (1979, p. 41)

As early hunter/gatherers settled down around 6000 BCE, silk production emerged and the practice of embroidery flourished. Chinese tradition attributes the discovery of silk to Empress Xiling, in approximately 2640 BCE. According to written accounts, a cocoon fell into her cup of tea and began to unravel, revealing a silk thread. However, Chung argued that silk weaving was actually introduced much earlier, probably by the beginning of the fourth millennium BCE, as evidence revealed the discovery of knife-cut cocoons found among artifacts dated to that time. More significant than the exact date of silk's discovery is how this material became the most important resource for China, creating the conditions of possibility for the founding of an empire. Silk was prized all over Europe and middle Asia and became a form of currency as early as the second century BCE. China's ability to control the market on silk production for centuries was due to its ability and desire to keep the cultivation of silk worms a jealously guarded secret. The silk industry began to take hold and created enormous prosperity for China during the Shang dynasty (1600–1000 BCE), at which time the weaving of silk grew from a domestic cottage industry into a vast, centralized, and efficient enterprise administered under state control. Fine silks came to symbolize leadership and, as Chung writes, "gifts of silk bolts, garments, and even mosquito nets were presented by Shang kings as tokens of royal favor" (2005, p. 76). Excavated textiles found dating from the Zhou or Warring States Era (475–221 BCE) have been found in a good state of preservation.

From these artifacts, as well as from writings such as the *Chuchi*, a second-century compilation of earlier poems and shamanistic songs from the Chu kingdom of this period, a great deal was discovered about the style and sources of embroidered images, which mostly featured "twining foliage, fantastical birds and other mythical creatures that blend into each other in sinuous curves" (Chung, 2005, p. 89). The Qin dynasty (221–206 BCE) that followed was the first to unite the Chinese people into one vast empire, with a central industry of farming and weaving. By this time, the tasks of farming and weaving had been divided along gender lines with men responsible for farming and women in charge of weaving and embroidery. In this way, having good embroidery skills became a female virtue in Chinese culture.

Chung pointed out that China's cultural heritage survived through its successful transference from one dynasty to the next. This continuity accounted for "the empire's long survival and the steady endurance of its craft traditions" (2005, p. 97). The Han dynasty (206 BCE–220 CE) further solidified the Chinese empire, making it into a highly influential regional power. Within its high-functioning administration, the silk industry, which included embroidery, grew and prospered.

The arrival of Buddhism in East Asia at the end of the Han period had a major impact on Chinese culture and heavily influenced imagery in artistic practice. In the textile arts, needle-workers began to produce technically accomplished compositions representing Buddhist themes, such as depictions of the Buddha's life, his attributes, and the sacred number "8." During the Tang Dynasty (618–906 CE), the economic and military expansion of the empire developed alongside silk production and consumption. Textile designs became highly complex, "with floral wreaths replacing pearl roundels, geometric rosettes opening up into realistic flower medallions and butterflies and birds, often holding auspicious branches or ribbons in their beaks, flying amid elaborate floral compositions" (2005, p. 105). Han records also show that a bolt of embroidered silk was worth twenty-five times the price of a bolt of non-embroidered silk, demonstrating the intrinsic value of this material and medium. Throughout the Song Dynasty (960–1276 CE), embroidery practice began to take on a pictorial realism that Chung suggests had resonance with Renaissance painting. For example, Song embroiderers began to employ shading techniques that allowed them to heighten the changes of light through subtle gradations of color. The embroidery techniques developed were considered to be so refined that they were often mistaken for painting. The Ming Dynasty (1368–1644 CE) saw the emergence of the Gu school, which adopted Song Dynasty embroidery styles and techniques and became regarded as the most prominent style for Chinese embroidery. As the Qing Dynasty unfolded (1644–1911), the value of Gu School embroidery began to decline as embroidered pieces of dubious quality began to appear on the market bearing forged Gu School marks or brandings. Despite the counterfeit activity, four main regional embroidery styles or schools emerged during the Republic Era (1911–49) and became established in the areas of Suzhou, Hunan, Sichuan, and Guangdong. Suzhou embroidery became known for its refined patterns, subtle colors, variety of stitches, and accomplished level of craftsmanship. Hunan embroidery is distinct for its starkly elegant black, white, and gray coloration, which puts an emphasis on contrasts of light and shade to suggest a three-dimensional effect. This type of embroidery utilizes negative space in a similar way to approaches in Chinese ink painting. Guangdong embroidery, crafted in Chaozhou, is composed of intricate, symmetrical patterns and makes use of primary colors, light and shade, varied stitches, and a defined weave, reminiscent of techniques and styles of Western painting. Sichuan embroidery (Gu School) is the oldest known style in Chinese embroidery history, and is recognized for its even stitching technique, delicate coloration, and landscape inspired imagery.

This very brief synopsis of the history of embroidery offered some insight into the magnitude of this art form and its contribution to Chinese culture. Embroidery's deep roots as a practice and a medium provided a vehicle through which to explore my questions and incarnate their findings. The various examples of Chinese embroidery I have seen in person and in books convinced me of the exciting possibilities that the medium could offer, both conceptually and formally, keeping the central focus of Canadian-born women of Chinese heritage in mind. In order to investigate ideas for possible embroidery designs, I examined symbols used in embroidery patterns, as well as their function throughout China's history. Chung (2005) explains that embroidery patterns were informed by symbols that emerged through totemic and tribal customs, mythology, and religion, which were then adopted by imperial sumptuary codes. The symbolism and codes established for the "rank badges" of government officials, the Emperor's "dragon robe," and the roots of embroidery design in tattooing, provided essential information for how I might employ embroidery in the creation of the three dresses.

For each of the cheongsam created for this piece, I worked with various fabrics, motifs, linings, fastenings, colors, cuts, and the central element of embroidery to manifest the perspectives and questions raised in the interviews. Accompanying the dresses was a sound montage of selected excerpts taken from the audio recording of each interview. Two lounge chairs were placed inside the kiosk for visitors to sit and contemplate the dresses while listening to the audio piece on headphones.

Sim Dynasty Dress

With the *Sim Dynasty Dress* I attempted to express the disparaging attitudes described by some of the women interviewed towards a store-bought dress. While some women found their dresses in Chinatown stores, there was an equal number of women who felt that the dresses available in stores in Canada were "loud" and of poor quality and, therefore, unsuitable to wear. I used embroidery as an interventionist strategy for this as well as the notion of artist Marcel Duchamp's *readymade*,[5] which consists of working with a found object, in this case a cheongsam that my mother received from a white American friend. The friend had purchased the dress during a trip to Beijing and when it no longer fit her, she gave it to my mother. Back in 1992, when I mentioned to my mother that I had a formal event to attend, she passed this dress on to me. A bright red silk satin brocade fabric, very heavily adorned with large flowers, bats, longevity and happiness symbols and scrolls, in purple, blue, green, and most strikingly, heavy-gauge metallic gold thread, it is a sleeveless, full-length dress with typical s-curve that would be appropriate for a bride. My initial thoughts towards this cheongsam are echoed by the comments about the "gaudiness" of store-bought cheongsam made by the women I interviewed. To me this was a prime example of the ubiquitous cheongsam, where the red color, the over-the-top brocade motif, floor length, and form fitting silhouette all came together. To me this dress was also representative of the essentialized concept of Chinese femininity as typically understood in a North American context. As a person who is not recognized as Chinese, wearing a dress such as this would be demonstrative of my desire for an "authentic" Chinese appearance, no matter how illusory. Displaying this dress on its own may have been sufficient. However, my interest in using embroidery led me to investigate how I might intervene with the *readymade* dress with needle and thread. The very busy motif encouraged me to think about the pervasiveness of Chinese symbols that I have encountered throughout my life, either in the furnishings at home, the decor of Chinese restaurants, or the gifts I received for Chinese New Year. I thought about my desire to be acknowledged by the Chinese community and to situate myself within this culture. Remembering my teenage pride in displaying the Chinese character of my surname on various pieces of clothing, it occurred to me that I might hand embroider this symbol in gold thread onto the dress, in any available space within the charged motif. I asked my father to write the Sim name in Chinese character on paper at a specific size, which I made into a stencil. I traced the stencil onto the dress everywhere I could, with respect to the motif in order to find balance in the composition. Over the course of six months I undertook this embroidery, taking cues from Chung's books. Starting from the bottom of the dress, I grew more confident as I worked my way up. While the overall look of my embroidery work is very much that of an amateur, I found this a fitting analogy to my experience as a Canadian-born person of Chinese heritage trying to find her confidence and footing in a community that is at once familiar and estranged. To acknowledge my Canadian cultural upbringing, I complemented the Sim characters on the front of the dress with an embroidered outline of my given name across the back of the dress in reference to the T-shirt I received at the Sim family reunion. Growing up in the 1970s and 1980s, iron-on T-shirts that could be customized with one's name were a big part of popular culture. The ability to wear one's name on a T-shirt was incredibly empowering for kids and teenagers. I ordered iron-on letters in the desired size and iconic Cooper Black font (the most typical lettering for iron-on letters when I was a growing up) and used them as a stencil for the embroidered outline.

Both the "Sim" characters, of which there are eighteen in all, and the embroidered outline of my given name on the back of the dress, simultaneously blend in and hide in the busy motif, as if Chinese culture and symbolism are too heavy to accommodate any other ideas, and where there does not seem to be space for anything else but a singular Chinese identity based on the "Central Country Complex." My intention and hope was that my names would be found, upon closer inspection, when taking the time to see past the motif and beyond the complications, in order to see the details.

My first attempt at hand embroidery was quite a moving experience. This came as a surprise, as I do not consider myself particularly gifted with the needle. I remember my mother trying to teach me needlepoint when I was eight years old. I lacked patience and precision, and eventually abandoned my first project. My eighth-grade attempt at making sweatpants for Home Economics class did not fare any better. These experiences left me with a serious lack of confidence about my ability to take on embroidery. But as I began, I enjoyed the sound and feeling of the thread as it was pulled through the fabric. I thought about the Chinese women who had practiced this ancient art form and about my grandmother, a pillar of society, an excellent business person, and a loving mother, who was also very talented in all manner of sewing. I recalled that her last business was an Irish linen manufacturing company that created beautiful machine embroidered napkins and tablecloths and cotton embroidered dresses and blouses. My grandparents bought that business from a Jewish family in New York with whom my grandmother kept ties well into the 1980s. My uncle Alfred also had a ready-to-wear fashion line of high quality polyester dresses for women in the late 1970s, simply called Alfred Sim. It dawned on me that my interest in fashion, textiles, and embroidery was not superficial but, rather, part of a family history.

DNA Dress

DNA Dress worked principally with the idea of not being recognized as a person of Chinese heritage, despite my DNA. I wanted to work with a visualization of my DNA as a decorative motif for the dress which would underscore how the un-readability of the pattern, despite being displayed on the dress's outer surface, would be analogous to my experience as a person whose ethnicity is difficult and at times impossible to ascertain on a visual register. Through my concept of primary colors, I determined that this dress would be blue—in particular, a darker, royal blue, which is the shade that makes direct reference to the male *changpao*, appropriated by female students in the early 1920s. I wanted to combine this aspect of the cheongsam's history with the DNA concept, as a way to link my feminist reading of the dress with my search for recognition within the Chinese community. Embroidery was the perfect technique to incorporate the DNA pattern, not only for its historic and cultural significance, but also for how the stitches physically mesh with the fabric in an additive move to make it stronger. In this way, embroidery interlocks with the fabric the way that my DNA is integral to my physical and biological make-up. To add to the reality of the illegibility of my ethnicities, I decided to embroider the DNA pattern in a thread color that was exactly the same as the fabric of the dress.

In order to generate the stencil for the embroidery I had my DNA visualized by a now defunct company called DNA2ART.[6] This company was one of several that would visualize a sample of your DNA, which could then be printed onto different objects, including canvas for wall display, mugs, and even mousepads. Far from the image presented in "Photo 51," the first x-ray image of DNA credited to Rosalind Franklin, DNA2ART proposed two "styles" of visualized DNA to choose from—Genestripes™ and DNA Dots™ which could be ordered in a variety of color schemes.[7] I selected the Genestripes™ pattern for two reasons. The first is formal, as I was drawn to its graphic simplicity in addition to its organic, bioscience aesthetic. The second reason was that it resembled a kind of Morse code, which lent itself well to the concept of language and symbol.

DNA2ART's process of visualization was comprised of two steps. First, the DNA sample was visualized through a process of electrophoresis, which caused the pieces of DNA to become visible on a laboratory gel. DNA2ART then used their custom software and presumably a camera to capture the pattern so it could become a digital picture file. The DNA2ART website, which is now off-line, described the process in more technical terms:

> Most of the single nucleotide polymorphism (SNPs) can be detected using a method called restriction fragment length polymorphism (RFLP). RFLP makes use of the many different biological enzymes called restriction endonucleases and their ability to cut the DNA at predetermined sites for detecting specific genetic variants. DNA will be amplified to get millions of copies followed by the actual digestion by the selected biological enzymes and actual output will be visible after visualizing the pieces of DNA on a laboratory gel. One can actually see different stripes on an image and when you compare two persons you might see the differences in the pattern that correspond to the genetic composition of a particular individual.

The result is what looks like a grid pattern of horizontal stripes that are a visual representation of my unique, genetic code that provides information about my ancestry as well as my physical and biological traits.

In the context of art history, George Gessert (2010) explained that DNA was used as a medium by Edward Steichen as early as 1936 in a work called *Delphiniums,* while Salvador Dali was one of the first artists to employ the image of the double-helix in his 1958 painting *Butterfly Landscape (The Great Masturbator in a Surrealist Landscape with D.N.A).* My interest in DNA is first and foremost in what it offers conceptually and formally, in the spirit of works by artists such as Kevin Clarke, Gary Schneider, Dui Seid, and Marc Quinn. *Genetic Self-Portrait* by Gary Schneider (1997–8) is a series of photographs of the artist's body that range from an x-ray of his skull to microscopic views of his cells and DNA. As the title indicates, Schneider proposed that a true likeness can only be revealed through the presentation of images of what is inside his body—what he is literally made of, rather than the surface of his body. Marc Quinn's work *Sir John Sulston: A Genomic Portrait* (2001) featured visualized DNA taken from a sample of Sulston's semen displayed in agar jelly. Like Schneider, Quinn argued that the depiction of Sulston would be more true to life than a patent depiction of his outward appearance. Dui Seid, an American artist of Chinese heritage, believed that a person's DNA is a portrait of his ancestry and possibly his descendants. In *Blood Lines*, he displayed frosted test tubes of blood with the digital images of his DNA, along with images of his parents. In an accompanying video, his family portrait dissolved into his own image then into a multitude of ethnically diverse people before finally dissolving into an image of his own DNA. In the late 1980s, Kevin Clarke used DNA sequences to create what art historian Ingeborg Reichle (2009) called "conceptual genetic portraits." In these photographic works, he combined the linear arrangement of genetic sequences in code (ACGT—Adenine, Cytosine, Guanine, and Thymine, the four nitrogenous DNA bases) based on DNA samples from his subjects, with an object carefully selected to symbolize his sitter. Through these portraits, attention is brought to a reflection and meditation on the individual, and his or her hereditary physicality.

The ideas and concepts expressed through these artists' works resonated with my desire to use DNA as an embroidery design. To literally wear my visualized DNA is to display my ancestry, and would be, as Reichle notes in *Art in the Age of Technoscience: Genetic Engineering, Robotics and Artificial Life in Contemporary Art*, "to bring the innermost essence of an individual to the surface and make it visible for all to see" (2009, p. 74). The difficulty of deciphering this message, however, made it analogous to my experience growing up in Canada. As revealed by the interviews, this double-edged feeling of marginalization is a commonly shared experience among Canadian-born people of Chinese heritage. An embroidered design of my DNA would therefore convey my attempt to assert and connect to my Chinese heritage, while making a statement about the illegibility of my ethnic heritage to others. Furthermore, the centuries-old medium of embroidery, combined with the non-prescriptive look of the visualized DNA, made for a supplementary strategy of hybridity that combined Chinese (ancient/culturally specific) and bio-scientific (modern/universal) signifiers.

Once I had my visualized DNA pattern in a software-readable format, I brought it into a program utilized by an Embird embroidery machine. The original image of the DNA I received was in grayscale and made up of short, horizontal lines of various thicknesses and shades. Through a very slow, manual process of tracing these lines through the software, a pattern was made for the embroidery machine to follow. Given my tone on tone concept, I decided not to replicate the variations in shade.

The use of machine over hand embroidering was also strategic. On the one hand, I wanted this pattern to be produced with a very clean, graphic aesthetic, which my amateur hand would never be able to achieve. On the other hand, the use of a machine also made reference to my presence in the West, which was looked upon by China as the model of modernization during the Republic Era, but also raised the topic of mass manufacturing and labor which has been one of the major building blocks for China's rise to economic prominence.

Given the opportunities to explore visibility and invisibility in this dress, it made sense to play with the lining, which is a practical element of the cheongsam, as well as a more subtle aesthetic field in which to intervene. Normally, the lining of a garment is hidden from view. But because of the cheongsam's side slits, it is possible to catch quick glimpses of it as the wearer moves. As my DNA, and therefore the proof of my Chinese heritage, passes imperceptibly on the outside of the dress, I decided to bring some actual proof of my heritage to the inside of the dress. I scanned passport photos of my Chinese grandparents, George and Charlotte Sim, that were taken in the 1950s, and cropped their images into circles into order to create a fabric motif that referenced the round medallions of an Emperor's robe. I then printed this pattern onto silk using a large-scale fabric printer and gave it to the same local dressmaker that had been making cheongsam for me in recent years, for incorporation into the final art piece.

A final feature of *DNA Dress* is its cut and shape. I wanted this dress to resemble the man's *changpao*, the male version of the cheognsam, as a way to address how the typical close cut of the cheongsam imposes an idealized and unrealistic body type on women. With this in mind, I asked the tailor to employ a a straight cut for this dress so that it would look and fall more like a shift and where there may only be darts at the bust. I also provided him with a photo of a 1992 dress designed by William Tang, which had influenced my vision for this cheongsam. As I briefly mentioned in Chapter 4, I was very disappointed when I came for the fitting, as the dress was not a loose shift at all, but instead featured a form-fitted bodice. The skirt portion was not cut straight, but instead flared into an A-line shape with thigh high slits. The modification of the cut of the dress from what I had asked confirmed the existence of entrenched design rules that impose a form-fitted dress shape onto the body, further proving how this dress as a cultural form falls prey to dominant aesthetic conventions. Rather than have the dress re-made, I used it as evidence of these tendencies.

Banana Dress

In the case of *Banana Dress*, I wanted to examine what I call "the banana syndrome," which was described in the "Banana Blog" passage in Chapter 1. As described, "banana" is often a pejorative term used amongst Canadian-born or raised people of Chinese heritage, to describe the ambivalence of having "lost" one's ethnicity due to attempts at assimilation into dominant culture. Rather than express the guilt and shame for not being Chinese "enough," which is a feature of the "banana syndrome," I chose to make this dress in the spirit of reclaiming and celebrating my "banana-ness" through an acknowledgement of my hybridity. I chose to have this cheongsam made from a cotton fabric with a polka dot motif, as cotton is practical and casual enough to be worn every day. The tiny polka dot pattern reminded me of dresses I wore for Sunday School picnics when I was a kid growing up in Ontario, and represented freshness and youth. Yellow is not only the most obvious choice for the color of this dress, it completes the primary color concept and it also, as mentioned above, was the color most revered and worshipped in Chinese culture between the establishment of the Han dynasty in 206 BCE and the end of the Qing dynasty in 1911, and was reserved for the Emperor. What better color to use for a dress that aims to affirm and assert one's Chinese heritage, in spite of the marginalizing barriers that are up on either side of the Chinese-Canadian hyphen? Furthermore, the use of the color yellow would subvert and disrupt the campaign-like catch phrases such as "yellow peril" and "yellow fever" that were meant to denigrate Chinese Canadians. The concept for this dress also brought about an irresistible opportunity to use the lining. In the interviews, many women shared their fear of being exposed as imposters in the Chinese community. Their shame in being labeled "banana" is therefore something that was deeply embedded. With this in mind, I found a graphic image on the internet of a banana shedding its peel. I manipulated this image in Photoshop and then used it as the basis for a motif. The end result is a field of bananas that resemble birds flying up somewhat defiantly in a bid for freedom. I printed my customized pattern onto silk, and as a finishing touch, hand embroidered the outline of a few of the bananas in gold thread, as a way to symbolize how Canadian-born people of Chinese heritage are transcending this syndrome and transforming this experience into wisdom and knowledge. My main regret with this piece is that I did not push for a more innovative cut for this dress as a way to bring the tone of the exhibition more into a present day critique. This will have to wait for a future iteration.

Given that the three cheongsams were statically displayed on dress mannequins, I hoped that viewers would make the connection between these dresses and my performance in them in order to appreciate their activation in the real world.

Hybrid Dresses: Audio Montages

As a key element in this part of the installation, I took selected excerpts from the interviews and created an audio montage, one with the English interviews and another with the French interviews. I set up a listening station in close proximity to the dresses so that they might be viewed by the visitor while listening to the women who influenced the choices and elements that made up these dresses. This approach articulated my strategy of presenting a multiplicity of viewpoints about the cheongsam and never letting the discourse settle, while giving voice to the women who participated in these interviews. Choosing to record interviews in audio only was a strategy I began to use in 1998 with an experimental documentary called *Ode to the Chambermaid*. Separating the video from the audio was meant to privilege the voice with its grain, cadence, and mode of expression. A close listening experience was also employed as a de-essentializing strategy, as the appreciation of the individuality of a woman can be greatly overwhelmed by the visual register.

The Fitting Room

Elizabeth Wilson's 1985 book, *Adorned in Dreams*, looks candidly at the impact of clothing and fashion from a feminist perspective. Wilson celebrates how clothing provides possibility and reassures us that taking clothing seriously is not contrary to feminist concerns. Wilson also explains that clothing, like art, is itself a terrain of self-expression constitutive of social, cultural, historical, geographical, and climatic factors. Choosing what to wear becomes a public cultural statement, where what is disclosed and what is concealed can say a great deal about a person's age, socio-economic background, or psychological state. The question of choice, negotiation, and experimentation when it comes to what we wear brought me directly to the site of the fitting room found in clothing stores. When trying on clothes, we are inhabited by questions, fears, hopes, and desires. This room therefore serves as a liminal space for the ongoing construction and creation of identity. For this piece, I collaborated with a fabricator to create a stand-alone fitting room with transparent sides. I used transparency to underscore the feeling of vulnerability and ambivalence we may experience when trying on clothes. Transparency was also employed to elicit the idea that while the fitting room is a private space, we are actually testing and dressing for the public, outside, world. As a result, my aim with this piece was to link the commonly held experience of trying on clothes with the hestitations felt by Canadian women of Chinese heritage in regards to wearing the cheongsam. To further explore how we use clothing to represent who we are and what we want to say to the world, I activated the fitting room with a video montage that was projected onto the body of the visitor when she/he stepped inside. The mirror that faced them allowed the viewer to see the projection cast directly onto the body. The transparency of the fitting room also allowed onlookers to see the person inside, contributing to the tension between public and private.

The video projection presented on the inside of the fitting room structure employed the "super cut" editing approach. The "super cut" is a technique employed by artists such as Christian Marclay in which images with similar content or action are taken from existing films and edited together.[8] The montage I created was made up of excerpts from Hollywood films of people choosing clothes, dressing, and looking at themselves in a mirror. Echoing my use of clips from the film *In the Mood for Love*, the use of excerpts here reinforced the impact of cinema on our imaginary in terms of another universal experience, that of trying on clothing. The clips selected were all from films I saw when growing up during the 1970s, 1980s and 1990s. They therefore spoke to the past, and might bring about other memories and newer associations for viewers. The ten-minute video explored in a different way how the concept of identity construction can take place through the almost ritual process of the selection of clothes and dressing.

Over the course of the exhibition, I discovered that there were two states of reading and activation involved in this work. People approached *The Fitting Room* piece with a lot of curiosity and found the projection emitting from the work onto the floor very beautiful, which was a happy accident for me. Observing *The Fitting Room* from the outside could therefore first be read as a place to hide and reveal—a structure in which projections occur based on a person's own fantasies, ideas, or fears, which are equally fueled by social, psychological, environmental, and media-influenced images. Once inside, there was a second stage of the reading process. Initially, there was the moment that the eye observed the body in the mirror which then scrutinized the body. Then there was the moment when the eye focused on the projection itself to discern the video content. This action took the viewer's focus away from their own body and into the mind where they might be absorbed in another set of associated reflections.

As the act of choosing clothes is an almost universal experience, I hoped the fitting room structure would serve as a familiar site that could transcend gender, age, and ethnicity. In this way, my aim with this work was ultimately to make use of this space/object as a transcultural device that would connect with all visitors.

Reception: A multiplicity of patterns

In concert with the ideas that emerged as artists became critical of modernist regimes that dicated how art was to be viewed, visitors were free to approach the three works that made up the whole of *The Fitting Room* in any order. At the same time, I did have a proposed path for the visitor that I felt best activated the relationship between the works that could enhance the experience for the visitor. Starting with *(Chinese) Screen*, the work presented the history of the cheongsam as it evolved in China and eventually made it over to Canada. In this way, it spoke of my Chinese ancestors including members of my own family. Moving onto *Hybrid Dresses*, this work played with the concepts of hybridity, the construction of identity, and the design discourses that govern the cut, style, and decoration of the dress while imparting the current ideas and attitudes towards the cheongsam held by Canadian women of Chinese heritage. This component brought the story of the cheongsam into the present and enlivened the issues related to this dress for the visitor. Ending with *The Fitting Room*, the main intention of this piece was to transcend the cultural specificity of the cheongsam. The trying on and choosing of clothing is presumably an experience shared by all visitors regardless of ethnicity, gender, or age, and was meant to connect people together in the gesture of trying on identities in order to feel out aspects of who we are and who we would like to be. Hundreds of people came across these works over the one-month period and they solicited a multiplicity of reactions, based primarily on my observation and direct interactions with visitors, in combination with those of an invigilator I hired who was also of mixed Asian heritage.

The viewers who were drawn to the installation can be separated into two groups: those who knew about the exhibition and those who did not. For the sake of this analysis, I identify those who knew about the exhibition as "intentional visitors" and those who did not as "accidental visitors." As described earlier, some people who came specifically to see the exhibition expressed having a difficulty finding the works as they seemed to blend into, and were even camouflaged within, the context of the mall. One viewer described the work as infiltrating the space, and another, who knew me personally, felt my strategy was analagous to my desire to fit into the context of Chinatown. Overall, the reaction by "intentional visitors" to the insertion of this art installation into a non-art space was positive. Feedback on the use of the Swatow Plaza as a site for this exhibition confirmed the utility of a non-art space for supplementing the thematics and questions related to the subject of the cheongsam and its relationship to Chinese ethnic identity. The placement of artworks directly within a real world context proved, in this case, to greatly enhance the reception of the work for intentional visitors on both formal and conceptual levels.

The situation was quite different for "accidental" viewers. I would describe the great majority of their reactions to the exhibition as consisting of a combination of confusion and curiosity. During the run of the exhibition, I noted that the Swatow Plaza was frequented by a surprisingly wide demographic. Based on my observation, there seemed to be a slight majority of Asian shoppers issuing from a variety of communities, among them Chinese, Filipino, Vietnamese, and Korean. The balance of non-Asian visitors also seemed to be made up of a wide variety of ethnicities. Among the "accidental viewers" I engaged with were a trio of teenagers of Moroccan heritage, two different sets of white, francophone *Québecois* young adult males and three mixed Asian/Caucasian couples. There also seemed to be an equal ratio of female to male shoppers, as well as a broad representation of ages, from small children to senior citizens. Very generally, "accidental viewers" disregarded the exhibition, or gave it a very cursory glance. I looked after the exhibition on weekends and evenings, and I would conclude that approximately one out of twenty people who came by spent somewhere between five and ten minutes trying to understand the works and their presence in the mall.

The amount of time spent with any one work varied greatly. Most often, children gravitated towards *The Fitting Room*, first mesmerized by the projection on the floor. Once they realized that they could enter the booth freely, they would start to play a "peek-a-boo" game, ducking inside and outside of the booth. *The Fitting Room* also attracted the teenage son of a *Québecois* family of four. I observed them from a distance as they examined the booth. The son finally went inside, and when the projection hit his body, he exclaimed, "Cool!" At that moment, I approached the family and talked to them about the work. They listened politely, thanked me for the explanation but then hustled away. I could only surmise that this was a very strange and unexpected intervention for them, and perhaps they were concerned

163

that I might try to sell them some art! As I have explained, the goal of this work was to engage with an intercultural strategy. However, in an attempt to bring the trying on of clothing into the realm of universal experience through excerpts from Hollywood films, I did not include images of Chinese women or the cheongsam. This decision I feel may have evacuated the primary subject and object and its attendant questions from this piece, which may have unintentionally disrupted the cohesion of the three works. This is something I would address in a future iteration.

Senior citizens of Asian heritage, both male and female, seemed to spend the most time with the (Chinese) Screen work. There were stools to sit on, and on a few occasions all three would be occupied. Women would watch and then comment to each other, while men mostly stayed silent. Perhaps the mix of archival footage, the nostalgic air of the clips from In the Mood for Love, and the familiar look of family photographs kept them engaged. My instinct was to not intervene and simply to let them view. However, if I had the ability to speak Cantonese, Toisanese, or Mandarin, I may have had the courage to ask them about what these images meant to them.

As there was approximately twelve feet between the screen and the back wall of the kiosk space, people often passed behind the screen, oblivious to the work or the projections onto which they cast their shadows as they walked by. As I watched people do this, I thought through how this unconscious involvement added a layer to my experience of the work, somehow bringing people in the present into contact with the past images linked with Chinese culture—never physically touching but converging all the same.

A final notable reaction towards the four-screen video installation came from a young anglophone white male in his twenties, who asked if the work was part of an advertising campaign for the goods on sale in the mall. This reading never occurred to me, but it made a lot of sense when I considered the presence of screens in malls in general. Indeed, most of the content on typical mall screens is geared towards advertising for certain stores, brand name items, and also to announce events and sales inside the mall. I thanked the man for his observation as it greatly informed an aspect of my understanding of the language of mall constructs and experience that I had not fully grasped until then. In the way that calendar girl images were actually advertisements in their original framework, this art exhibition could easily be interpreted as a display to enhance the appeal of the Chinese "goods" available for purchase and consumption. I can readily imagine that screening a film like In The Mood for Love in a shop selling cheongsam would be a very good way to attract buyers, fueling the factors of fantasy and nostalgia that surround the dress. At the same time, the clips from that film mixed with my family photos, archives, and new content were all there to serve or sell my idea of the history and evolution of the dress as well as its cultural value. While I was not offering art in exchange for money, the colliding of my art intentions with the commercial environment provided another layer of consideration of the political economy of the art market on the one hand, and fashion merchandizing in relation to a search for ethnic identity or an engagement with "Asian chic" on the other.

Hybrid Dresses presented an interesting challenge, specifically to accidental viewers. The placement of the three dresses on mannequins, prominently displayed in the space as they might be in a storefront window, attracted passers-by who examined the works as if they were simply dresses for sale. A few women asked for information about them, asking how much they cost, why there were only three and if I had any more. If they were Chinese-speaking, I would give them the Chinese handout, and there would be a nod of acknowledgment, a smile, and they would be off. One set of accidental viewers was a mixed heritage couple (the woman was of Chinese heritage, the man of Anglo-Saxon heritage) who stopped to look at the dresses, again thinking they were for sale, and asked for information. I started off with a general explanation and, as they grew more curious, I explained further. They seemed very moved by the work, as the woman felt an acknowledgment of her experience as a North American-born woman of Chinese heritage, and the man gained more insight into his partner's life. As for the audio component, the two listening stations were constantly occupied during the opening. Someone I had known for many years came to me in tears, having been deeply moved by some of these testimonies. During the run of the exhibition, however, only intentional visitors spent time with the audio component, listening for anywhere from five to thirty minutes.

The exhibition received some scholarly attention in the form of a review by Sean Metzger in the journal "Asian Diasporic Visual Cultures and the Americas" (2015), and an essay by Alice Ming Wai Jim in the book *Desire Change: Contemporary Feminist Art in Canada* (2017). Their written insights provided a deeper reading of the works and revealed a few surprising interpretations and helpful observations. As one of the stronger aspects of *The Fitting Room*, Metzger mentioned the video sequences in the four-screen work, in which I walk through various landscapes wearing the three cheongsam that made up the *Hybrid Dresses* work.

Perhaps the most intriguing, because they remain the most enigmatic, are sequences of a woman in qipao traversing different environments from woodlands to sidewalks (when Sim is present, the viewer would recognize the figure as the artist). These images work not only to stress but also to defamiliarize the cheongsam's associations with urbanization [...] In what context is this dress a naturalized fit for an Asian woman's body? (Meizger, 2015, p. 215)

The original impetus for these images was to trangress specific terrains in and around the city of Montreal as someone who, for many years, wished to make my ethnicities as ambigious as possible. Moving through these locations and being filmed while wearing the different dresses was a choreographed action wherein I indeed "traverse" or cross over the invisible thresholds that attempt to demarcate and limit the complexity of the experience of women of Chinese heritage. Wearing these dresses, I was physically constrained while asserting my desire to transcend the normativity of an essentialized Chinese identity through the expression of messages sewn into and printed onto the dresses' fabric. This simultaneous acceptance of constraint while covertly asserting freedom is a characteristic mode of *being* that is illustrative of the condition of Canadian-born children of visible minority immigrants. One effectively becomes comfortable with discomfort. Metzger's reading is remarkably insightful despite his mention of the hermetic aspect of these images. In another unexpected reading of the works, he considered the role of the invigilator as a point of artistic intervention.

The fifth part of the exhibition was the artist (or her representative), who served as a guide to the various facets of the installation. Without a guide, the disparate elements would be much more disjunctive. The exploration of how a dress might fit its wearers into commercial, cultural, and national contexts could in the absence of explication work more in the sense of a changing room ... that circulates less stable narratives of belonging and becoming in relation to Chineseness. The guide, however, maintains continuity across both time and the installation's various components. (2015, pp. 217–18)

As a curator who works for a medium sized contemporary art institution, I reflect regularly on the use of didactic texts in exhibitions as well as the role of invigilators. In a recent exhibition, I included only one short introductory paragraph on the wall and for each work, indicated only title, year of production, materials, and required acknowledgements. While a gallery guide was offered to visitors that included some entry points into the works, there were no descriptions or interpretation of the works on the walls, as a way to encourage visitors to develop their own readings of the works and to enjoy that process. Invigilators provided another mode of dialogue with the visitor in that they would be there to discuss works and related ideas with the visitor, which invested their role with the task of cultural mediation as opposed to surveillance. For *The Fitting Room* exhibition, however, I had not actively considered the role of invigilator as part of the work itself. The way we operated was to allow visitors to approach and contemplate the works on their own and to remain approachable, ready to answer questions rather than to guide visitors. It would seem that the intervention of a guide did not deter Metzger from coming away with his own readings of the works. But what drew my attention was his mention of how the works might be read without such a presence. Despite his own assessment about the heterogeneity of the works, it seems that with or without a guide, they could be read as an ensemble that spoke to the instability and mutability of ethnic identity as it is informed by a wide range of influences, among them the fashion industry, one's family upbringing, and popular culture.

Alice Jim's analysis puts an emphasis on the current state of agency for Canadian-born women of Asian heritage. She described how each of the three dresses presented in the exhibition displayed a manifestation of the desires and insecurities that punctuate the second-generation experience. She read into the messages that were disguised as the dress's ornamentation to ascertain that this generation of women is in a process of evolution.

> Collectively, their voices articulate an insistent diasporic belonging in the Canadian context that not only aesthetically manifests in the customized design on the fabrics of the three cheongsam, but also signals generational transformation. (Jim, 2017, p. 83)

The notion of being "in between," as the child of immigrants born in the host country, has been well documented. What I and other researchers have noted is the lack of knowledge around what happens to an individual over time as a result of this experience. What the interviews revealed is that learning from the space "in between" is valuable and productive. Many of the women who had endured racialized treatment in their formative years were compelled to eschew their Chinese ethnic heritage. Later, as they were able to prove their own worth and abilities within the Canadian context, they came to see their ethnic heritage(s) as a strength even if the bulk of its expression such as the speaking of the language had been lost. As our parents had the courage to come to a new country and forge a different life, we had the courage to become something unprecedented—not fully Chinese or Canadian, yet something entirely new. What we did not realize when we were children was that our existence would become part of a major transformative force in society—an experience that radiates beyond our national boundaries and connects us to a hugely significant population of Asian people born of immigrant parents in cross-cultural contexts all over the world.

Jim also discussed the exhibition in relation to the changing depiction of the Asian female.

> The archetypal Asian (Canadian) woman has shifted from being ridiculed, tragic and poor to being hypersexualized and over-domineering, making Sim's *The Fitting Room* and its array of diverse voices that counter the stereotypes imprinted on ethnic apparel all the more resonant. (2017, p. 000)

Jim's use of the term "ethnic apparel" as a critical term distinguishes it from terms such as *world fashion, ethnic dress,* and *national dress.* Picking up on definitions that often mark ethnic apparel as non-fashion, her observation also took into consideration the recent appropriation and instrumentalization of ethnic apparel by mainstream culture for its exotic currency, which only serves to further embed Orientalist stereotypes within the realm of dominant perception. One way to unmoor these viewpoints is to gather and share divergent viewpoints on ethnic apparel such as the cheongsam, as a way to claim space in the general cultural conversation. This is what I attempted to do with this exhibition. Not to change minds, but, as Gayatri Spivak (1993) has said, "to rearrange desires."[9]

Activating the public site of the Swatow Plaza presented challenges to the overall reception of the work that I had not anticipated. If one of my goals was to generate an intercultural and intergenerational dialogue, the exhibition's virtually anonymous insertion into the context of this Chinatown shopping mall may have required additional concerted cultural mediation. For the intentional visitor, the works' fusion with their environment for the most part evoked a productive reading. However, the delineation between art and the mall environment was too subtle for accidental visitors. If I were to re-mount this exhibition in a similar non-art space, I might make use of an introductory didactic text that would delineate the space of the mall from the space of this non-selling, non-profit art exhibition. Second, I would work with cultural mediators that would be able to connect with people in the predominant Chinese languages. Finally, I might employ a few museal devices, such as the vitrine or light box, that could further denote the informational and dialogic goals of the exhibition. The employment of a non-art space is useful for bringing works into contact with a general public. But reaching the general public could be a missed opportunity without an adequate framework that takes their expectations into consideration, and then builds on them.

Plate 1 Installation view of *(Chinese) Screen* (Photo: Victor Sim)

Plate 2 Installation view of *Hybrid Dresses* (Photo: Victor Sim)

Plate 3 Installation view of *The Fitting Room* (Photo: Victor Sim)

Plate 4 Inside *The Fitting Room* piece. Detail of projection on visitor's body (Photo: Victor Sim)

Plate 5 *Sim Dynasty Dress* (Photo: Victor Sim)

Plate 6 Detail of *Sim Dynasty Dress* featuring hand embroidered Sim family name in Chinese character (Photo: Victor Sim)

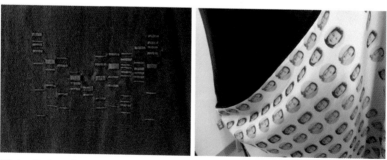

Plates 7, 8 and 9
Top: *DNA Dress* (Photo: Victor Sim)
Bottom left: Detail of DNA embroidery pattern (Photo: Victor Sim)
Bottom right: Detail of lining printed with passport photos of Charlotte and George Sim (Photo: Victor Sim)

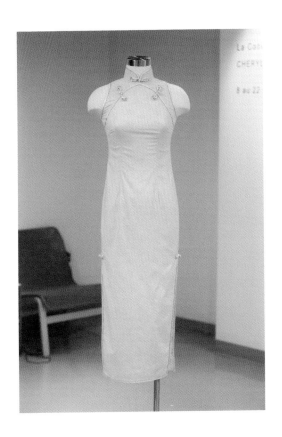

Plates 10 and 11
Top: *Banana Dress* (Photo: Victor Sim)
Bottom: Detail of *Banana Dress* printed lining (Photo: Victor Sim)

Plates 12, 13 and 14 Still images from the video component of *(Chinese) Screen*

CHAPTER 6
CONCLUSION: CHEONGSAM 2.0 / MAKING ALTERATIONS

Despite its focus on a specific ethnicity, gender, nationality, generation, and cultural artifact, this exploration enriched a discussion on the long term effects of migration as cultures come into contact with one another. This study also exposed the power dynamics that inform interests such as nation building and re-building, and outline how those dynamics play out in public and private spheres to affect one's representation and conduct of self in everyday life. The story of the cheongsam and its relationship with Canadian-born women of Chinese heritage radiates outwards to shed light on how a garment can maintain significance after traveling from its country of origin to a new country, through an engagement with memory, emotion, and desire. The art installation that was inspired by this relationship attempted to speak to the ideas, attitudes, and wearing practices of Canadian-born women of Chinese heritage for the purposes of opening up dialogue about the diasporic condition, its impact on ethnic identity, and the role that ethnic clothing can play in identifying with one's ethnic heritage(s). Ultimately this study aimed to contribute to a deeper appreciation of ethnic clothing and its relevance to women of the Chinese diaspora in Canada, given the effects of advanced globalization, intense media saturation, and late capitalism.

A highly recognizable form, the cheongsam is riddled with complexity, informed by history, culture, politics, and economic concerns. In China during the Republic Era it was adopted by women as both a political and a stylish sartorial statement. It was also instrumentalized by the government to promote a new female representation of national identity. By the 1930s the cheongsam was taken up by fashionable women in China's major urban centers. After falling out of favor upon the establishment of the People's Republic of China in 1949, it was banned as a symbol of bourgeois excess during the Cultural Revolution. In places like Hong Kong, Taiwan, and Singapore, the cheongsam remained popular into the 1960s and then lost ground with societal changes and the desire for Western modeled modernity that manifested itself in a fervor for new clothing items, in particular the mini skirt. In the 1990s, as part of a strategy to rebuild the country's economy,

China revived the cheongsam to stimulate the fashion industry. But for Chinese women, the effects of the cheongsam ban ran deep as the garment continued to give off a conspicuous and antiquated air. By 2007, however, initiatives such as the Shanghai Cheongsam Salon and the Festival of Traditional Cheongsam dress in Hangzhou have greatly increased the worldwide appeal of the dress in addition to uncovering Chinese women's secret desire to wear it. Furthermore, a new generation of Chinese designers and entrepreneurs are working with the cheongsam, inheriting the skills of master tailors and innovating the form.

Photographs show that the cheongsam came to Canada through the immigration of Chinese women who wore both Western and Chinese clothing. The reasons behind the decline of the cheongsam in Canada are closely tied to what happened in China. But the perception of the cheongsam by Canadian women of Chinese heritage was further complicated by a history of xenophobia and racialization beginning with the vilification of Chinese migrants who built the CPR and continuing through to the Second World War. Beginning in the 1970s, government sanctioned events that exemplified Canada's policy on multiculturalism, such as Toronto's *Caravan* festival, brought the cheongsam into more mainstream view. But these culturally specific events would relegate the cheongsam to the realm of the folkloric costume. The large wave of Chinese immigration from Hong Kong and Taiwan in the 1970s and 1980s added to the cheongsam's presence in Canada. But as it was worn mostly by older, newly arrived immigrants, the cheongsam was largely perceived as part of the past. In concert with the country's dominant societal norms for behavior which include dressing, the cheongsam, as it was popularly understood, survived primarily as a garment reserved for formal occasions, a practice which is reflected in the type of cheongsam available in Canadian Chinatown stores today.

What I have argued throughout the course of this book is that the cheongsam exemplifies the characteristics of a technology that imposes a specific set of practices and techniques of the body. The experiences of Canadian-born women of Chinese heritage inform a complicated relationship with the cheongsam that can be characterized most aptly as ambivalent. All of the women I interviewed perceive the cheongsam as a beautiful, iconic garment that commands respect and appreciation. As an artifact of Chinese culture, it can be worn to affirm connection with one's family and to indicate affiliation with a larger ethnic community. Formally sumptuous and infused with history, wearing the cheongsam for many of the women has been a pleasurable experience. At the same time the cheongsam continues to inspire apprehension, fear, and feelings of intimidation. Women who feel unknowledgeable about Chinese culture have avoided wearing the cheongsam out of a concern that doing so would be comparable to a gesture of cultural appropriation. Wearing the cheongsam in mainstream, public settings could also over-emphasize one's Chinese appearance, bringing about uncomfortable comments and questions evoking one's past experiences with racialized taunts and bullying. There is also the fear that the dress may charge its wearer with the responsibility of representing Chinese culture, providing the role of native informant. Despite the allure of the cheongsam, women are also wary of the dress's body-conscious cut that imposes on women a normative set of beauty ideals. The daunting task of "measuring up" is also imparted by an idealized image of Chinese femininity presented in movies, television, and advertising in both China and Canada, a concern that plagues wearing the cheongsam with the fear that it will perpetuate Orientalist stereotypes that objectify the Asian female. What this tangle of concerns points to is an enduring conundrum: how can a dress so imbued with a specific feminized racialism be reconciled with critical feminist analysis? The deep ambivalence that surrounds the cheongsam makes it an item of clothing that is worn contingently and negotiated on an ongoing basis. If we follow the idea that ethnic clothing is considered non-fashion, the cheongsam even transcends this designation. As a paradox, the cheongsam's ability to defy logic contributes to its durability as a fascinating idea.

I have also endeavored to prove that the ambivalence of the cheongsam is further infused with a pre-occupation with the notion of authenticity. This troublesome aspect governs a set of discourses that indicate when, where, how, and by whom it should be worn. In an era of advanced globalization and intensified migration, the marks of authenticity in cultural forms ranging from food to clothing become increasingly impossible to pin down. In relation to the cheongsam, the most commonly held image of the dress that finds stability today consists of a form-fitting dress with high collar and side slits, made from red shiny brocade fabric and decorated with intricate fastenings. For all of the women interviewed for this study, these are the characteristics of a ubiquitous cheongsam, where the meaning of authenticity is determined more by its materials and appearance than its provenance. The term "authentic" was also used to indicate an essential Chinese quality. However, referring again to Ien Ang's "Central Country Complex" (Ang, 2001) the "authentic" cheongsam takes on the quality of surrogate for a singular manifestation of Chinese identity, elusive for Canadian-born women of Chinese heritage and by extension women of the Chinese diaspora around the world. Depending on a number of specific factors, the wearing of the ubiquitous cheongsam can be positive, negative, or both simultaneously. For some women, there can be no substitute for the ubiquitous cheongsam, as it most aptly denotes elegance and respect for Chinese culture, pays homage to one's family, and represents Chinese values. The main caveat however is that this cheongsam should only be worn for formal occasions that preferably take place within one's Chinese family or community. For other women, wearing the ubiquitous cheongsam in the Canadian context implies physical and psychological discomfort. The wearing of hybrid clothing items produced by the mainstream Western fashion industry as Asian cultures became chic was preferred, as it maintained a woman's insistence on her diasporic status while drawing a controlled amount of attention to her ethnicity. Furthermore, women are divided among and within themselves about whether the dress can be worn by anyone regardless of ethnicity or if it should be worn only by women of Chinese ethnicity. While each woman has reconciled her relationship to her Chinese heritage to varying degrees, their collected attitudes, ideas, and wearing practices of the cheongsam reveal a great deal about their acknowledgment of ethnic identity as a constantly evolving concept where the baseline understanding of how their ethnicity factors into that identity is always shifting over time. The existence of overlapping and contradictory discourses that govern the cheongsam, in particular the pre-occupation with the notion of authenticity, further complicates wearing practices in Canada.

My third argument is that the study of the cheongsam and its relationship with Canadian-born women of Chinese heritage shows that women are beginning to wear the dress as a tool of agency to express an evolved, mutable ethnic identity manifested by experiences growing up and living in a diasporic context. The cheongsam's characteristic hybridity can allow women the power to shape and fashion new representations of Chinese femininity that reflect their knowledge and deft negotiation of cross-cultural and intercultural environments with an awareness of patriarchal norms and the effects of racialization. Olivia Khoo's concept of the "Chinese exotic" provides some insight into how changing power dynamics between China and the West have affected a shift in perception of the Asian female that takes on the qualities of cosmopolitan, mobile, and therefore modern citizen. Wearing the cheongsam in ways that reflect this more progressive image can be part of fashioning new representations for Chinese diasporic women, but as Khoo indicates, "although exotic discourses now appear in new, updated forms, their orientalist underpinnings haven't entirely disappeared. What *have* appeared are sources of potential empowerment, or agency, in these representations, which are a product of their modernity" (Khoo, 2007, p. 2). The cheongsam can be taken up to affirm and transcend stereotypical archetypes, with the understanding that these productions are always subject to a variety of readings. I have struggled throughout this study with how the realization that my desire to wear the cheongsam is wrapped up in nostalgic fantasy and a longing to incarnate some degree of idealized Chinese femininity. This susceptibility was noted by Alice Jim in her writing on *The Fitting Room* with her assessment that the exhibition "*unavoidably* resuscitates the durable 'Suzie Wong' stereotype . . . heightened by sequences from *In the Mood for Love*, where the lead actress, in multiple versions of the dress, appears in various fantasy scenarios" (Jim, 2017). What I glean from this remark is that the story of the cheongsam can never be fully evacuated of its commodified past. The seduction, longing, and desire fostered by images like these are truly difficult to deny. But these desires are matched equally by a belief that the cheongsam can be worn consciously and powerfully to connect with the disparate, hidden, or erased senses of oneself to express an empowered representation of a diasporic woman of Chinese heritage. In this way I have argued throughout this book that incorporating the cheongsam into everyday dressing can greatly contribute to the decolonizing of the garment and a diffusion of the male gaze. As I have described, women are exercising strategies such as altering and accessorizing, so that wearing the cheongsam, despite its ambivalences, ultimately becomes a gesture of empowerment, experimentation, assertion, and joy.

A fourth contention of this book was to examine how the cheongsam and its relationship with Canadian-born women of Chinese heritage could be further explored through the creation of artworks and their public dissemination via the strategic use of art installation. The ethnographic and autoethnographic methodologies that mixed the personal stories of the women I interviewed with my own, the use of historical research on the origins and evolution of the cheongsam in China and its arrival in Canada, the focus on significant pop cultural texts, the employment of multiple and single channel video projection, an audio piece, and the making of three cheongsams that incorporated the narratives and concerns voiced in the interviews and a strategy of inclusivity aimed to seek out the poetics of this dress and its place in women's lives. The materiality of the sculptural and video-based works combined with the ephemerality of the exhibition set within a Chinatown mall created a space for a mulit-dimensional and sensorial expression of the complex and layered meanings of this garment.

As I began researching for this project in 2011, I found out about a newly published book entitled *The Measure of a Man* by Canadian journalist J.J. Lee. This moving account chronicles the relationship with his late father via the social history of the men's suit. As Lee is also of Chinese heritage, I wondered why it seemed that Canadian-born men of Chinese heritage had not engaged with any ethnic clothing items such as *changsam* or *ma gua* as a way to rediscover or assert their heritage. What I had noticed was that men tended to manifest this desire more through food or martial arts, with the exception of one friend. On a recent sojourn to Hong Kong to meet relatives from his father's side, Lee came back with a beautiful contemporary *changsam* jacket and some excellent Chinese disco LPs from the 1970s. For J.J. Lee, however, it was the altering of one of his father's Western suits in order to make it his own that provided the healing he needed to reconcile their turbulent relationship. This book highlighted the power of clothing's ability to preserve memory, to live out fantasy, to protect, to express, and to evoke and even exercise demons, as in J.J.'s case:

> There's more work to be done. The lapel stitches are uneven. I could shave another inch off the shoulders. The waist could be tighter. I can see in the suit all its shortcomings, its deficiencies. It is incomplete, but he's still there and now so am I. At this moment, I am occupying the same space as my father. We remain entangled. (Lee, 2011, p. 283)

Lee's story articulates perhaps the strongest undercurrent in the understanding of what the cheongsam means for Canadian women of Chinese heritage. It is a garment that emanates an enigmatic and charismatic persona. It inflames as much controversy as delight, and it is as ancient as it is part of a representation of the new. The investigation into the wearing practices of the cheongsam contributes to a growing wave of self-interrogation, as new generations of Canadian-born people of Chinese heritage are finding their own voices, and adding to those of pioneers that have been calling for the liberation of narrow definitions of ethnic identity for quite some time now.

Wearing the cheongsam becomes a strategy of hybridity that embodies politicized sensuousness. The cheongsam can withstand endless variations and combinations to allow the wearer to play and experiment with the communication of multiple, imbricated messages while maintaining signification as a Chinese garment. As Canadian-born women of Chinese heritage continue to discover and claim this dress for themselves, they are finding ways to declare and own the productivity of an ethnicity in flux. For me, inhabiting the cheongsam has always consisted of reaching back while simultaneously reaching forward. When I wear the cheongsam I channel my grandmother's spirit, paying homage to the grandeur and rigor of this Chinese woman. At the same time, wearing this dress mindfully as I wish while campaigning for new varieties of cheongsams, is the way forward to the acknowledgment of the multiplicity of ways to live and *be* of Chinese ethnicity in the Canadian diaspora today. Wearing the cheongsam is alive with all of these tensions and, like any love affair, it involves intimacy, risk, exchange, and courage.

NOTES

Chapter 1—*One size does not fit all*

1. This was the mandate stated by the National Film Act of 1950 and had not changed at the time of my employment. The mandate has since been reinterpreted the following way: "The National Film Board's mission is to provide new perspectives on Canada and the world from Canadian points of view, perspectives that are not provided by anyone else and that serve Canadian and global audiences by an imaginative exploration of who we are and what we may be."

   http://onf-nfb.gc.ca/en/about-the-nfb/organization/mandate/

2. The history of Studio D at the National Film Board of Canada is well documented in Elizabeth Anderson's 1999 book *Studio D's Imagined Community: From Development to Realignment*. Studio D was founded by Kathleen Shannon in 1974 to be a studio dedicated to the production of films by women from a feminist perspective. In 1990, The New Inititatives in Film (NIF) program was established and run by an external Advisory Board while administered at arm's length within Studio D. This new program would address the under-representation and mis-representation of women of color and aboriginal women in film and video through a range of professional development activities. The women who worked for this program added to the very low number of people of color and aboriginal people employed at the NFB. My first job out of university was Production Coordinator of the New Initiatives in Film Institute, a two-week, intensive film and video production workshop developing new talent.

   According to The Canadian Encyclopedia website, the term "Aboriginal" in the Canadian context refers to descendants of the first peoples of this land and includes First Nations, Métis, and Inuit peoples.

   https://www.thecanadianencyclopedia.ca/en/article/aboriginal-people

3. At the time of my initial research for this project in 2009, this was the wording that appeared on the official Government of Canada website below. This formulation has been quoted in a variety of published texts including Andrew Griffith's 2015 book *Multiculturalism In Canada: Evidence and Anecdote* and Fethi Mansouri's 2017 book *Interculturalism at the crossroads: comparative perspectives on concepts, policies and practices*.

   Citizenship and Immigration Canada, "Canadian Multiculturalism: An Inclusive Citizenship" (2012) www.cic.gc.ca/english/multiculturalism/citizenship.asp.

   This link is no longer active, and the formulation of the policy's mandate has been revamped to include a series of bullet points, now found under the heading "laws"

Notes

tab on the Government of Canada website: http://laws-lois.justice.gc.ca/eng/acts/C-18.7/page-1.html

Chapter 2—*Determining the "fabric"*

1. My main reference for the chronicle and critical analysis of the situation of Canadian cultural politics and artists of color and aboriginal artists in Canada during the late 1980s and 1990s is *Other Conundrums: race, culture and Canadian art* by Monika Kin Gagnon published in 2000.

2. Banana Blog: Echoes of the *Jook Sing* Generation www.drivel.ca/banana/topic01.html. Accessed 10 September 2014.

3. An often cited example of installation art that is conceived for and rooted to a specific, often public space is Richard Serra's 1981 work *Tilted Arc*. This art installation was displayed in the Foley Federal Plaza in NYC from 1981 to 1989. Consisting of a 120-foot long, twelve-foot high, solid curved plate of unfinished, rust-covered COR-TEN steel.

4. See Elizabeth Anderson's 1999 book *Studio D's Imagined Community: From Development to Realignment*.

5. Chow, Rey, 1995. *Primitive Passions: Visuality, Sexuality, Ethnography and Contemporary Chinese Cinema*. Columbia University Press, New York.

Said, Edward W., 1978. *Orientalism*. New York, Vintage Books.

6. http://www.ninalevitt.com

Chapter 3—*The cheongsam: A complex garment*

1. Clark, Hazel, (2000). *The Cheongsam*, Oxford, New York, Hong Kong: Oxford University Press.

2. Ibid.

3. Trouillard, Pascale, (2010). "Shanghai women revisit 'In the Mood for Love'" http://www.telegraph.co.uk/expat/expatnews/7138842/Shanghai-women-revisit-In-the-Mood-for-Love.html. Accessed 14 October 2017.

4. Schmitt, Kellie, (2007). "Work it sister: The Chinese qipao is back" http://travel.cnn.com/shanghai/play/work-it-sister-chinese-qipao-back-668610/. Accessed 14 October 2017.

5. People's Daily (2012). "Cheongsam culture booms in Shanghai" http://www.china.org.cn/travel/2012-05/29/content_25505568.htm. Accessed 17 October 2017.

6. Cang, Wei and Tang, Yaochang, (2017). "Women show off the beauty of Chinese *qipao*" *China Daily* http://www.chinadaily.com.cn/china/201705/26/content_29518556.htm. Accessed 17 October 2017.

7. Information on the website for the Shanghai Cheongsam Salon is written in the Chinese language. An address, telephone number, and email address are listed in English. My inquiries sent via email were unanswered.

www.sh-qpsl.com.

8. Bardsley, Daniel (2012). "China's qipao in fashion revival as women cling to traditions" *The National*, https://www.thenational.ae/world/asia/china-s-qipaoin-fashion-revival-as-women-cling-to-traditions-1.443172.

9. Vickery, Nina (2014). "Qipao Comeback" http://www.chinatoday.com.cn/english/culture/201402/17/content_596877.htm. Accessed 18 October 2017.

10. Feng, Rebecca (2016) "Chinese Girl Drops Out of Brown to Bring New Life to Qipao" https://www.forbes.com/sites/rebeccafeng/2016/08/01/chinese-girl-dropsout-of-brown-to-bring-new-life-to-qipao/#71e9261b5e12. Accessed 18 October 2017.

11. https://www.yi-ming.asia.

12. http://www.classicsanew.com.

13. Siu, Elky, (2016). "In the Mood for Cheongsams: Where to get a qipo taliored in Hong Kong" https://coconuts.co/hongkong/lifestyle/mood-cheongsams/. Accessed 18 October 2017.

14. *The Hindu* (2017). "Reviving the dying art of qipao-making in Taiwan" http://www.thehindu.com/todays-paper/tp-life/reviving-the-dying-art-of-qipao-making in-taiwan/article19766172.ece. Accessed on 18 October 2017.

Chapter 4—*Wearing practices in Canada: ambivalence, authenticity, and agency*

1. The high cost of rent forced the tailor to give up his storefront atelier and to move his business to his home in 2014.

2. This assessment was based on visits to Chinatown shops selling cheongsam in Montreal, Toronto, and Vancouver in 2009. In Montreal, little has changed in terms of the kind of cheongsam one can buy in stores in Chinatown.

Chapter 5—*Getting inside "The Fitting Room"*

1. Catherine Grenier, *When History Encounters Aesthetics*, 2011

2. Saheen Merali, *Clash of Ignorance (After Said), 2009.*

3. Rachel Kent, *Time and Transformation in the Art of Yinka Shonibare MBE*, 2014.

4. Ibid.

5. Alice Jim, *Fashioning Race, Gender and Desire: Cheryl Sim's Fitting Room and Mary Sui Yee Wong's Yellow Apparel, from the anthology Desire Change: Contemporary Feminist Art in Canada*, Toronto: McGill-Queens's University Press and Mentoring Artists for Women's Art (MAWA), page 86, 2017.

Notes

6. *Mary Sui Yee Wong's Velvet Apparel*, Fibre Quarterly ISSN 1916-534X http://www.velvethighway.com/joomla/index.php?option=com_content&task=view&id=103.

7. Rebecca Duclos, *Mary Wong and the Burden of Semiotics*, 2008

   http://www.velvethighway.com/joomla/index.php?option=com_content&task=view&id=104.

8. *Fusionable Cheongsam And The Mêlée Of Fashion* Christian Huck (2007) Exhibition publication.

9. http://www.tate.org.uk/art/art-terms/r/readymade.

10. DNA2ART www.dna2art/have-your-dna-data/about-reverse-engineering. Link no longer active.

11. https://blogs.scientificamerican.com/observations/rosalind-franklin-and-dna-how-wronged-was-she/.

12. http://www.tate.org.uk/art/artworks/marclay-video-quartet-t11818.

13. Jim, Alice Ming Wai (2008) *Rearranging Desires: Curating the "Other" Within*, Gail & Stephen A. Jarislowsky Institute for Studies in Canadian Art, Concordia University, Montreal.

REFERENCES

Anderson, Elizabeth (1999). *Studio D's Imagined Community: From Development to Realignment*. Eds. K. Armatage, K. Banning, B. Longfellow, J. Marchessault. Toronto: University of Toronto Press Inc.

Ang, Ien (2001). *On Not Speaking Chinese*. London and New York: Routledge.

Araeen, Rasheed (2000). "A New Beginning Beyond Postcolonial Cultural Theory and Identity Politics," *The Third Text Reader On Art, Culture and Theory*. Eds. R. Araeen, S. Cubbitt, and Z. Sardar. London: Continuum.

Bannerji, Himmani (2000). *The Dark Side of the Nation: Essays On Multiculturalism, Nationalism, and Gender*. Toronto: Canadian Scholars' Press.

Bardsley, Daniel (2012). "China's qipao in fashion revival as women cling to traditions," *The National*, https://www.thenational.ae/world/asia/china-s-qipao-in-fashion-revival-as-women-cling-to-traditions-1.443172

Bhabha, Homi K. (1994). *The Location Of Culture*. London and New York: Routledge.

Bhachu, Parminder (2003). "Designing Diasporic Markets: Asian Fashion Entrepreneurs in London," *Re-Orienting Fashion: The Globalization of Asian Dress*. Eds. S. Niessen, A. Leshkowich, C. Jones. Oxford and New York: Berg.

Bishop, Claire (2005). *Installation Art: A Critical History*. London and New York: Routledge.

Bolton, Andrew (2010). *Anna Sui*. San Francisco: Chronicle Books LLC.

Cang, Wei and Tang, Yaochang (2017). "Women show off the beauty of Chinese *qipao*," *China Daily* http://www.chinadaily.com.cn/china/201705/26/content_29518556.htm

Case, Sue Ellen and Foster, Susan L. (2005). *Cruising the Performative: Interventions Into the Representation of Ethnicity, Nationality and Sexuality*. Bloomington: Indiana University Press.

Chung, Young Yang (1979). *The Art Of Oriental Embroidery*. London: Macmillan.

Chung, Young Yang (2003). *Painting With A Needle: Learning The Art Of Silk Embroidery*. New York: Harry N. Abrams.

Chung, Young Yang (2005). *Silken Threads: A History of Embroidery in China, Korea, Japan And Vietnam*. New York: Harry N. Abrams.

Citizenship and Immigration Canada (2012). "Canadian Multiculturalism: An Inclusive Citizenship" Link no longer active.

Clark, Hazel (2000). *The Cheongsam*. Oxford, New York, Hong Kong: Oxford University Press.

Cornwell, Rebecca (1974). *Projected Images: Peter Campus, Rockne Krebs, Paul Sharits, Michael Snow, Ted Victoria, Robert Whitman*, Minneapolis: Walker Art Center.

References

Craik, Jenny (1993). *The Face of Fashion: Cultural Studies in Fashion*. London: Routledge.

Curdt-Christansen, Xao Lan (2004). *"Made in China." Not Just Any Dress: Narratives of Memory, Body and Identity*. New York: Peter Lang Publishing.

Daniels, Dieter (2005). "Before and After Video Art." *Present Continuous Past(s). Media art. Strategies of Presentation, Mediation and Dissemination*. Eds. Ursula M. Frohne, Schieren and Jean-François Guiton (pp. 96–111). Vienna: Springer-Verlag.

DNA2ART. www.dna2art/have -your-dna-data/about-reverse-engineering. Link no longer active.

Eicher, Joanne B. (1995). *Dress And Ethnicity: Change Across Space And Time*. Oxford: Berg.

Eicher, Joanne B., Mary-Ellen Roach-Higgins, Kim K. P. Johnson (1995). *Dress and Identity*. Oxford: Berg.

Fanon, Frantz (1967). *Black Skin, White Masks*. New York: Grove Press.

Feng, Rebecca (2016). "Chinese Girl Drops Out of Brown To Bring New Life to Qipao," https://www.forbes.com/sites/rebeccafeng/2016/08/01/chinese-girl-dropsout-of-brown-to-bring-new-life-to-qipao/#71e9261b5e12

Feng, Zhao (2005). *Chinese Silk Art History*. Oxford, New York, Hong Kong: Oxford University Press.

Finnane, Antonia (2008). *Changing Clothes in China: Fashion, History, Nation*. New York: Columbia University Press.

Forney, Judith C. (1980). "An Investigation of the Relationship Between Dress and Appearance and Retention of Ethnic Identity." Diss. Purdue University.

Franklin, Ursula (1989). *The Real World of Technology*, Toronto, Ontario: House of Anansi Press.

Fung, Richard (1990). "Multiculturalism Reconsidered," *Yellow Peril Reconsidered*. Ed. P. Wong, Vancouver: On Edge on the Cutting Edge Society.

Garret, Valerie M. (1987). *Traditional Chinese Clothing in Hong Kong and South China 1840–1980*, Oxford, New York, Hong Kong: Oxford University Press.

Gessert, George (2010). "Recent Art involving DNA," *Green Light: Toward an Art of Evolution*, (pp. 111–24). Cambridge, MA; London, England: The MIT Press.

González, Jennifer (2008). *Subject to Display: Reframing Race in Contemporary Installation*, Cambridge, MA: The MIT Press.

Hall, Stuart (1994). "Cultural Identity and Diaspora," *Colonial Discourse and Post-Colonial Theory, a Reader*. Eds. Patrick Williams and Laura Chrisman, (pp. 392–401). London: Harvester Wheatsheaf.

Hall, Stuart (2000). "Conclusion: The Multi-Cultural Question," *Un/Settled Multiculturalisms: Diasporas, Entanglements, Transruptions*. Ed. B. Hesse. London: Zed Books.

Hall, Stuart and du Gay, Paul (1996). *Questions of Cultural Identity*, California: SAGE Publications,

Hollander, Anne (1993). *Seeing Through Clothes*. Berkeley: University of California Press.

Hua, Mei (2011). *Chinese Clothing*, Boston, MA: Cambridge University Press.

Jim, Alice Ming Wai (2008). *Rearranging Desires: Curating the "Other" Within*, Gail & Stephen A. Jarislowsky Institute for Studies in Canadian Art, Concordia University, Montreal.

Jim, Alice Ming Wai (2017). "Fashioning Race, Gender and Desire: Cheryl Sim's *Fitting Room* and Mary Sui Yee Wong's *Yellow Apparel*." *Desire Change: Contemporary Feminist Art in Canada*, Toronto: McGill-Queens's University Press and Mentoring Artists for Women's Art (MAWA).

Keenan, Randall (1999). *Walking on Water: Black American Lives at the Turn of the Twenty-first Century*. New York: Alfred A. Knopf.

Khoo, Olivia (2007). *The Chinese Exotic: Modern Diasporic Femininity*. Aberdeen, Hong Kong: Hong Kong University Press.

Kondo, Dorinne (1997). *About Face: Performing Race in Fashion and Theater*. New York: Routledge.

Kwon, Miwon (2000). "One Space After Another: Notes on Site Specificity," *Space, Site, Intervention: Situating Installation Art*. Ed. Erika Suderburg (pp. 38–63). Minneapolis and London: University of Minnesota Press.

Lee, J.J. (2011). *The Measure of a Man*, Toronto, Ontario: McClelland & Stewart Ltd.

Li, Peter S. (1988). *The Chinese in Canada*, Oxford: Oxford University Press.

Li, Peter S. (1990). "Race and Ethnicity," *Race and Ethnic Relations in Canada*. Ed. Peter S. Li, (pp. 3–15). Toronto, Oxford, New York: Oxford University Press.

Lurie, Alison (1983). *The Language of Clothes*. New York: Vintage Books.

Mackey, Eva (2002). *The House Of Difference: Cultural Politics and National Identity in Canada*. Toronto: University of Toronto Press.

Mah, Bonnie (2005). *Ethnic Identity and Heritage Language Ability in Second Generation Canadians in Toronto*, (Master's Thesis). Retrieved from Theses and dissertations. (74).

Manovich, Lev (2002). *The Language of New Media*. Cambridge, MA: MIT Press.

Mauss, Marcel (1973). "Techniques of the Body," *Economy and Society* Volume 2, Issue 1, pp. 70–88.

Maynard, Margaret (2004). *Dress and Globalization*, Manchester: Manchester University Press.

Mercer, Kobena (1994). *Welcome to the Jungle: New positions in Black Cultural Studies*. London: Routledge.

Metzger, Sean (2014). *Chinese Looks: Fashion, Performance, Race*. Bloomington, Indiana: Indiana University Press.

Metzger, Sean (2015). "La Cabine d'Essayage (The Fitting Room): Cheryl Sim," *Asian Diasporic Visual Cultures and the Americas*, Volume 1, Issue 1–2, pp. 214–18.

Minh-Ha, Trinh T. (1991). "Bold Omissions and Minute Depictions," *Moving the Image: Independent Asian Pacific American Media Arts*. Dir. R. Leong, pp. 83–92. Los Angeles: UCLA Asian American Studies Center Press.

Mondloch, Kate (2010). *Screens: Viewing Media Installation Art*, Minneapolis, MN: University of Minnesota Press.

Multicultural History Society of Ontario (2010). *Chinese Canadian Women, 1923–1967: Inspiration – Innovation – Ingenuity*. Retrieved from http://mhso.ca/wp/multi-faceted-websites/

References

Mulvey, Laura (2003). "Visual pleasure and narrative cinema," *The Feminism and Visual Culture Reader*. Ed. Amelia Jones. London and New York: Routledge.

Narumi, Hiroshi (2000). "Fashion Orientalism and the Limits of Counter Culture," *Postcolonial Studies*, Volume 3, Issue 3, 311:330.

Ng, Erica (2014). "Alice Ko: The Art of the Cheongsam," *FG Magazine* http://www.thefashionglobe.com/author/ericang/page/2

Nguyen, Thi Phuong (2012). "The Discourse of *Wenming* ('Civilisation'): Moral Authority and Social Change in Contemporary Shanghai" (Doctoral dissertation).

Niessen, Sandra, Jones, Carla, Leshkowich, Ann Marie (2003). *Re-orienting Fashion: the Globalization of Asian Dress*. UK, USA: Berg: Oxford International Publishers Ltd.

Palumbo-Liu, David, (1999). *Asian/American: Historical Crossings of a Racial Frontier*. Stanford, California: Stanford University Press.

People's Daily (2012). "Cheongsam culture booms in Shanghai," http://www.china.org.cn/travel/2012-05/29/content_25505568.htm

Pratt, Marie-Louise (1992). *Imperial Eyes: Travel Writing and Transculturation*, London: Routledge.

Reichle, Ingeborg (2009). "When Life Becomes Art," *Art in the Age of Technoscience: Genetic Engineering, Robotics and Artificial Life in Contemporary Art*. Eds. Ingeborg Reichle, Gloria Custance, Robert Zwijenberg (pp. 63–95). Vienna, New York: Springer.

Russell, Catherine (1999). "Autoethnography: Journeys of the Self," excerpt from: *Experimental Ethnography*. Duke University Press. http://www.haussite.net/haus.0/SCRIPT/txt2001/01/russel.HTML

Ryan, Anne B. (2006). "Post-Positivist Approaches to Research," *Researching and Writing your thesis: a guide for postgraduate students* (pp. 12–26). MACE: Maynooth Adult and Community Education.

Said, Edward W. (1978). *Orientalism*. New York, Vintage Books

Sánchez, Rosaura (2006). "On a Critical Realist Theory of Identity," in Linda Martin Alcoff, Michael Hames-Garcia, Satya P. Mohanty (Eds.), *Identity Politics Reconsidered* (pp. 31–52). New York: Palgrave MacMillan.

Schmitt, Kellie (2009). "Work it sister: The Chinese qipao is back," http://travel.cnn.com/shanghai/play/work-it-sister-chinese-qipao-back-668610/

Sharif, Farha (2008). "Straddling the Cultural Divide: Second-Generation South Asian Identity and The Namesake," *Changing English*, Volume 15, Issue 4, pp. 457–66

Shohat, Eil and Stam, Robert (2004). *Unthinking Eurocentrism: Multiculturalism and the Media*. New York: Routledge.

Siu, Elky (2016). "In the Mood for Cheongsams: Where to get a qipo tailored in Hong Kong," https://coconuts.co/hongkong/lifestyle/mood-cheongsams/

Spivak, Gayatri (1993). "Can The Subaltern Speak?" *Colonial Discourse And Post-Colonial Theory, A Reader*, Eds. Patrick Williams, Laura Chrisman (pp. 66–111). New York: Columbia University Press.

Tarlo, Emma (1996). *Clothing Matters: Dress and Identity in India*, Chicago: University of Chicago Press.

The Banana Blog: Echoes of the Jook Sing Generation (2002). "Topic One: What is your definition of 'banana' as it relates to Chinese-Canadians?" www.drivel.ca/banana/topic01.html

The Hindu (2017). "Reviving the dying art of qipao-making in Taiwan," http://www.thehindu.com/todays-paper/tp-life/reviving-the-dying-art-of-qipao-making in-taiwan/article19766172.ece

The Women's Book Committee, Chinese Canadian National Council (1992). *Jin Guo: Voices of Chinese Canadian Women*, Toronto, Ontario: Women's Press.

Trouillard, Pascale (2010). "Shanghai women revisit 'In the Mood for Love'," http://www.telegraph.co.uk/expat/expatnews/7138842/Shanghai-women-revisit-In-the-Mood-for-Love.html

Tu, Wei-Ming (1995). *The Living Tree: The Changing Meaning of Being Chinese Today*. Palo Alto, CA: Stanford University Press.

Vickery, Nina (2014). "Qipao Comeback," http://www.chinatoday.com.cn/english/culture/201402/17/content_596877.htm

Weir, Alison (2013). *Identities and Freedom: Feminist Theory Between Power and Connection*, Oxford and New York: Oxford University Press.

WESSIELING (2007). *Fusionable Cheongsam*, Hong Kong: Hong Kong Arts Centre.

Wickberg, Edgar (1982). *From China to Canada: A History of the Chinese Communities in Canada*. Toronto: McClelland & Stewart.

Wilson, Elizabeth (2003). *Adorned in Dreams: Fashion and Modernity*. New Brunswick: Rutgers University Press.

Wu, Amanda (2017). "HK Women's Cheongsam: From Tradition to Innovation," http://www.womenofchina.cn/womenofchina/html1/culture/lifestyle/1707/2559-1.htm

Wu, Juanjuan. (2009). *Chinese Fashion from Mao to Now*, Oxford, New York: Berg.

Yang, Chui Chu (2007). *The Meanings of Qipao as Traditional Dress: Chinese and Taiwanese Perspectives* (Doctoral dissertation).

INDEX

Page numbers followed by *f* denote illustrations.